Trail Magic

Creating a Positive Energy Home

CARL N. MCDANIEL

Sigel Press

For

David, Don, Joe, Mary, Mike, and Scout

Sigel Press
4403 Belmont Court
Medina, Ohio 44256

51A Victoria Road
Cambridge CB4 3BW
England

Visit us on the World Wide Web at www.sigelpress.com

Cover and internal design by Harp Mando
Cover Images: Photos of Trail Magic by Carl N. McDaniel
Back Cover Image: Photo of Trail Magic at Night by Joseph Ferut

ISBN: 978-1905941-16-2

Printed in the United States of America

Printed on 100% recycled, 100% post-consumer waste paper.

Contents

Acknowledgments   vii

Prelude   ix

Chapter 1:   Deciding to Really Do It   1

Chapter 2:   Size Matters   11

Chapter 3:   Wants and Needs   23

Chapter 4:   Matching Personalities   33

Chapter 5:   Oberlin Mud   43

Chapter 6:   Where's the Dumpster?   53

Chapter 7:   Deadline   65

Chapter 8:   The Big Decisions   81

Chapter 9:   Performance   89

Chapter 10:   Trail Magic and Oberlin—Gesture and Challenge   105

Coda   113

Appendices

     A. Owner's Programs   129

         Initial Owner's Program   130

         Final Owner's Program   134

     B. Architectural Diagrams   141

     C. Photographs   155

     D. Cost Analysis   163

End Notes   169

Indices

     Name   177

     Subject   178

Sidebars

Sidebar 1:   McDaniel Energy Use in Troy, NY   13

Sidebar 2:   East College Street Project   16

Sidebar 3:   Human Fantasy and Biophysical Reality   21

Sidebar 4:   Carbon Dioxide Released from Energy Sources   29

Sidebar 5:   Economic Growth and the Keeling Curve   41

Sidebar 6:   Ecological Footprint   45

Sidebar 7:   Emerald Ash Borer   48

Sidebar 8:   Value of Botanical Knowledge   51

Sidebar 9:   Birth of The Oberlin Project   55

Sidebar 10: Positive Energy and Climate Positive Homes   62

Sidebar 11: Lumber from Trail Magic Trees   76

Sidebar 12: Plug Load, Baseline Operating Energy, and   91
             Phantom Load

Sidebar 13: Water Conservation Reduces Energy Use and   97
             CO_2 Release

Sidebar 14: Average Household and Trail Magic Operating   100
             Energy

Sidebar 15: Tenth Anniversary of the Lewis Center and The   109
             Oberlin Project

Sidebar 16: Bioclimatic Design Features Embodied in Trail Magic   118

Acknowledgements

David and Harriet Borton's passive solar home in Troy, New York, inspired us to build Trail Magic. I have written the story of that creation to educate and to advocate the use of solar energy. The energy crisis, in large part, resulted because we have not strived to employ the sun's free energy to run not only our homes, but also to power much of the human enterprise.

First and foremost, I thank David Sonner (Scout) for finding the perfect site, for helping us settle in Oberlin, and for his leadership in having the city of Oberlin abandon coal as its energy source for electricity; Doren Portman, not only for selling us his family's longtime home, but also for his tremendous help thereafter; Donald Watson for his true friendship and architect expertise, par excellence; Joe Ferut and his associates for translating Watson's schematic design into the home we now inhabit and for never failing to be there when needed; Mike Strehle for his exceptional building skills that made Trail Magic the tightest house he'd ever built and for his unflappable personality that played a major role in creating a cooperative, can-do team; and my wife, Mary, who lived through it all making contributions too numerable to list. She was there to do what needed to be done and without her it would have never happened.

My colleague and best friend, David Borton, is in his own class: he did his best to teach me practical physics for three decades, persisted for most of that time to tell us that we had to prepare for a future of fewer resources, was with us every step of the way in making and assessing the performance of Trail Magic, and then provided support and useful input during the writing of *Trail Magic*.

In addition to the central characters in the Trail Magic story mentioned above, innumerable trades people, suppliers, and others in the community merit my thanks. Two, in particular, stand out: Mike Foraker, whose company installed our solar hot water system, helped me prove it was a mistake; and George Ficke whose woodworking skill and artistic flare transformed merely functional floors, shelves, bookcases, balusters, beams, and countertop into objects of true beauty.

Writing for me is a team effort. Harriet Borton, Margaret and Howard Stoner gave encouragement and comments on early draft chapters. Kirk Jensen reviewed the entire first rough draft, providing insightful criticism that shaped subsequent versions. I am deeply indebted to Kelly Viancourt who enthusiastically supported this project and who thoroughly edited the best draft I could produce. She cut with no mercy that which didn't belong and used her superb editing skills to make what remained into a coherent, readable story. David Orr has been an invaluable colleague for the better part of two decades and gave input that greatly improved the presentation here, particularly his suggestion of sidebars to provide information and perspective. Rumi Shammin read the final draft spotting technical and factual errors. David Benzing, as a master writer and critic, edited the entire final draft, offering suggestions that allowed me to improve significantly the text and correct errors of fact. Bruce Laplante expertly reproduced the Keeling Curve. Thomas Sigel then used his considerable talent and experience to polish the text and oversee the assembly of the book before you.

The people mentioned above, and many others, did their best to have me write only that which is true, but errors and misstatements remain for which I am responsible.

Prelude

We hiked up the north side of the narrow valley following a stream for a mile or two before spotting the ruins on the other side of the valley. We descended across the stream into the December sun. The Anasazi dwellings were under an overhanging south-facing cliff some 100 feet above the flowing water. Snow covered the northern slopes, but the ruins were dry and bathed in sun. We climbed up a stone wall and peered down a dozen feet into a thousand-year-old corn crib to see small cobs long relieved of their kernels by rodents.

It was lunch time. We jumped down from the corn crib, dropped our daypacks on a big, flat rock, and shed our winter coats. It was delightfully warm. We ate our simple lunch of tuna fish, carrots, potato chips, and water flavored with sugar and tea mix, sitting amongst the ruins abandoned 800 years earlier.

My wife and our pre-teen children, Stuart and Virginia, wandered off to explore. I lay back on a rock and closed my eyes to bask, much like a native rattle snake on a chilly morning. Snakes do it by instinct; humans do it by choice. So why did the Anasazi build their homes under south-facing cliffs— and not cliffs that faced north or east or west? If they'd had been in the real estate business, the mantra would be as it is today: location, location, location. But unlike today's developers, the Anasazi understood that the sine qua non was, "Where is the sun?"

In 1981, the year of that southwestern experience, our good friends, David and Harriet Borton, broke ground for a passive solar home in Troy, New York. Located near Albany in the east-central part of the state, Troy faces nine months of below-freezing temperatures, along with several weeks of sub-zero temperatures. Despite the climate, our friends' house was built without central heating. A small woodstove warms their home the several degrees needed when the sun does not shine. The house does have several backup, baseboard electric heaters that were required then by code. The standard practice was— and still is—to have conventional heating in northern climates.

My family spent our last 23 years in Troy in a 1930s center hall colonial house with 2,300 square feet of living space. During our last decade in the house, our winter heating bill for natural gas equivalents ranged from $1,150 to $1,650 (in 2008 prices). The Bortons' cost for heating their similar-sized, passive-solar home ranged from $75 to $150. The key features of their house—long axis facing south; thicker, well-insulated walls and roof with low infiltration; triple-paned windows; added thermal mass to take on and release heat; many windows on the south side and few windows on the other sides— cost them just three percent more than standard construction. This premium in up-front cost was paid back by their substantially reduced heating expenses within several years.

The design principles that enabled the Bortons to heat their home with the sun's energy for free have been employed by humans for thousands of years. In the last century we were beguiled by the development of modern heating and cooling technologies, combined with the widespread availability of inexpensive fossil fuels, to abandon traditional ways of doing the same thing without such artificial assistance. Today, fully a third of the energy generated in the U.S. is used in buildings.

As the years passed, we came to covet the Bortons' house. With the century drawing to a close, my wife and I began to think about building a passive solar house. We initiated conversations with a Borton neighbor who had several suitable acres, but they weren't interested in selling.

Retirement—previously considered a distant phase of life—was upon us. Mary and I contemplated our future. Our son had married and grandchildren were in the offing; however, his education as an academic scientist was still in progress. Our daughter's fire-ecology work with the national parks would likely require her to relocate several more times. Their future locations were uncertain.

Although we had spent half our lives in Troy, I felt the need to create a new life after three decades at Rensselaer as an academic scientist. I had had various associations over the years with Oberlin College, my alma mater. In the early 1990s, soon after political scientist David Orr came to Oberlin to jumpstart its fledgling environmental studies program, I began to advocate for his vision there—to create an environmentally sustainable college and an ecologically grounded curriculum that turned out environmentally aware citizens in addition to competent professionals.

In 1992, Rensselaer asked me to develop and direct its new environmental science degree program. This career change from experimental scientist to environmental science educator coincided with Orr's early years at Oberlin and fostered an exchange of ideas between us.

Within a year of coming to Oberlin, Orr wrote an article for the student newspaper titled "What good is a great college if you don't have a decent planet to put it on?" In it, he outlined educational responses to environmental issues that we must address if our descendents are to have desirable choices. The list now is unchanged from then: over consumption, over population, pollution, extinction of species and destruction of ecosystems, and climate destabilization. Oberlin's first major response to this manifest call for action was the Adam Joseph Lewis Center for Environmental Studies, designed and built under Orr's leadership just before the turn of the 21st century. When dedicated in 2000, the center was the greenest classroom/office building in the United States, perhaps the world. Within several years it became a national icon for ecological design.

In 2002, I formed EnviroAlums, an Oberlin alumni group dedicated to support the college's sustainability initiatives. In 2004, Oberlin approved an environmental policy—perhaps the most comprehensive for any college at the time. Oberlin's president, in 2006, signed the American College & University Presidents' Climate Commitment, an obligation by colleges to take short- and long-term actions and develop a comprehensive plan leading to climate neutrality. At the same time, Oberlin's city council adopted a policy to pursue environmental sustainability within the community.

Although I had been involved in various environmental initiatives and programs at Rensselaer and at the local and state level, Oberlin had unique appeal. Orr's leadership there had given the college national presence, and both the college and the city were in serious conversation about taking on the challenge of achieving climate neutrality. With a combined population of just over 8,000, the college and city were sufficiently large and diverse to provide a meaningful model, yet small enough to actually accomplish something.

From afar I had immersed myself in Oberlin's environmental initiatives, enabling my wife and me to appreciate the opportunities offered by a small college town. In 2006, we decided that Oberlin would be our next, and most likely, final home. I fancied we'd go there and build our own mini Lewis Center. This book is the story of our brass tacks grounded demonstration that creating a home that runs on sunshine is, contrary to popular belief, attainable with off-the-shelf technology and affordable to any homeowner or builder who seeks to achieve that goal.

Chapter I:

Deciding to Really Do It

I've never designed or built much of anything. My specialty in building, if you could call it that, is shelves. In the basements, closets, and garages of the three homes we've owned, I added storage shelves that should have been there from the start. I did build a roofed, open storage shed to shelter the five cords of wood that we used to supplement the oil we burned to heat our first Troy house, and a simple deck for our second house there. Needless to say, I had little experience and few qualifications for our house-building adventure. Thinking about overseeing the design and construction of a solar home was intimidating. My wife, however, had no reservations. We'd just do it.

Oberlin is a small town nestled among farmland and rural homes. With Oberlin more than 500 miles from our upstate New York home, it was clear that we'd need a real-estate broker. With plans to attend an Oberlin Alumni Council Executive Board meeting the first weekend in March 2007, I arranged a lunch appointment with Oberlin school superintendent Geoff Andrews, who I had met in New York City at an Oberlin College event. After having grown up in Oberlin and been away for a number of years, Andrews had returned recently with the goal of not only improving Oberlin's schools but also "greening" them. Thinking he must know someone to approach about Oberlin real estate, I emailed him and he responded, "Real estate is done oddly in Oberlin, so a traditional agent may not be the best move. I'll have suggestions for you when we meet in March."

Over lunch we discussed our histories and the formidable challenge of transforming Oberlin to climate neutrality. As we finished, Andrews said he couldn't recommend any particular brokerage, but he did, however, believe he knew the perfect person to help us.

"David Sonner is eccentric, perhaps a bit strange to many with his unusual history here, but he knows Oberlin real estate like nobody else," Andrews said. "I grew up with his kids, so he's on the older side. He's been in Oberlin some 40 years and championed open-space and other environmental concerns. I guess you'd call him an environmentalist. I can't say if you'll hit it off, but it's the best I can do for you. I've arranged for him to meet us at the Oberlin Inn."

A man with graying hair and beard was sitting alone reading the *New York Times* as we entered the lobby. We caught his eye. With intent, he organized his lean, six-foot frame and rose to greet us. With the briefest of introductions, Andrews departed. Sonner and I stood for a moment sizing each other up and then sat as we moved quickly to what Mary and I sought. We wanted to live close to Oberlin, if not within city limits. Our first choice was to build a passive solar house on an interesting piece of property with enough space to plant a garden for raising much of our food. But we'd certainly consider a house that we could upgrade. Our budget was $300,000. We expected a bit more than $200,000 from the sale of our house in Troy and could add another $100,000 from savings.

Sonner took it all in and asked, "How much time do you have for a tour?"

"About an hour," I replied.

"Not enough time for the grand tour, but I'll show you the prospects."

We walked to Sonner's office—a 1992 Lincoln Continental Town Car—and headed out. He noted for sale a stately, early-twentieth-century house with a deep lot. Further down the road, he slowed as we approached a split rail fence, behind which stood two houses in disrepair. "The houses are a disaster, but this is a nice piece of land, four or five acres, that aren't on the market, but might be available," he said. "The talked-about price had been $275,000, but it's now $225,000."

I smiled and exclaimed, "David, you've got to be kidding! That's a budget breaker. What kind of house can we build with the remaining $75,000?"

He drove out of Oberlin city limits to the east and then south and west, but still within Oberlin jurisdiction. Off Route 20, and down a muddy quarter-mile driveway, he showed me a burned-out house on twenty acres of land with a pond. It was located just behind the commercial corridor and about three miles from the center of Oberlin. Not much of a neighborhood, but an attractive setting. We headed further west, and then north, passing several new houses growing out of a recently vacated corn field. One house stood half finished. Sonner remarked, "Developer just walked away. Ran out of money."

Turning east, Sonner commented on the beautiful fields and wooded hills, all owned by Oberlin College and not for sale. Just before reaching the city limits, he pointed out twelve acres that were for sale, six of scrub growth and six in open field. Less than half a mile from the town center green—known as Tappan Square—the site's location was quite appealing. We stepped from the vehicle and walked the length of the property, considering the possibilities. It was close to town and to the college's athletic facilities and had abundant space for a house and huge garden. The land was flat, with the east side bordered by a busy north-south highway. Through the scrub I could see the wreckage of an abandoned gas and auto-repair station. Lord knows what treasure of contamination lay in wait for the new owner, but the property was certainly worth further consideration.

We drove past Tappan Square and then west on Elm Street. Sonner pulled onto the side of the road across from the Lewis Center. All during his not-so-grand tour, we talked about our histories in Oberlin, his career as a book salesman, his efforts to preserve green space and to plant trees, and his overall concern for sustainability while attentively supporting appropriate businesses. He was an environmentalist for sure. Andrews had gotten it right. If anyone were to find an ideal site for us, it would be Sonner.

"I want you to find us our place," I said.

With a beguiling smile, he agreed. "I'll be your scout."

"Scout it will be," I affirmed, stepping out of his office.

As I walked to my car, I thought, "First step accomplished; we've got eyes and ears in Oberlin." It felt great! I'd found a kindred spirit to hold our hands into the unknown. Scout hadn't shown me anything that felt right, but Mary and I had only the vaguest image of what we wanted—we didn't even know if our dream home was possible in Oberlin.

What we did have were images of utopia—a small homestead with woods and open space, including a large garden to raise our food. We'd have fields to mow for mulching the garden. There'd be a sustainable yield of firewood that would provide the little energy necessary to heat our well insulated, passive solar house. We'd have a pond, or dig one, to raise fish and to provide water for the garden. Our new home would be a natural paradise where we'd reconnect with nature and share adventures with grandchildren.

Like the Bortons' house, ours would be dug into a hill; only the south side of the ground floor would be visible. The other sides would benefit from the earth's constant 55°F. The first floor, our living space, would be at grade on the north side. As we aged or became incapacitated, we'd have no stairs to climb. And we'd be within walking distance of downtown Oberlin and the college's many activities.

Looking back on our first meeting, Scout was polite and kept his assessment to himself. We had given him an equation with no solution. Oberlin's city limits form an irregularly shaped rectangle enclosing 4.4 square miles. For almost 200 years, people have been carving the space up for businesses and homes. The best of the not-so-desirable acreage of pin oak, elm forest on poorly-drained clay loam soils that became Oberlin had long been built upon or otherwise taken. The flat terrain proved ideal for bicycle transportation, but Mary, a native of Proctor, Vermont—the heart of the Green Mountains—didn't want her home in flat country. The highest hill in Oberlin is 25 feet, a dirt pile created in the 1930s by the excavation to install the college's old swimming pool. Scout had to have known that he'd be unable to deliver our dream home on a $300,000 budget. He could have broken the bad news at that first meeting, but I guess he'd been down this road before. He knew his new clients would figure it out soon enough.

Back in Troy, we exchanged emails as Scout prepared for our next visit in April. I arranged for us to stay with my longtime colleague and friend, David Benzing, a botanist and noted authority on bromeliads. Benzing came to Oberlin College in 1965, the year after I graduated. We got to know each other well when our son, Stuart, attended Oberlin in the early 1990s, and when I began to embrace David Orr's environmental vision. It was Benzing's class on plant systematics that captured Stuart's curiosity. Benzing recognized his potential and invited him to be his teaching assistant the next year. Stuart is now an evolutionary biologist at the University of Florida. As the years passed, Benzing and I came to appreciate our similar academic experiences and worldviews.

Spring had arrived when Mary and I drove into Oberlin and to Benzing's home. The several thousand daffodils that Benzing had planted in his woods were in bloom. It was raining, but the green and bright patches of yellow were uplifting, a sharp contrast to the dull gray-brown atmosphere of early March when I had met Scout.

We joined Scout the next day to learn about his findings. He had five houses and several pieces of land for our consideration. The land possibilities were mostly "not-yet-for-sale" parcels, except for the 12 acres just east of town and a block outside of Oberlin's city limits where no sewer would be available. However, the electrical utility companies that serve Oberlin proper and the surrounding areas do accommodate small renewable electrical systems such as solar photovoltaic panels (PV) or a wind mill.

This was significant, because we needed to have net metering; that's when the electric meter runs backwards or forwards depending on whether the house is exporting or importing electricity to or from the grid respectively. Photovoltaic panels are the most cost effective in northeastern U.S. climates with net metering because the best sunshine is from March through October. During those months, a modest 3 to 5 kilo Watt (kW) PV system can produce more electricity than is required. From November through February, however, grid power is necessary to make-up the shortfall.

We decided to return to the 12-acre plot to investigate. Scout iterated the pluses and minuses that he had pointed out on my tour six weeks earlier, and we walked the western boundary twice. Later, Mary and I went back to more carefully examine the neighborhood. We peered into scrub growth and at the occasional maturing tree, but the ground was too wet and the vegetation too dense to explore further. We really liked the six open acres—a fantastic garden site. We could become farmers! The plot was also close to town, a ten-minute walk. But it was extremely flat. The real deal breaker was the old auto repair shop. We didn't want toxic surprises.

Scout then drove us to another site, the northern edge of the $225,000 parcel he had pointed out in March.

"These five acres might be available," he said. "Doren Portman needs the money. He just sold his business property south of town, so the pressure may have eased, but I could pursue it if you want."

We got out of the car. It was cool and gray, but the rain had stopped. We looked at the two vacant houses nestled in the northwest corner, set back 30 feet from the road. To the south, the land sloped ever so gently toward Plum Creek, a small stream that flows through the south part of town, and then east into the Black River and on to Lake Erie. Plum Creek is channeled and difficult to access at this location, and has no eatable fish.

Perhaps two dozen trees, some exotic ornamentals and others native to Northern Ohio, grew around the houses and to the east in the area nearest the street. A meadow a few dozen feet wide ran down the east side to a wall of trees some six hundred feet to the south. West of the meadow, islands of trees blocked the view south, except for a narrow break through which another meadow was visible. The grass was tall and wet. We just looked. "Nice, but too expensive," I thought. Getting back in the car, Scout pulled out of the driveway and headed east.

Earlier, when we'd first joined up with Scout for lunch, he was apologetic. "Well, I'm afraid I haven't located anything that meets your requirements. I do have something that might work, but let's save it for last."

At this point, we had seen the several houses (too big, too small, poor orientation for solar) and the land (out of Oberlin city limits, too isolated, too flat, too expensive). The time had come for the surprise. With twinkling eyes, Scout smiled with the delight of a child about to reveal a just-found treasure.

"I was driving by here a week ago," he began. "Just ahead at the corner I saw a dumpster behind the house. I stopped and looked around. Nice property—almost two acres with about an acre of grass in the back that you could make into a garden. A local developer, Larry, bought it a few months ago and is fixing it up, making the original four apartments into three. The largest one that occupies the second floor would appear to meet your needs."

It, said Scout, had a large kitchen-dining room that was separated from a big living room by a fireplace that opened to both areas. South-facing picture windows offered beautiful views. Off the living room were three rooms for guests and two full baths while on the other side of the kitchen was the master bedroom and bath. Scout continued, "Larry is willing to sell as-is, but needs to know if you're interested because he's got crews working to make it ready to rent in June."

We parked in the drive. From the front, only the second floor was visible; it was dug into the hill above Plum Creek. Walking past a one-car garage, we saw a wide, deep expanse of grass ending in woods, with a pond to the east. It was exactly what we imagined; unfortunately, the pond wasn't part of the property.

Inside, several men were working on kitchen cabinets, plumbing, and wiring. Soon Larry arrived. He greeted us warmly and said he'd be around for an hour if we had questions. The dwelling was big: about 2,000 square feet on the second floor and 1,500 square feet on the first. We absolutely loved the second-floor layout; the kitchen-dining-living room complex was what we would have designed ourselves, and with a beautiful view to the south. The sun porch and deck off the master bedroom and dining area were in poor structural condition and needed to come down. Not a problem. We didn't need a sun porch and could replace the deck.

The first floor, however, was not what we wanted. The space was dark. Water damage was apparent, and we noted mold. A toilet had backed up and not been cleaned. Each of the apartments had its own furnace and hot water heater. Outside, the steps from the front entry down to the garage had shifted from ground movement, and a wall of the garage had been stabilized by vertical iron I-beams. The one-car garage had a low ceiling and was a jumble of junk; we wanted a two-car garage.

Although we observed the negatives—along with the warning signs of deeper trouble—we rationalized them away as manageable. We were bewitched by the land and the perfect layout of the second floor. The location, within Oberlin city limits and a mile from Tappan Square, could hardly be better. We loved Scout's surprise. He grinned with satisfaction.

We talked with Larry about what he had done and what we needed to do to achieve our vision. His position was clear. He would sell for a price that covered his investment, but he needed an answer in days, not weeks. He had a renovation schedule to meet because prospective renters were looking at the apartments. We promised to return the next day.

Over the following three days we counseled with David Benzing and Nathan Engstrom, Oberlin College's newly hired sustainability coordinator, and visited the house several times. Everybody loved the view and the possibilities. We talked of ways to make the house energy efficient. There was plenty of south-facing roof space for PV panels and a solar hot water system. We could increase insulation in the walls and roof to reduce heating requirements, which we could then meet with an airtight fireplace insert. We agreed that the sun porch had to go and that a new deck would be spectacular. Blindsided by the positives and possibilities, the first floor didn't get much attention. Nor did the structural issues we had noted on the first visit. On Monday evening we agreed on a price of $202,000.

We were excited, but guardedly so. This was happening fast and we were plagued by many unknowns. Again, that night I didn't sleep well. As dawn broke, I knew we had to follow up on Scout's suggestion and schedule an inspection.

Scout's inspector colleague was out of town, but after much effort he had chanced upon Bill Kozusko. Kozusko was booked for weeks, but luck was with us: he'd had a cancelation for Wednesday morning. It would cost $300.

The positives dominated our spoken analyses, but my subconscious had been working overtime. Tuesday night it reached a conclusion: we were stepping into a quagmire. We had been naïve—baited our own trap and stepped right into it. I don't know what had transpired in Mary's mind, but when I woke that Wednesday morning and gave her my assessment, she concurred.

Kozusko provided exactly what we needed. Fifteen minutes into the inspection, we all knew the house would fail with flying colors. Never before had Kozusko completely filled the defects space on an inspection form, but this time he needed the margins, too. I am a frugal person never wanting to waste my or anybody's money, especially hundreds of dollars. I was delighted this time to write Kozusko his $300 check.

We were back to where we were five, long days ago.

"How about a walk," I said to Mary and Scout. "I need to clear my head. Let's go down the street to Portman's place and look around."

We walked the short distance and down the driveway between the split rail fence. We glanced at the two vacant houses and headed into the rain soaked grass. Two mature oak trees over 3 feet in diameter dominated the western edge 100 feet south of the derelict houses. A huge upturned oak stump lay between the two and, to the south, a narrow alley of grass opened on a steeper slope down to more trees and patches of low vegetation. We walked through the alley and then left across a rise to the meadow that bordered the eastern edge of the property. Our feet were soaked. Mist rose from the vegetation, and the air was heavy. We didn't say much, just looked. I held Mary's hand and then put my arm over her shoulder. "That was close," I said softly. "You'd think we'd know better after all these years."

That night I slept well for the first time in days. During our nine-hour drive home, Mary and I replayed the week. Mistakes are easy to make.

Over the next days we came to accept that desirable land and house choices in Oberlin were few. Scout had shown us a teardown house that had a typical Oberlin inner-city lot—a narrow 66 feet wide by 240 feet deep—but if we removed the huge black walnut tree in the backyard, a decent garden became possible. Benzing had lived there in the 1970s and liked the location, a ten-minute walk from the college and the town center. The asking price was $80,000, plus another $10 to $15,000 to tear down the house.

And the Portman land might also be available. A spectacular property, the five-acres were a 20-minute walk or a five-minute bike ride from Tappan Square.

Everything else was out of town and mostly flat. Further away from Oberlin, all kinds of possibilities opened up. But in the end, we gravitated to being in town, where we'd have to drive little and be close to everything as we aged.

Perhaps building a solar home was not to be. Home values were similar in Oberlin and Troy, so it made good economic sense to simply buy a quality house in Oberlin and do what we could. Mary, however, was clear on her position: "If we are ever to build a solar house, it's now. We've talked about building a house like the Bortons' for years. We'd only have regrets." She was right, of course, but it would still be a monumental undertaking.

Perhaps Portman would be reasonable and come down a bit. After all, $45,000 an acre was pricy for Oberlin, where a quality house on a one-acre lot was selling for $250,000. We asked Scout to see what kind of offer Portman might entertain. He stuck to his price. Scout thought that $180,000 would be a fair price, so we offered $165,000, which included a 10 percent commission for Scout. Portman rejected the offer with nary a word, just disgust. He wanted $225,000. Period.

Mary and I returned to Oberlin for Memorial Day weekend. It had become clear to us that if we wanted to live within Oberlin city limits for net metering and city services—while still having a close connection to nature—the Portman land was the best possibility. Scout drew up another contract with an offer of $180,000 which Portman rejected again with no counter offer. Two days later we asked Scout to verbally offer the Portmans $190,000. They accepted the offer, but we would have to pay to take down the two houses and pay Scout's commission. We agreed to meet Portman on the property Monday morning, Memorial Day, to discuss the details.

It was a spectacularly beautiful spring morning. Portman and Scout were talking when we drove into the driveway. All of our dealings with Portman had been through Scout—terse, to the point, perhaps even gruff. I had no idea what to expect. I brought a jar of our "signature" blackcap jelly, a rather special treat for those who like it. Blackcaps are an early fruiting raspberry with small, black fruits composed mostly of seeds that get stuck in your teeth—the seeds are screened out in the jelly-making process. The taste is unusual, and it's virtually impossible to buy.

Portman was a big man, more than 6-feet tall and with the muscular frame of a physically active person. He greeted us with a warm smile, and I handed him the jelly, explaining that we'd made it from berries that grow behind our garage. He was clearly pleased. We chatted about gardening and our desire to have a large garden to grow much of our food. He was easy-going and not at all gruff. We agreed on the previously stated terms. We shook hands.

"You are the right people," Portman told us. "This is the best piece of property in Oberlin, and you're going to like it. If you need any help with trees, just let me know."

From an earlier conversation with Scout, we knew that Portman was hoping to keep his tree service trucks and equipment on the property for a while. I told him it was fine.

"I'd appreciate that," he replied. "Until you get here, I'll keep the grass and fields mowed."

Mary and I smiled. "That'll be great."

The Portmans had been shrewd negotiators and had gotten their price. Beyond the purchase price, we'd pay $13,500 to have the houses demolished and removed, and another $13,300 to Scout, for a grand total of $216,800. If Scout hadn't reduced his commission, our payout would have been just $2,500 shy of their asking price. We were paying a hefty price, but I couldn't fault the Portmans for not wavering—they knew well the treasure they had.

We drove back to Troy with a sense of amazement. It had been just six months since we'd made the decision to move to Oberlin, and we'd had the sketchiest of plans. Now, we were about to own the last of the best land in town.

Chapter 2:
Size Matters

Shaking Doren Portman's hand was a small gesture, but a big event. I liked him and sensed he was a good person who would become a friend. Little had we realized that beautiful Memorial Day morning just how much he would do for us—cutting down and trimming trees; chipping brush; hauling leaf-compost soil and cow manure to enrich our dense, clay soil; asking his friends to lend us a helping hand; and serving as a good natured companion and wise elder.

We were on an emotional high when we returned to Troy. With excitement, Mary and I shared our news, but it meant we were leaving our home, the place where we had spent half of our lives. Although our children were not born in Troy, they came of age there. It will be different now. Stuart and Virginia will visit our Oberlin home, but never again will they come home. Like a salmon swimming up the wrong stream, their senses will not call forth the deep memories of home. For them, the smells, the sights, and the lay of the land will just not be right.

We are sad for this, but our sadness was more distressing. After 33 years, our roots in Troy were deep. Many friends, especially those with whom we shared intimately in life's most meaningful relations, felt their pending loss as we did ours. Our exuberance was awkward, really out of place, as we began to disengage from a lifetime of commitment.

Deep friendships, however, are just that. Our closest friends immediately took an interest and provided advice. David and Harriet Borton became fully involved, offering a wealth of ideas and suggestions. They reviewed with us the most important things to get right. Orient the long side of the house to face south in order to maximize the availability of solar energy. Install the best windows you can afford to increase durability and to reduce energy use. Put the appropriate amount of mass in the house to make it more comfortable by dampening temperature swings. Create a very tight envelope—the floor, wall, and roof that surround the living space—with little air leakage and well-insulated walls and roof to curtail heat loss and gain.

I asked the Bortons and others about architects who were competent in passive solar design and green architecture, but nobody could provide fruitful suggestions. Then we had a stroke of good fortune when I emailed a colleague, the former Dean of Architecture at Rensselaer, who had returned to his home in Connecticut to continue his life's work of designing in nature's image and writing about it. Don Watson had been among several architects invited to bid on the environmental studies center at Oberlin. I had wanted him to land the job, but his student, Bill McDonough, did. Perhaps Watson would see my dream of making our house a little Lewis Center as a way to put his mark on Oberlin's architectural landscape. Watson agreed to brainstorm ideas. Over the phone, I sketched out our nascent plans for the house.

"What's your timetable?" he asked.

I told him we wanted to design the house within the next six months and begin building the following spring, with the goal of finishing at summer's end. Dead silence. I waited. Nothing.

"Don, are you there?" I asked.

Finally, he responded, "If everything goes exactly as planned, you'll be lucky to finish before winter."

Having no idea of what was involved, it seemed doable to me, but he was telling me that our schedule was overly ambitious. We talked more and Watson agreed to meet with us in a few weeks. He asked us to think about how we lived and how our house would accommodate our lifestyle. I set about writing an overall program for the project and a detailed room-by-room description—size, furniture, and uses of each room.

Even before our second and last child, Virginia, had left for college in 1992, Mary and I had friends and colleagues live with us for periods of time—sometimes several months. As Director of Environmental Science at Rensselaer, I would ask our long-term guests to make a donation to Rensselaer's environmental education endowment in return for free room and board. We'd enjoyed our guests and had simultaneously raised over $8,000 for the endowment. Having space in our new home for family, friends, and colleagues was a must.

In thinking about our future needs, I mentally evaluated our current home—a center hall colonial with a full basement and two attic bedrooms that had way too much space for the two of us. The two main floors provided 2,300 square feet of living space. On the first floor we had a large living room, a pleasant dining room, a horrible kitchen (with seven doors and two windows), a half bath, and a sun porch and deck. The second floor comprised four bedrooms, an unheated sun porch, and two full baths.

Mary and I pretty much lived in just four spaces: the bedroom/bathroom, the kitchen, the study (a bedroom), and, depending on the season, either the living room or the sun porch and deck. In the living room, we'd installed an airtight fireplace insert that provided half of the heat for our home. In cold weather, the living room was the only room we kept over 60°F; we sealed the rest of the house during the winter to reduce carbon emissions and to conserve energy and money.

> **Sidebar 1: McDaniel Energy Use in Troy, NY.**
>
> The bounty of our lives in the United States relies on enormous amounts of energy, mostly supplied by fossil fuels. Energy is a complex topic, and people do not easily understand the relationships among its units of measure (gallon of gasoline, barrel of oil, ton of coal, therm or hundred cubic feet of natural gas, kilowatt hour [kWh] of electricity, British thermal unit [BTU], joule, etc.). To allow comparisons, although imprecise, we can convert different energy uses to a common unit: the BTU, the amount of energy to raise one pound of water one degree Fahrenheit.
>
> To grasp the amount of energy used to create our lifestyles, let us consider million-BTU-equivalents: 1 million BTUs = 293 kWh of electricity = 10 therms of natural gas = ~8 gallons of gasoline = ~ 80 pounds of coal = ~ work one very fit human can do in a year. That is, a person steadily turning a generator by pedaling can light a 100 Watt bulb, and in a year produce 1 million BTUs (100 Watts × 10 hours per day × 6 days per week × 50 weeks per year × 3.412 BTUs/Watt hour = 1,023,600 or about 1 million BTUs).
>
> In 2007, Mary and I personally used about 380 million BTUs: electricity, 10 (3,000 kWh); natural gas, 90 (900 therms); wood, 80 (4 cords); gasoline for car and truck, 55 (440 gallons); gasoline for air travel, 40 (13,000 miles ÷ 40 passenger miles per gallon = 325 gallons); food, 80 (5,000 calories per day that take 10 calories of fossil fuels per calorie to put on our table); other, 25 (entertainment, clothes, health care, house repairs, and insurance at 1,000 BTUs per dollar spent). Of these 380 million BTUs, 180 were for operating our house: 10 from electricity produced by our PV system, 80 from the wood burned in our fireplace insert, and 90 from natural gas. The average household in the U.S. purchases 110 million BTUs.

It struck me that it was this pattern of living that had resonated with Mary and me in the house we'd almost purchased in Oberlin. As it turned out, that tumultuous experience was most serendipitous; the second-floor layout we had loved became our proposed design: we'd put our living space on the main floor, and guest rooms and work space on the ground floor.

The design brought together everything we had learned over the years and, more recently, from the Bortons:

- two floors;
- no basement or attic;
- rectangle of about 30 by 60 feet;
- a ground floor with earth built up on the west, north, and east sides about to the level of the second floor;
- adequate window area on the south side of both floors for sufficient passive solar energy to heat the house on sunny winter days;
- minimal window area on the north side;
- some window area on the east and west sides to provide daylighting, but limited to reduce heat gain in summer and heat loss in winter;
- south-facing roof windows in ceiling to provide daylighting in north end of spaces (kitchen, living room, bedroom) [we learned later these "roof windows" are called clerestory];
- deck at level of first floor, extending from middle of east side around 1/3 of south side with entrances from dining room and north end of east side;
- free standing garage about 20 ft by 30 ft with space for 2 cars and yard equipment, including small tractor;
- storage space above cars with access steps; and
- metal roof on house and garage.

The ground floor rooms for guests would include two bedrooms, a full bath, and a small kitchen, along with a root cellar and work room. The first floor—our living space—would have a master bedroom with a walk in closet and full bath, a kitchen, a dining area, a living room with a wood stove, a study, a half bath, and an entryway and closet. The kitchen, dining, and living rooms would have cathedral ceilings.

I sent a three page owner's program to Watson in late July in preparation for our meeting in Connecticut two days later (see Appendix A).

Watson's response, laced with dry humor and positive, insightful comments, was to become typical of hundreds of email exchanges over the coming two years.

"Carl and Mary: How thorough! Terrific! Only thing left out is to have you generate your electricity with that bike exerciser. And access off laundry to greenhouse and sundeck to allow fresh-air solar drying of clothes! There are actually many ideas that will come from designing the house to be self-sufficient in energy that is available on-site. ... Don."

Watson had arranged for us to see a high-performance green home in Bethany, Connecticut, that he had recently designed. Driving up a dirt road on the side of a glacial ridge, we turned into the driveway and up to the crest where the house stood, facing north. It was two-and-a-half stories with an attached two-car garage that had a loft connected to the house. An open field sloped away to the south from the edge of the woods that had been cleared to site the house. The regenerating forest that surrounded the imposing structure, except on the south, lessened its visual impact. Watson arrived. We walked around the house and down the field to a new horse barn, talking all the while.

This green project had started off at a modest 1,800 square feet, with the goal to obtain a LEED platinum rating (Leadership in Energy and Environmental Design). Watson had worked diligently with the owners to incorporate everything they'd wanted within the space constraints. As the project unfolded, however, its size grew and grew, eventually becoming 4,200 square feet on two floors in addition to a finished basement and an attic study, all for two people. The house was beautiful, with many green features—passive solar design; a tight, well-insulated envelope; bamboo floors; Hardiplank siding; and a deck made with plastic boards. Watson wanted us to see these features, but I sensed he had an additional message: size matters.

Over lunch in New Haven, Watson introduced us to the design process, sketching out several options based on the program I had sent to him with a footprint of 1,800 square feet. Then he got to the heart of the matter: cost. He literally did a back-of-the-napkin calculation and delivered his assessment: "You can't afford this on your budget of $300,000."

We didn't know the range of costs per square foot in Oberlin, but it was easy to see that Watson was right. The math was simple. Based on costs ranging from $100 to $150 per square foot, our 1,800-square-foot first floor, combined with a 1,000-square-foot ground floor (mostly for guests) set the range at $280,000 to $420,000. And we hadn't considered site preparation, landscaping, the barn, or fees for architectural and other services. Watson continued, "Now's the time for discipline. The pressure will only rise to increase the budget. Keep the belt tight. Let me work on it."

We continued in earnest that most procrastinated task—sorting through a lifetime of acquisitions and finding homes for things still useful. During much of the summer, Mary had been hauling things from the attic for our children and friends, with the rest going to charity. We packed our Toyota truck with items for our son's family: mattress and box springs, dresser, table and chairs, a huge container of Lego, dress-up clothes, and more. Despite serious efforts to avoid accumulating stuff, 40 years of family living have a way of filling attic, basement, garage, closets, and drawers to overflowing with all too often unneeded possessions.

The next day we headed west for St. Louis. We spent two days in Oberlin to close on the property and to check on the demolition and recycling of the two derelict houses. Portman procured a bid of $9,994 for the standard procedure of demolishing the houses and paying the landfill tipping fee. I thought that recycling seemed more appropriate, but how to do it?

I had been following the saga of three recent Oberlin graduates who were inspired by David Orr's teaching to take on the formidable task of revitalizing a block in downtown Oberlin that came to be known as the East College Street

Project. I contacted them for guidance. Ben Ezinga offered to oversee the demolition of the houses. The cost would be $11,500—a 15 percent premium over conventional demolition. But supporting the nascent, demolition-recycling effort in northeast Ohio seemed the right thing to do; it would be a net benefit to the larger society.

As it turned out, we were able to recycle 150 tons—or 60 percent—of the houses. It should have been closer to 80 percent, but a miscommunication resulted in 50 tons of clean plaster and wood ending up in a landfill. In the end, the price of demolition increased by $1,500 for fill necessary to make the old foundation holes safe.

We returned from St. Louis to Watson's simple diagram of our plans and his more complete financial analysis. His previous back-of-the-napkin assessment held water. Even at a modest $130 per square foot for the finished space and $43 per square foot for unfinished space, deck, and barn—construction costs totaled $375,700. That didn't include $25,000 in fees and thousands more for special features such as a metal roof, solar electricity, a central vacuum cleaner, and a heat recovery ventilation system.

Watson suggested we contact local builders for the current and projected cost range of residential construction. "If my assumptions are correct," he wrote, "the project program and 1,800 ft² footprint are not affordable within the $300,000 budget, but could be accomplished, with discipline, within a $400,000 budget."

He continued, "If push comes to shove (it always does), you might consider the following economical alternatives: (1) Make the house plan smaller, more compact in footprint. Reduce the footprint to 1,200 ft² or less. (2) Delete the garage and provide a carport. I hope this is a helpful reality check early on in the planning, when the greatest economies are found in such brainstorming discussion."

Sidebar 2: East College Street Project

David Orr's teaching and vision have influenced innumerable students across the country and at Oberlin. Most notable for the local community are Oberlin graduates Ben Ezinga (2001), Josh Rosen (2001), and Naomi Sabel (2002), who, even before graduation, were inspired to take on the formidable task of revitalizing a 2.5 acre site in the heart of Oberlin. In 2001 they began with no experience, no money, and no idea of the project's challenges. In Fall 2010, the East College Street Project was formally dedicated and won the Lorain County Beautiful Award for a new building with a budget over $3 million dollars—the actual budget was $17 million. It was the first major commercial development in the town center since 1958.

The three became known in town as "the kids" over the eight years it took to make their idealistic dream a reality. With majors in Economics, Environmental Studies, and Politics, but mostly captivated by the teachings of David Orr, they emphasized environmental sustainability and social values in the project. Some buildings on the site had been an eyesore for decades, but provided a unique opportunity to initiate revitalization in Oberlin that traditional commercial development had been unable to seize. The project comprises 32 residential units, with 21 condominiums and 11 units rented to households with the income limit being 60% of the median income; 18,000 square feet of street level retail office space for local businesses, including the Oberlin College Alumni Office and a college art gallery; and 10,000 square feet of open space for public use, as well as garage parking for residents. The project will most likely receive U.S. Green Building Council's LEED gold certification.

Richard Baron, a 1964 Oberlin graduate and chairman of a St. Louis development firm that specializes in mixed use urban development, worked with Sustainable Community Associates, the corporation the three formed, to devise an unbelievably complex financial package, including philanthropic financing to subsidize rental of low income housing, federal new markets tax credits for commercial projects in low income areas, and Oberlin's first tax increment financing bond in which taxes pay off the bond with taxes from increased property values resulting from the project.

The East College Street Project focused attention on renewal of Oberlin's downtown and may very well be looked upon in decades to come as the project that turned the corner for the city and college toward a more environmentally sustainable and equitable future.

Clearly, our budget and owner's program were drastically mismatched. We were beginning to fathom the costs for quality construction and how they compared to existing home prices. Our house in Troy was insured for 95 percent of replacement cost at $419,000. This total replacement cost of $440,000 for 2,300 square feet of living space in a market similar to that of northern Ohio should have been a wake-up call.

The brain, unfortunately, doesn't work that way. Fantasy dies slowly. For months, we had entertained the assumption that if our spacious, quality Troy house was worth $200,000, then adding another $100,000 should provide nicely for a smaller house in Oberlin with a few special features.

Watson's reality check was a clear call to scale back. His Bethany, Connecticut, clients had scaled up in the pattern typical of 20th-century Americans. We imagined building a house for the 21st century—a house that would last for more than 100 years and not be responsible for forcing climate change. Watson's recommendations were pretty severe: reduce the footprint by at least 33 percent and postpone or eliminate the barn. Our next owner's program went halfway with a footprint of 1,500 square feet and a reduced living space of 2,100 square feet: 1,500 square feet for us on the first floor and 600 square feet for guests on the ground floor. We delayed building the barn for a year, but kept the deck, metal roof, solar electricity, and a few other upscale features.

We circulated our updated owner's program to friends in Troy and Oberlin for comments and suggestions. The Benzings encouraged us to install a security system (easier to do during the construction phase), and urged us to consider a central heating system (we couldn't heat the house with the wood stove if we traveled in the winter) and central air for the increasingly hot summers that will come with global warming. They recommended ceiling fans for all bedrooms, a recycling area in the kitchen, and a wine cellar was an absolute necessity.

Other friends warned us of Oberlin's heavy clay soils that cause flooding in over 80 percent of basements, and suggested major attention to drainage around the foundation. The Bortons discouraged floor-to-ceiling windows because they let in too much light (heat) and require extensive roof overhang for summer shading. They suggested we install a variety of window sizes with some, but not all, operable because operable windows are likely more expensive and leak sooner than fixed windows; ceiling fans in all living spaces; and a central vacuum cleaner. Some suggested radiant heat in the ground floor cement slab and others recommended it for tiled floors, especially in the full bathrooms. Thus began the endless process of evaluating options, often about which we knew little to nothing.

I had been invited by Bluffton University to give a convocation address in August, so we again returned to Ohio and Oberlin. I had been asking friends in Oberlin about local builders. Several people had highly recommended Mac & Sons, including John Petersen, chair of Oberlin College's Environmental Studies program, so I scheduled a meeting. Mac & Sons specialized in major renovations, but Mac was interested in our project even though he had no passive-solar or green project experience. I asked about construction pricing in the area. "You can get junk for $90 per square foot," he replied. "A hundred fifty dollars per square foot gives you quality. Of course, if you get fancy, it will be more." His prices would be on the higher side, he said, but he guaranteed quality work.

Our impressions of Mac were good, and we promised to get in touch when we had more detailed plans. Conversations with other contractors yielded similar ranges, with $150 per square foot as the cost for conventional, quality construction. At $130 per square foot, Watson's estimate was low.

After a wonderful time at Bluffton, we arrived back in Oberlin. I wanted to finish fixing the split rail fence that had fallen down in several places. As we drove past the local elementary school, Mary said, "Stop! It's the first day of school. I want to see the school and meet some of the teachers. I'll walk to the land when I'm finished."

An hour later, as I was completing the fence work, Mary arrived with positive feelings about the school and more builder news. She had talked with the teachers who shared with her some builders' names. She also met the principal, Brian Carter, who interestingly, was building an Energy Star house. He had met a green builder, Mike Strehle, at Cleveland's Home and Garden Show.

"Brian thinks he's good, really knows what he is doing," Mary said.

"Is Strehle building a passive solar house?" I asked.

Mary was unsure, so I wondered, "How can he be a green builder without doing passive solar?" I doubted if Strehle was building LEED type houses, but the energy efficiency attained in an Energy Star house is a big part of green. I added him to our list of possible builders.

That afternoon, before we flew back to New York, we had scheduled a meeting with Chris, the most promising green builder we'd found. He had connections to the George Jones Farm, a not-for-profit organization dedicated to local food and sustainable farming practices that David Orr had been instrumental in founding. It was run by Brad Masi, a 1993 Oberlin graduate. Chris did energy-efficient building with an emphasis on local materials, including straw-bale construction, and had agreed to meet us at our site. Just before the appointment time, however, he called and canceled because of unexpected problems with one of his projects. We scheduled another meeting in September, but again a conflict interfered and he canceled. Disappointed, we concluded that Chris didn't have the time for or interest in our job to create the kind of builder-owner relationship we sought and believed necessary.

How would we find a competent green builder? Earlier in the spring an acquaintance of Portman's, Don Daily, had stopped by our site to introduce himself and Reddi-Wall, a type of insulated concrete form (ICF) made of expanded polystyrene blocks that are assembled like Lego and then filled with rebar reinforced concrete. I had heard of ICFs, but knew nothing about them. He showed us how they were assembled and gave us literature to read. It seemed worth further consideration.

We discussed our project and then a major concern I'd had about buying the property—how far from the street could the house be sited and still have access to the sewer? Scout and I had already conducted a simple check with a rope and level, but Daily offered to use his laser and send us precise measurements of the slope. This kind offer was among many that came our way from trades people, city officials, and others interested in our project. His measurements established that we could site the house as much as 150 feet from the street.

We appreciated Daily helping us out, and because he was pushing Reddi-Wall, I met with him several more times and sought his bid on the project. I had also met, through Ben Ezinga, Nick Zachos, a 28-year-old builder who was considering settling in Oberlin to build green houses. He liked our project, especially the possibility of using on-site trees to build the barn. Portman had told us that two mature red oak trees on the property and near a neighboring house required removal. Each was more than 3 feet in diameter and 75 feet tall, so we discussed making a post and beam barn from them.

The desire to lumber these oaks led to conversations with Scott, who lives in Oberlin and has a portable sawmill. I knew nothing about milling trees or building a post and beam structure, so I asked many questions of Scott and others. Over the fall, Scott came to the site several times, and we laid plans for him to mill the oaks on-site for the barn. Responding to Don Watson's insistent advice to reduce costs, we talked with several people about having a community barn raising. They liked the idea and the community rapport it would foster. The straw bale barn at the Jones Farm was a recent community project fondly remembered.

Driving to the airport, I felt good about the Oberlin community and the generous, helpful people we were meeting. Nevertheless, I was anxious and worried about finding a builder. Chris had been a major find, but my vibes about him were not positive. We'd had good interactions with Mac & Sons, Don Daily, and Nick Zachos, and Mary had just found Mike Strehle. But could any of them build a solar house that was climate neutral within our budget? We had to make so many decisions about things for which we knew nothing. It was great to be an optimist, but we all know horror stories. Things can, and do, go wrong. Living 500 miles away and having full-time jobs certainly wouldn't help.

Fall semester had begun for Mary and me, drastically diminishing our discretionary time. My teaching load had been doubled for reasons never adequately explained, but likely because those in charge needed someone to teach the course and considered my educational and environmental research of minimal or no value. Needless to say, the juggling act became ever more problematic: major educational and writing projects were jettisoned, and all things associated with preparing for retirement and moving were curtailed. Teaching and house design consumed the fall.

Watson had held our hands for about two months and convinced us to shrink our footprint to 1,500 square feet. We had checked each other out and liked what we saw. In early September, we signed a Memorandum of Agreement with Watson to provide an Initial Design and Energy Analysis (IDEA).

> *The following items will be addressed in the IDEA Study:*
>
> *(1) Design studies showing options of plan (room locations and furniture sizes), sufficient for square foot budget comparison of options.*
> *(2) Design sketches indicating options for design and appearance of the home.*
> *(3) Outline specifications of recommended materials and systems.*
> *(4) Energy 10 analysis of options, indicating options of % glass, mass and insulation.*
> *(5) Outline "green checklist," referring to LEED-H and comparable rating checklists.*
> *(6) Preparation of Preliminary Contractor Set including drawings and outline specifications sufficient for contractor review. This set will allow contractors to provide estimates and for you to select a contractor for a negotiated construction contract. This also enables you to define follow-on steps required to complete contract documents (architectural services, engineering, construction administration and related fees). Subject to requirements to be defined, the follow-on steps may be contracted through a local professional or through the office of Donald Watson.*
>
> *My fixed fee to accomplish the IDEA study: $6,000.*

He would begin in mid-September and finish by mid-November.

At this time, Watson also responded to our second owner's plan based on $150 per square foot for high-quality space on the first floor, and $100 per square foot on the ground floor. We could achieve substantial savings on the ground floor by using the concrete slab as the floor surface and by foregoing upscale features like a full kitchen and tiled shower—giving an estimated cost of $399,000. The cost did not include barn, construction documents, administration, filing fees, site preparation, or landscaping, estimated at another $61,000. We also needed to consider a 10 percent overrun as standard. These estimates put our completed project, not including land, at $506,000!

On September 7, we sent the first of many update emails to Watson. This included 12 items summarizing suggestions and queries from colleagues, questions on radiant heating, expense for various types of deck material, the idea of a central vacuum system, a pantry next to the kitchen, a mudroom only on the ground floor, and ceiling fan locations.

I didn't expect a response that evening, but checking email before hitting the sack, I found a detailed message sent at 11:25 PM. After a few general remarks about process, Watson had answered each question. He was more than clear on his view of a central vacuum system: "Just thinking how thermo dynamically absurd it is to pick up thinly disbursed dust and blow it through little pipes to a central tank. Uses much more power than the sun provides compared to ease of cleaning with conventional methods. How about a Shaker broom?" Radiant floor heating didn't fair well either. Watson viewed that as a costly luxury.

Watson never ceased to amaze me with the speed of his responses; so much that Mary and I began to venture guesses—not in days or hours, but in minutes—as to when he'd email back. If I didn't know better, I'd swear he had his computer hardwired into his brain.

Watson's latest cost estimate of $506,000 called for major scale-back; however, it wasn't getting much traction on our side. Fantasies, after all, are beliefs fashioned by the brain for the convenience of the believer. I'm sure Watson knew change would come: the pot had to get bigger or the house smaller. The problem, and beauty, of an open mind is that demonstrable facts have a way of eroding false beliefs, especially if the brain is forced to place the fantasy against brass tacks.

In the spring of 2007, at a green-building fair in Troy, I had purchased a book, *Your Green House: A Guide to Planning a Healthy, Environmentally Friendly New Home* by Alex Wilson. Summer had passed without reading it, but then I received an email announcing a book signing by Alex Wilson at a Troy bookstore.

Wilson and his wife are deep into sustainable living. Their newsletter and website are a premier source of information on green materials for the building industry. After his talk, I told Wilson about our plans and asked him to rank order the most important things we needed to consider to be as green as possible.

"First and most important is to make it as small as possible," he said. "No matter what you do with a four or six thousand square foot house, it isn't green. Second is the envelope. Make it as tight as possible and insulate it very well. After that, everything else pales by comparison."

Sidebar 3: Human Fantasy and Biophysical Reality

Continual population and economic growth are impossible on a finite planet. At the present annual growth rate of 1.2%, the human population will equal the mass of the Earth in about 2,500 years. The value of a dollar invested at the time of Christ at 3% annual growth would today be greater than the current economic wealth of all humanity. Exponential growth and its consequences are understood by few people.

Ten thousand years ago, several million hunter gatherers used about 0.001% of the energy acquired by plants on the land, while today seven billion people use about 40% of this plant energy. That is, modern humanity has 40,000 times the impact of hunter gatherers on Earth's ecological resources.

Hunter gatherers used no commercial energy (fossil fuels, hydro, wind, nuclear) while modern people use 500 quadrillion BTUs (a quadrillion, or quad, is 10^{15}: 1 with 15 zeros after it). The use of this commercial energy enables each person today to be 60 times more effective in using Earth's resources than hunter gatherers. Overall, the human impact has exponentially increased to be now 2,400,000 times (60 × 40,000) greater than it was 10,000 years ago.

Hunter gatherer societies had the capacity to alter local ecosystems and to play a major role in the extinction of the large animals (megafauna) in Australia, North America, New Zealand and numerous other smaller islands, thereby radically altering continental and island ecosystems. Modern humanity's impact is global: climate destabilization, destruction of innumerable ecosystems, mass extinction of plants and animals, release of lethal amounts of untold pollutants, and rearrangement on a continental scale of the circulation, occurrence, and distribution of water. Our implausible belief in unlimited growth will likely undo civilization and much of Earth's bountiful life among which humanity has thrived.

My long relationship with David Borton had led me to place energy use and envelope at the top. For Alex Wilson, size trumped everything. For a moment I pondered this and then realized that Wilson, Borton, and Watson had no conflicts in their assessments. The bigger the house, the more one needs, not only to build the house, but also to live in and maintain it. As Watson had instructed, cost is inversely proportional to size; the same is true for energy to heat, cool, and light the house. Perhaps the envelope is not quite as important as size; however, because heating and cooling consume most of the energy we use over the lifetime of a house, including the energy embodied in the materials that make up a house, the envelope stands far above all other considerations, except size.

Four days later we rendezvoused with Watson in Winsted, Connecticut. It was a Norman Rockwell autumnal day—temperatures in the low 70s, wisps of high clouds with ever so slight a breeze, and trees just beginning to reveal the reds and yellows of the season. We met on the town green under a large maple tree, where we placed a folding table with chairs, and feasted on a tasty lunch, mostly consisting of produce from our garden. We exchanged gifts. Don presented us with his classic book, *Climatic Design*, inscribed, "At the beginning of the great adventure! Don Watson 9-21-07." We gave him recently harvested potatoes, squash, and carrots, along with a jar of our blackcap jelly, like the one that sealed the deal with Portman.

After lunch, Watson took out three options for our consideration. Option A was the initial design with an 1,800 square foot footprint. We had moved on—fantasy was meeting brass tacks. Holding the other two unrolled options, he explained, "I've been able to get you everything you wanted except your study on the main floor. But I've found a solution, a cozy dormer study above the front entryway."

He unrolled Option B, a compact, split-level, two-floor design on a 1,056 square foot footprint with the upper level as our living space and a tiny study in a dormer over the front entryway. Option C was similar to B in footprint, but with our living space on the lower level and a cathedral ceiling in the lower level living room with upper level guest facilities overlooking the living room. Watson explained the cost savings with the smaller footprint and split-level design. He had edged us close to our $300,000 budget with Option B. Option C struck us as a summer cottage with its openness between floors. This openness had appeal, but it wouldn't give us or our guests the degree of privacy we sought. Watson wanted us to thoughtfully consider Option C because, among other things, we could most likely implement it on or under budget. But, we really liked B.

We were excited and overwhelmed. It was a magical moment—the kind you can never plan, but must treasure, for they are rare. Our emotions and intellects had harmonized—I knew we'd make sweet music. Watson was the master I believed him to be, not only as an architect, but also as facilitator. He had created a design that honored our desires within budget. It was compact—he had reduced our footprint by 40 percent and brought the cost down significantly. But would it really work for us?

As we drove home in a euphoric state that memorable fall afternoon, I'm quite sure that neither Mary nor I grasped the implications of the size decision we'd just made. Oberlin building code requires a minimum footprint of 1,000 square feet. We were just 56 square feet above that minimum. And with foot thick walls for adequate insulation, our inside footprint was 924 square feet or 60 square feet less living space than conventional construction with the same footprint. We wouldn't appreciate fully the joys and constraints small bestows until much later.

Chapter 3:

Wants and Needs

B y the time we arrived home in Troy, Option C was out. We wanted greater privacy for us and our future guests that distinctly separate floors would offer. For our living space, we wanted the better view and daylighting on the upper floor. We had also rejected a split-level design. First, and for reason enough, Mary disliked split-level houses. It also meant climbing a half-flight of stairs to reach our living space. This certainly was not a problem now, but we intended to grow old and die in this house; it made sense to make our living space as accessible as possible. We knew the budget would go up and that major design changes were required, but we also understood that time and effort to modify drawings were minimal compared to the costs of physical changes later.

We cleared the drop leaf table in our living room and unrolled Plan B. Mary had a partly used notebook left by one of her students that we placed on the table and labeled "Floor Plan: Comments and Suggestions." We showed everyone who came to our home the plan and asked them to log their suggestions or ideas. Whenever I had a few spare minutes, I'd review the notebook and plans, enter anything new that came to mind, and make pencil changes where appropriate.

I had to be in Oberlin the last weekend in September for Alumni Council weekend. I stayed with Marta Laskowski, a plant biology colleague whom I'd met when she was at Williams College, and her husband, Ken Stanley, a former computer programmer who shifted his career to education and obtained grant funds to facilitate the transition of at-risk, preschool children into grade school. Stanley was keen on Mary coming to Oberlin because he wanted to involve her in his program.

Good citizens with environmental concerns, they have only one child and were the second family in Oberlin to put a PV system on their roof. And they walk or ride their bicycles everywhere.

While in town, I was also to meet with Peter Crowley, an Oberlin resident who was about to break ground on an energy-efficient house that Joe Ferut designed and Calvin Smith was to build. Scout had brokered the sale of the five-acre plot the previous spring and had introduced me to Crowley via email.

Crowley and I arranged to meet Saturday at one of his children's soccer games. It was a brisk morning, and we huddled on the sidelines to examine design plans, energy calculations, and costs. I was overwhelmed; Crowley exuded excitement.

His wall design was similar to the Bortons' house, built almost three decades earlier. Two 2×4 walls were separated by five inches, for a total width of 12 inches of insulation. The five inches of insulation in between the studs of the two walls would significantly reduce heat loss by thermal bridging (heat loss through the studs).

The insulation comprised one inch of closed cell foam to seal the wall and prevent air movement. Inside the foam were 11 inches of damp spray cellulose, giving the wall an R value of 48. R value is the resistance of a material to heat flow; the larger the R, the greater the resistance and the smaller the heat loss. A standard 2×4 wall with fiber glass insulation has R-13 and major thermal bridging.

The roof was similarly insulated, but with 15 inches of cellulose to give an R-65. Ferut's engineer had calculated energy for heating the 3,500 square foot house to cost $380 annually—less than 20 percent of the cost to heat the average U.S. home this size. Crowley was also incorporating other green features—bamboo flooring, an energy recovery ventilation system, structurally insulated panels—but he did not design it for passive solar. As with the Carter house that Mike Strehle was building, I wondered, "How can it possibly be truly green and not be passive solar?" Nevertheless, I was interested in talking with Smith and Ferut. I scheduled a meeting with Smith for Monday morning.

I drove to our site on Sunday afternoon. Fall was in the air, warm and sunny, and I walked down the side of our property to the grassy knoll situated above a small prairie of grasses and autumn wildflowers. I lay in the grass, soaking up the sun's warmth and gazing idly into a blue sky broken by puffy clouds. Birds flew overhead and in the field below butterflies and other insects gathered the last of the year's pollen and nectar. I could hardly believe this was ours. I lay quietly communing with the simplicity and elegance of the nature about me. Soon I longed to share the emotions that swept over me. I sat up and called Mary, Stuart, and then Virginia. It was a magical moment of innocence that I treasure for its emotional truth. But, all too quickly I abandoned quiet rapture for the required.

Portman had kept animals in the past, and a small corral and shed remained at the edge of the wooded area that separated the meadow from the break in the trees. The shed's roof kept out rain and the door sort of closed. It had become my place to stash tools, water, and working clothes. I walked to the shed, changed into work clothes, and set to seeding the ground area that had been disturbed with the removal of the derelict houses.

Monday morning I headed for Smith's home in LaGrange, a small town southeast of Oberlin. His house is in the style of a southern mansion, with tall pillars in the front that seemed ostentatious and a bit out of place. Welcoming me with a big smile, Smith cordially ushered me into his office off the main entryway. He is a big man with a presence that conveys confidence and authority. You know he is in charge. I told him what we sought to accomplish, and he related his building career.

Until recently, Smith had been a big-time developer responsible for hundreds of homes, and he had organized the construction of several buildings that demonstrated solar and green design. But things came undone; his marriage fell apart. He was now returning to where he started and doing what he loved: building individual custom homes. A hands-on supervisor, he subcontracted most of the work, but was on-site at least once a day. His own house had been in his family for a long time and, rather than build a new one, he had renovated it. Immaculate with exquisite craftsmanship, beautiful furniture and art, the home's style may have been out of place in LaGrange, but it and Calvin complemented each other.

I departed elated and relieved, convinced that I had finally found a builder with the background to understand what we wanted, as well as the connections and experience to guide our aspirations to reality. I liked Smith's forthrightness, and although he appeared a little too much like the boss who knew what to do, I believed we could develop a productive working relationship.

I drove back to Oberlin, changed clothes, and finished seeding and spreading straw. A week later Scout reported that a lush carpet of green concealed the bared earth where the houses once stood.

Meanwhile, Don Watson wanted our feedback on his floor plans by mid-October. The notebook in our living room had half a dozen pages of comments, and we had marked up Plan B with modifications. I translated these and our numerous conversations with friends into six pages of single-spaced comments, suggestions, and questions. We moved, eliminated, and added doors. We relocated the ground-floor kitchenette to make the piping system more compact. We expanded the study to accommodate a fold-down bed and moved the stairs to provide an entry hallway into what we called the "great room"—a living-dining room combination with a cathedral ceiling. We addressed our concerns about insufficient storage space by adding a ladder-accessible storage area over the master bedroom closet and the bathrooms on the second level and suggested widening and lengthening the house by several feet to give us a bit more space. We eliminated the counter separating the kitchen from the great room, replacing it with a moveable cart. We suggested ash for our hardwood floors because we loved the flooring in Oberlin's Black River Café that we thought was ash (it's actually hickory). With these changes, and many more, we transformed Plan B into a layout we really liked.

I emailed the six-page document to Watson. True to form, he sent his reply 16 minutes later. "Thank you, Carl. Really nice job, clear and helpful. I will need a few weeks before getting the second round to you, but I hope to be able to get something to you prior to Nov 1. All best wishes, Don."

Eleven days later, we sent Watson a written description for the barn. He replied, "Carl: All duly noted. Room for squirrels in garage? DW."

Aside from the humor, these simple replies were much different than Watson's earlier ones. He gave no commentary nor provided specific responses. Without realizing, Mary and I had moved into the next phase of design. The owner's programs, phone conversations, email exchanges, and our input to Plan B had provided him with all he needed to create floor plan options for us to consider and iterate until we optimized all trade-offs.

In early November, a package arrived from UPS—an 11 X 17 inch booklet of site plans, floor plans, cross sections, and elevations. Watson had included the three options he'd presented at our September meeting under the maple tree in Connecticut, plus two more floor plans, D and E. We studied the new options carefully, but didn't see them as improvement; we still really liked Plan B with our modifications, and I emailed Watson to that effect.

His immediate response was instructive, "Carl and Mary: I took a chance in sending the plans without a full description, which I prefer to communicate verbally. May I ask that you withhold judgment until I have a chance to fully describe the options? There are advantages in each of the four options. I try not to favor one or the other, but to let each one teach me something I had not seen previously. The agenda for [our phone call] tomorrow night should simply be a chance for me to communicate the options. Then, you and Mary will have as much time as you need to mull these over, and more. DW."

The next evening, during a 90-minute phone conversation, Watson walked us through the four plans, explaining his choices and how each informed the design process. Mary and I tried to have open minds, but we had gone into the phone call convinced that our modified Plan B was the one we wanted. Again, Watson revealed his skill as a facilitator and his capacity to integrate our multiple ideas into an optimized outcome. After our conversation we wrote, "You have provided another most creative and appropriate design. We'll continue digesting and blending. I do believe we'll have a composite design soon, as we have spent many hours thinking on the design and site."

Six days later we emailed our response to the four floor plans. "Mary and I have spent many hours talking about the plans. Your creativity has again delivered an exquisite design that embodies all that has gone before. We really like what you've created in Plan E. We have several modifications and would like to transfer a few aspects of Plan D as indicated below."

Watson's response revealed that we had redeemed ourselves. "Thank you. I am booked solid… I cannot focus on your project until week of Thanksgiving. I looked quickly at comments and all good, helpful, and on its way to a great design that suits." The design was, indeed, progressing. Our response was down by half from the last time to three, single-spaced pages with 29 specific changes or recommendations.

Watson had offered to be our architect for the entire project, and I really wanted him. We had developed an excellent working relationship. Even more to the point, I knew we would never find another architect with his facilitation skills and depth of knowledge about solar and green building. I was, however, uncomfortable about not having an architect near Oberlin. If we did contract Watson, he'd be in Connecticut and we'd be in New York—with no one on-site in Ohio. We not only needed a builder, but also a local architect to hold our hands and guide the project.

Joe Ferut was Peter Crowley's architect. Highly recommended, I scheduled November meetings with him and with builder, Mike Strehle, in Oberlin. I drove to Strehle's house northwest of Oberlin off Portman Road, named for a relative of Portman's. Strehle lived by himself in a house he had built just before the recession and had been unable to sell. It sat in a typical cornfield development—two-story houses each on large flat lots, well separated from other houses.

Strehle was of average height, lean, and young. His cat greeted me as we walked toward the dining room table. He tersely described his background in building. He had begun learning the trade as a teenager and earned an associate's degree in building science, gaining an interest in energy efficiency at college. He worked for builders in several capacities, then earned a second associate's degree in business management and opened his own business, All Seasons Builders.

Strehle enjoyed having two projects going at the same time, and he usually had one or two people working for him. Although his expertise was carpentry, he was familiar with all aspects of house construction. Like Don Dailey, he advocated Reddi-Wall foundations and was using it currently in two houses he was building. All the houses he built were tight and Energy Star certified.

I showed him Plan B to illustrate what we wanted to do. He hadn't heard of LEED, but was curious. I don't think he'd thought much about green building practices or that he advocated for them, but neither did he scoff at them. It was clear, however, that he was interested. I told him I'd be in touch when we were further along in design.

Driving back to Oberlin, I realized that I didn't know what to make of Strehle. I wasn't completely familiar with the requirements of an Energy Star certified house, but Strehle understood the importance of energy and a tight envelope. He wanted to learn new things and LEED had caught his interest. At the same time, he wasn't a green builder like Chris, nor did he overtly promote green building practices. In temperament he was the opposite of Calvin Smith: soft-spoken and terse, and he didn't show his emotions. His disposition was so even that when Mary asked about him, I described him as "level, just level."

On Monday I met with Ferut and his colleague, Mark Hoberecht. Six-feet tall and lean, Ferut had been a conventional architect until several years earlier, when he realized that climate change and other environmental concerns demanded radical new approaches in architectural practice. Hoberecht, who has a day job as a NASA engineer, champions the passive house movement in the United States that is attempting to replicate the Passivhaus crusade in Germany, an advance that has made energy efficiency there a fine art. Ferut and Hoberecht were keen on using straw bale insulation to raise R values so high that "a candle could heat a house."

I showed them Plan B and discussed our interest in having a local architect take over once Watson completed the schematic design. We then drove to the site and walked the land. Ferut was impressed and sent an email the next day: "Thanks for all the time you spent with Mark and me yesterday. Great site; looking forward to discussing more with you and Donald Watson. I had a chance to look at Donald's website; it will be an honor to work with him." Ferut, at age 50, was in the prime of his career. A hard time to make radical changes; I knew he could learn much from Watson.

No other local architect who championed green building had come to our attention. Peter Crowley solidly recommended Ferut, and my interactions with him confirmed what Crowley had said.

Over the next two months, through numerous emails and phone calls, we worked out the contract details with Joseph Ferut Architects and Associates. Like the land-purchase-mortgage process, it was complex and in unfamiliar language. Mary and I did our best to understand the meaning of each item and heeded expert advice from Watson and Ferut. We signed in January, trusting all would go well.

Thanksgiving was upon us, and I had nine days free from teaching to spend in Oberlin.

The Saturday morning before Thanksgiving I headed west with our Toyota truck loaded with hardwood palates, a chain saw, maul, and wedges. If all went as planned, we'd be in our new home in a year, heating it with firewood from our land. Weather permitting, I'd begin clearing trees from the pond area and get next winter's firewood drying.

I arrived in time to drop the palates at the site before dark and then drove to the Benzings' home. They were in Florida, but were pleased to have us use their house for our Thanksgiving holiday. Over the next four days, when not on-site, I met with various people, including the four builders. Although all were pleased to see the updated plans, I sensed that Don Daily was more interested in doing a Reddi-Wall foundation than the entire project. Ferut and I discussed the project and contract, and made plans to visit an under construction, straw bale house they had designed in Cleveland.

As I did during all of my Oberlin visits, I had a meal or two with Scout to discuss environmental issues and the latest on sustainability in Oberlin. In the spring I had given him my two books, which he read. He then gave copies to Oberlin's public library and to a few people in town. I learned more of his environmentalism from articles he had written and our many discussions. During the summer, Oberlin's city council had voted 4 to 3 to commit the city to purchasing for 50 years electricity generated from a proposed coal-fired power plant. Scout had formed a coalition running for city council to reverse that decision and replace coal-produced electricity with renewable sources. And they had been elected. This was indeed good news. With coal electricity out of the way, the city and college could work on climate neutrality and other sustainability concerns.

The weather held warm and dry until Wednesday afternoon. I felled half a dozen trees, then cut, split, and almost stacked it all on palates before the rain began. I was tired and wet, but pleased; I had harvested the cord of firewood we'd need next winter. It was about 8 p.m. by the time I arrived at the Benzings' house. Mary, Virginia, and Virginia's friend Becky were due to arrive in Oberlin that night.

Virginia and Becky had come to see the land and to help clear trees from the future site of the pond, but the rain persisted. As we walked the land the next day, Virginia pointed out native plants and invasive species. Becky, a forester, marveled at the size of the trees—maple, oak, and ash—and commented on the number of board feet they'd yield. Virginia was more interested in the potential for making maple sugar; Portman had tapped several dozen maple trees in the past, and many were still there.

Friday was sunny, but cool for our introduction to straw bale construction. The home's walls were very thick, making

> **Sidebar 4: Carbon Dioxide Released from Energy Sources**
>
> Each basic type of fossil fuel (coal, gasoline, oil, and natural gas) releases a different amount of CO_2 per million BTUs and, within each type, there are differences; however, between-type-differences are much greater than within-type-differences. For one million BTUs, average values in pounds of CO_2 released are: coal, ~210; gasoline and oil, ~160; natural gas, ~120. Coal and to a lesser extent the other three also release a variety of additional substances and particulates, many of which are toxic.
>
> In addition to the CO_2 released by burning fossil fuels, the mining of the fuel and the facilities required to make useful energy from it consume energy and impact the environment and humanity.
>
> Nuclear, wind, hydro, and photovoltaic panels release no CO_2 in the actual generation of useful energy; however, each technology uses energy in making and operating the infra-structure employed for providing useful energy. And each has impact on the environment and risks for humanity. The analyses are complex; however, nuclear accidents are so catastrophic that no commercial insurer will take on a nuclear plant and nuclear waste disposal is a serious unsolved problem, thereby making nuclear energy economically not viable. Society cannot afford the risks, especially when other options are available.

for deep, 18-inch windowsills. Clay-plaster walls reminded us of southwestern architecture and Navaho pueblos. The house itself was stuffed into a small city lot—a country setting would have been more appropriate.

Neither Mary nor I knew exactly what to make of it. The straw-bale style was too unfamiliar, not what we were accustomed to in the northeast. At the same time, it utilized local materials, provided a high R value, and Ferut was using it in houses he designed. We decided to consider it.

Don Watson had taken a fancy to our blackcap jelly. In appreciation for all he was doing for us, I'd send him a jar from time to time. By mid-December he was overwhelmed with projects, and figuring he needed a pick-me-up, I mailed him a big jar.

"Hi Carl and Mary," he emailed. "Santa Claus delivered an advance jar of McDaniel jam, placing me deeper in debt to your gracious generosity. Our patient is still on the operating table, but doing well. The surgeon is remaining sober, despite holiDAZE, and is expected to finish up on or before December 21. And, I expect to be able to send progress sketches by JPEG for telecon discussion on or about Thursday this week. Don." HoliDAZE it would be.

Three days later another email came, accompanied by a file titled Floor Plan F. "Hi, Carl: In case you want to take a preview. Still fine-tuning plans. I THINK I have responded to each of your requested revisions per your November summary. See you tomorrow."

Five hours later, he sent another message. "I am working thru Saturday night and Sunday morning, continuing to study and refine. Therefore, don't waste too much time reviewing the plan I sent by email. I have since made additional revisions."

This time, he'd attached a cost analysis for Plans A, B, and C, as well as the new plan he labeled F for "FINAL!" For the house only, cost estimates were: A = $342,000; B = $288,000; C = $282,000; F = $342,000. Adding the costs for barn, deck, and basic landscaping (patio, berm walls, pond, etc.), Plan F rose to $484,000.

Watson cautioned, "Don't jump off the bridge just yet. The square foot cost comparison can be misleading and is principally useful to allow comparison between plans. But the high cost (present since the beginning) continues to force 'cut' and 'defer' decisions throughout."

The next day, before we left for Connecticut to meet with Watson, his newest version arrived. All changes looked great—a revised layout of rooms on the ground floor, a cathedral ceiling in the kitchen, an enlarged study, a bigger loft above the master bedroom, and bookcases on the staircase leading to the study. Watson concluded, "Alas, I have accounted for every square inch of space. More improvements to follow."

I had never been to Watson's house and was curious. What kind of place does a renowned award-winning architect have? I am not sure what I expected, but part of me had anticipated an architecturally unique, awe-inspiring dwelling. Instead, his home was a basic split-level at the end of an ordinary street located in the 100-year flood plain of the Pequonnock River. Watson's home embodied his worldview of simplicity and connectedness to nature rather than reflecting anything architecturally special. His deck overlooked the ponds of Twin Brooks Park. From conversations and emails, I knew he often walked the flood plain as he welcomed the dawn. It wasn't surprising that his architectural business is named *EarthRise: design inspired by nature*.

On the second level of his house, paperwork and evidence of various projects covered all surfaces. In the living room, near the airtight woodstove that warmed the house, his son worked on computer simulations for a joint project. Watson had cleared half the dining room table for our discussion of floor plans. He had, of course, tweaked the design sent earlier in the day. We liked it. Our only reservation was the loss of space in the great room caused by stairs placed on the south side of the house. We wanted to lengthen and widen the house by several feet. It was not to be.

Watson reminded us of the elegance and redeeming value of small spaces, and of our budgetary constraints. Based on our input, he was confident that the great room would be a fantastic space and accommodate 99 percent of our needs. During warm months, the deck would double our entertainment space, and in the winter we'd be a bit cozier. Although Watson could be direct, his style was story and humor. He didn't say he wouldn't do it. His message, however, was clear when he said, "How can we ever attain sustainability if we build to accommodate the one in a hundred event?" Wants are not necessarily needs.

With floor plans in good order, the ensuing week was a blur of emails and JPEG images of choices for the exterior of the house. Section and elevation diagrams illustrated window styles and placements, roof patterns, and how the house would relate to the ground. I had favored a simple roof line with no corners or valleys: easy to build, economical, and less likely to leak than more intricate designs. The elevations in our original plans had called for gable roofs for the study in the front and for the stairs to the study in the rear. But the complex roof was gone by December 28. The only complexity to the rectangular house and simple roof line was an overhang to cover the extension of the stair landing between the first and second floors that Watson had added for space for plants and a chair from which to enjoy the best view in the house.

The next day brought radical revisions. At 4:46 a.m. Watson wrote, "Midnight inspiration has prompted return of the design to OR [operating room]. A much improved elevation/section study in the works, saving lots of dough, more simpatico, and with gable roof for Mary."

This was followed at 10 a.m. with, "I am studying an alternate to the roof lines. My guess is that it will potentially save $30K. It is worth the additional study time, because Budget Meanie looms around the bend. Stay tuned."

Watson had discovered a major design flaw. We had wanted south-facing clerestory windows in the great room. To accommodate them, the ceiling was more than 19 feet high. As Watson wrote, "the volume of space created by the raised roof clerestory is too large, too costly to build, too much to heat, and too much a grand ballroom." We had to lower the roof.

Yesterday's elevation plan was gone, replaced by today's plan just sent, and Watson was working on tomorrow's. We studied each plan as it came, and immediately replied with an assessment. Detail-by-detail, Watson optimized the plans. He tried gable, shed, and hip roofs, as well as combinations. We settled on hip roofs. Watson made adjustments to the study, loft, and window placement and style. He removed the chair and plant space on the landing. We had a final phone conversation on New Year's Eve during which Watson revealed, "I've built your house in my mind three times, stick by stick. I love it."

He emailed us the final schematic design plans on New Year's Day. We called him with our approval. As we finished thanking him and discussing next steps, he commented, "It's time for a name."

Mary and I looked at each and said, "Trail Magic."

Trail magic is what leads Appalachian Trail thru-hikers from Springer Mountain in Georgia to the top of Mt. Katahdin in Maine. It's a long hike—2,280 miles. Most thru-hikers accomplish it in four to six months. Our son, Stuart, who hiked the AT in 1991, explained trail magic this way. "All north-bound thru-hikers have one dream: climb Katahdin. What makes the dream possible is taking the next step, ascending the hill, or crossing the stream in front of you. When that seems impossible—badly sprained ankle, sudden ice storm, rain-swollen stream with no obvious way to cross—someone offers to carry your pack to the next shelter, gives you dry gloves and a wool sweater, or shows up with a rope. The task is to just keep moving until trail magic kicks in."

Chapter 4:
Matching
Personalities

Don Watson sent disks of the final site plan, floor plans, elevations, and cross sections to Joe Ferut on January 2, 2008. Watson had not championed LEED, but he encouraged us to consider seeking LEED certification. I had been casually following LEED for commercial buildings and had sat in on parts of a LEED course in Rensselaer's architecture school. And although LEED had a pilot program for homes, I was initially inclined not to do it. It would be something else I'd have to oversee, and I was unsure of its value because we had the green building expertise of Watson and David Borton.

Watson nudged me to use the bid process to assess builder capacity for meeting LEED standards. He'd included a four-page document on green specification options to accompany the bid request, and we indicated our intention to seek LEED platinum certification.

The details were overwhelming. The mere thought of taking responsibility for researching and making green choices made me anxious. Nevertheless, I studied LEED's website and found the LEED provider closest to Oberlin. The U.S. Green Building Council (USGBC) contracts providers to 1) manage LEED applications and help applicants; 2) oversee and coordinate green raters who do the on-site inspections; and 3) certify a project on behalf of USGBC.

Only three green raters were available in Ohio, and none in the Cleveland area. I spoke with the rater in Columbus, who agreed to take on our project. Our application would require detailed design plans that Ferut would create once we selected the builder, so it would be several months before we could file papers.

Meanwhile, I looked over the 184-page guidebook, *LEED for Homes Program, Pilot Rating System*, January 2007. I assumed the technical aspects would become clearer to me as we launched into the detailed design and building process. Our architects and builder would know what they meant and could guide us into meeting the requirements for platinum certification. I knew we would be building a very tight, extremely energy efficient house that embodied many green aspects. Why wouldn't it merit a LEED platinum rating?

Mary and I had identified four builders to bid on the project, and Ferut added a fifth. Watson wrote the bid letter to which Ferut attached the supporting documents and mailed them on January 9, 2008, with the following cover letter:

Enclosed is a packet of Schematic Design Plans and Outline Specifications for a residence planned by Carl and Mary McDaniel. We are seeking preliminary budget proposals and expression of interest from qualified contractors, experienced in residential green building.

Based on the preliminary proposals and client references, we intend to select a contractor for a negotiated contract for construction, within a defined budget. A goal of the project is to build a home to qualify for a "platinum rating" in the LEED-H Pilot Program of the U.S. Green Building Council.

The following guidelines are suggested for preliminary construction budget estimates. Final selection of items and specifications to be included will be subject to budgeting.

For cost estimate purposes, assume the following outline specifications. You may elect to replace any of these items with an itemized alternate, for cost and quality comparison.

(a) Superior "Xi" walls for foundation and ground floor walls with foam insulation (R45 or better). Rigid insulation under entire slab; R20 or better.

(b) Exterior walls R45 or better, achievable by SIPs, double-frame walls with spray foam and wet spray cellulose, or composite 2x6/straw bale wall constructions. Sample wall sections are included for your use. The architect can assist in the budget pricing of the straw bale installation and earth plastering. When pricing the bale wall system, the overall dimension of the house should be increased 1'-6" as to not change the interior layout of the residence.

(c) Ceiling (roof) insulation R60 or better, achievable by SIPs, truss-joist cavity (foam insulation with wet spray cellulose)

(d) Steel metal roofing.

(e) Insulation in ceilings of Ground Floor and First Floor (for acoustic suppression).

(f) Fiberglass windows, R5 or better.

(g) No air-conditioning is contemplated. A whole-house ventilation system and energy recovery may be considered. Indicate as separate item.

(h) Various heating options will be considered. Indicate as separate item.

(i) A photoelectric (PV) panel system is indicated, as well as a two-panel solar domestic hot water system. Owner will supply all components of a PV panel system (3.12 kW). Mounting and wiring to be provided by contractor. These are to be indicated as separate budget items.

The attached "Green Specifications" provides recommended sources for the above specifications and additional items, subject to detailed budgeting in the negotiated contract process.

Proposals shall be submitted by Monday, January 28, 2008. The Owner and Architect will be reviewing proposals in preparation for interviews with contractors the weekend of February 9.

All questions shall be directed to the office of Joseph Ferut & Associates, Architects.

Several builders requested more information, so we sent an addendum on January 17.

The following is information that both supplements and clarifies project scope. Please use this information in the development of your project budget estimate.

1. *Pond:*
   a. *Location: Approximately 100 feet south of house site and just south of two oak trees and an Osage orange so that these trees are not killed.*
   b. *Size: ~90 ft by ~90 ft by ~12 ft deep (at middle) but give pond an irregular shape to be visually interesting.*
   c. *Earth from pond will be used to raise drive-way, to berm-up around house and barn, and to raise a little the area where two houses were removed. Bid to include this earth moving and leveling, but not planting of grass or shrubs.*
   d. *Drains from house site and under foundation to go into pond.*
   e. *Save top soil for around house site.*

2. *Ground Floor:*
   a. *Flooring will be finished, colored, concrete slab in all rooms including bathroom.*
   b. *Consider putting a floor drain in bathroom, mechanical room, and kitchenette.*
   c. *Cold Food Storage area well insulated from rest of Ground Floor.*
   d. *Interior walls sheet rocked and painted.*

3. *First and Second Floor Flooring:*
   a. *Kitchen, pantry and entry hallway to be durable material that can be wet and not slippery, and not marred easily.*
   b. *Tile in bathrooms.*
   c. *Shower in master bathroom tiled.*
   d. *All other rooms—bamboo, oak, ash, other and same in all rooms.*
   e. *Stairs open back and wood to match or complement wood floors.*
   f. *Consider putting a floor drain in kitchen and two bathrooms.*

4. *First Floor, other:*
   a. *Kitchen cabinets from commercial source with drawers of high quality and cabinets and shelves of good quality unless custom made of similar quality are less expensive.*
   b. *Major appliances of high energy efficiency and good quality.*

5. *Deck:*
   a. *Consider recycled plastic and tropical Ipe decking*

6. *Barn:*
   a. *Concrete slab well drained.*
   b. *Not insulated.*
   c. *Conventional framing or perhaps post and beam from oak trees lumbered on-site.*
   d. *Metal roof and siding as on house. Consider siding options including Hardiplank.*

Watson and Ferut employed the bidding process to gain information and input from builders. We were seeking their insights and expertise on how to build the house. This way, we'd know what each builder thought about the various options and what he knew how to do. I was unsure of exactly how the process would play out, but I saw that Watson was following through on his belief: "Builders do best what they have done, and therefore know how to do."

One builder withdrew. "Due to the time restraints and design criteria, we think it best that we pass on this project. Giving you a realistic bid would entail more time than we can afford to give." In a conversation with Ferut, the builder commented, "I would be surprised if anyone bid on it."

Another general contractor, who did submit a bid, wrote, "The sheer nature of this type of construction is not only new to me, it's new to anyone in Lorain County that calls himself a builder! If ANYONE says they are 'up to date' with all these different specifications and materials, or says 'Oh yea, no problem,' they are not being truthful! I think this is a great project, but I also think that it is so different that it requires a different thought process."

We were discovering the exact information that Watson had sought. The builder who had withdrawn was unfamiliar with the LEED agenda. The other builder understood the novelty and challenge of the project for local builders. Interestingly, the Bortons' passive solar house in Troy, almost 30 years old, had employed the same relevant features of our proposed house. Clearly, home builders in Lorain County are still building for the 20th century, as are most in the home construction industry in our country.

We received four bids. For the house alone they were: $328,775; $307,500; $293,000; and $291,500. Two of the builders had also offered to do a cost plus contract, meaning we'd pay for the materials, labor, and a fixed percent of these costs to the builder. Watson commented, "You are in the *very fortunate* position of having several viable options. I have rarely seen such a range of good choices." It was a great relief to have competitive bids.

Assessing and comparing the bids, it became clear that we had to focus on Calvin Smith and Mike Strehle. Foremost, these builders knew how to do what we wanted, and, because they understood the project, their two bids were the lowest. I was particularly impressed with the thoroughness of Strehle's bid. Eight single-spaced pages, it included pricing for four wall types, provided suggestions and recommendations, included homeowner and trade references, and was the lowest. Earlier, Strehle had told me that he had several pending jobs, but that ours was the house he wanted to build. His due diligence made this clear.

Because Strehle was new to Ferut, I called his references: two homeowners and three professionals. I asked the same questions to the homeowners and slightly different ones to the professionals. I pushed hard to identify any reservations they had. Uniformly, they were impressed by the quality of his work and with him as a person. The homeowners thought him an excellent builder. He worked hard and long hours, perhaps to a fault. He stayed on schedule, handled subcontractors well, and fixed any mistakes without fuss or cost.

The architect's reference was extreme: Strehle was the best contractor with whom she'd ever worked, bar none. The final reference was an Energy Star certifier who had tested five of Strehle's houses. Two were the tightest, and the others were in the top ten of about 200 houses he had examined. I was delighted!

Calvin Smith was confident that he could do the house well. He pointed out that we needed not a builder, but a project coordinator. He recommended that I serve as the "builder," specifying the materials I wanted, and he'd coordinate building the house. This could reduce costs by 10 percent.

We had two builders who knew green building. But who would do the superior job? With whom would I work best? We needed to interview Smith and Strehle.

I took a 6 a.m. flight to Cleveland for our Friday morning interviews in Ferut's office. The big issue to resolve was the basic structure of the envelope, and we wanted buy-in from the builders on our options.

Ferut's first choice was superior wall for the ground floor, and he encouraged us to consider straw bale for the upper floors.

Prior to the bid, Strehle had sent us information on Reddi-Wall and championed it for the ground floor, if not the entire wall envelope. An architect currently working with him used Reddi-Wall for the entire house and was convinced that it was the way to go.

In the bid, however, Strehle stated that structural insulated panels (SIPs) with expanded polystyrene would be "best for this particular project, because they are the simplest. They will not take on moisture and there is no outgassing."

This surprised me. Strehle had been so enthusiastic about Reddi-Wall earlier and was using it in the two houses he was currently building. Why not in ours?

Strehle arrived a few minutes before 9 AM. We discussed various aspects of his proposal, and the envelope in particular. He didn't champion SIPs, but for ease, performance, and cost he thought they would be the best choice.

Ferut was still leaning toward straw bale. He wasn't excited about SIPs; a colleague had had a bad experience with SIPs that leaked. But Mary and I had concerns about straw bale: 1) the cost would go up significantly if Mary, friends, and I were unable to install the bales, 2) a wall thickness of almost two feet was unfamiliar, and 3) we weren't sure how we would feel about the overall appearance of the Earth-plaster finish.

Mary and I had followed Watson's advice of going along with what the builder likes and does. We had researched Reddi-Wall and were amenable to it. We talked further, and Strehle said he would build with it if that was our decision.

I had met Strehle twice earlier, and we had spoken on the phone several times. The interview revealed nothing new, but affirmed my earlier assessments. He was quietly confident, knowledgeable, and to the point. I did, however, begin to notice that he'd reveal a charming smile to affirm something he had already concluded. We finished the interview just as Smith arrived.

Smith had not given a detailed cost analysis in his letter of response, and Ferut had asked him for some numbers. He reviewed his costs, for a total amount that was almost identical to Strehle's. He was open to whatever arrangement we wanted, but remained convinced that I knew enough about the materials to handle the project, with him managing subs and the actual construction.

We discussed envelope choices. Smith was comfortable with a superior wall foundation and double walls for the rest of the house; he was doing the same in Crowley's home. I liked Smith and believed he could do our project well, on time, and within budget. But he didn't appreciate my naiveté about house building, nor my superficial knowledge of building materials and systems.

It was an informative three hours. Ferut and I knew that both men could do the job, but how each would do it was quite different. We were surprised by Smith's approach and bid proposal. It was as atypical as the project itself, but clearly he had considered it seriously.

We were impressed also by the thoroughness of Strehle's proposal, and also with his low-key, but confident and knowledgeable interactions during the interview.

I felt that Ferut found himself in an awkward situation. He sensed that I was leaning toward Strehle, and while he, too, was impressed, he and Smith were working well together on the Crowley house. A pre-occupancy open house had attracted hundreds of people, as well as TV and print media who had come to see a house with a "projected annual heating cost of $380," and advertized as a "*true* green building." Ferut was on a roll and felt good about what Smith had done. Don Watson was right. We had excellent choices, but how to choose? We needed more time to digest and discuss our options.

I had a full afternoon ahead, but first I headed to Trail Magic to eat the simple lunch I had brought on the plane. I imagined how the house we had created was going to fit into the land. I estimated the positions of the house and barn. Three small black walnut trees and four, not-very-healthy pines needed to come down, but the remaining dozen or more mature trees—sugar and Norway maples, black walnuts, cherries, locust, and spruce—between the house site and the road would remain. Keeping the existing driveway would work well. I loved the rustic, but badly weathered split rail fence that Doren Portman had erected decades ago. The jury-rig, fix-up job I had done last summer was holding, but I wondered how long it would stay intact. Portman probably didn't care, but for me it preserved and respected the character of his family's tenure as we transformed the land with our aspirations for a durable pattern of habitation.

I headed into town and stopped at the local bank to pick up forms for making checking and savings accounts joint. Dawn greeted me as usual with her warm, friendly smile. I liked to drop by to say hello to her whenever I was in Oberlin; she always made me feel a part of the community. It's the way banking and business ought to be done; people get to know and trust each other so that rules become but guidelines, with each situation tailored to its particulars.

That afternoon, Portman met me at Trail Magic to discuss cutting down the two giant red oak trees that were at the end of their lifespan. One of their companion oaks had fallen on a neighboring house several years earlier. Scott, who had agreed to mill the oaks and other trees, joined us. With spring around the corner, I was keen on making a plan for lumbering the oaks and any other trees that required felling. Portman agreed to cut down the trees when the ground became frozen enough, or dry enough, for his bucket truck to reach them.

Scott was confident that he could lumber the oaks with his portable Lucas mill for a post and beam barn. He was ready to tackle this as soon as weather permitted, most likely in April or May. I loved the idea of making our barn from these massive trees, but was clueless about what would be involved or even its feasibility. Nevertheless, I pushed on, not wanting to use such magnificent trunks for firewood.

Later, I walked the land, pacing off several possible garden locations and the pond. How large could we make the pond while keeping intact the eastern meadow and the western cluster of trees?

Soon it was dark, and I headed into Oberlin for dinner. I was meeting friends to assess the consequences and actions resulting from the city council's recent vote to pull out of a 1,000 megawatt, coal-fired power plant. In an email in December, Scout, newly elected as Oberlin's mayor, summarized what happened:

"One of the first apocalyptic actions of the new council (taking office January 7, 2008) will be to consider the rescission of the city's agreement with American Municipal Power of Ohio, aka, AMP-Ohio, to participate in the to-be-built coal-fired power plant.

It is expected by some that, as an inevitable consequence of such a rescission, the lights will go out ten or twenty minutes later. Oberlin will freeze in the dark. Perhaps you would like to try to sell your property before this calamity? Alternatively, perhaps you will be so reckless as to further invest your lives toward helping Oberlin become a locally self-sufficient producer of clean energy, toward becoming a community that treads lightly on the Earth, leaving not the least smudge of a carbon footprint."

Kicking coal addiction is a big deal. Heat provided by burning coal generates some 80 percent of Ohio's electricity. It's an inexpensive source of energy if one doesn't consider the items not paid in cost: climate destabilization, particulate matter, the release of mercury and other noxious chemicals, diseases and deaths of those who dig the coal, pollution of water and soils, devastation of natural beauty, the impoverishing of lives when mountains are leveled, and the loss of biodiversity fostered by these consequences. A full accounting makes coal very expensive!

The January vote of the Oberlin City Council set the city and college on the same overwhelmingly difficult path of becoming climate neutral. Simply stated, all the activities of and resources used by the city, college, and their members must result in no net release of heat trapping gases into the atmosphere (carbon dioxide, methane, chlorofluorocarbons, etc.). Human activities are the major factor that led to the Earth's rise in surface temperature of over 1°F in the past 100 years. And the heat-trapping gases already released will

Sidebar 5: Economic Growth and the Keeling Curve

"The Chamber's Economic Growth Council is dedicated to establishing central Indiana as a place where businesses can grow and prosper and where new companies—both those moving from elsewhere and startups—can take seed and flourish." (Indianapolis Chamber of Commerce, 2010)

"The Professional Developers of Iowa (PDI) is a statewide non-profit organization representing more than 340 practicing economic development professionals dedicated to expanding the economy of the State of Iowa." (2010)

"Japan Aims to Cut Company Tax to Spur Economic Growth" (Bloomberg Business Week, 18 June 2010)

Locally and globally, the mantra and metric for humanity's success is economic growth. A consequence of this growth in the past century has been an increase in fossil fuel use, resulting in higher concentrations of atmospheric CO_2.

In 1957, climate scientist Charles Keeling began measuring the atmospheric concentration of CO_2 at Mauna Loa Observatory which is located 11,140 feet above sea level on the island of Hawaii. The plot of these monthly measurements is known as the Keeling Curve.

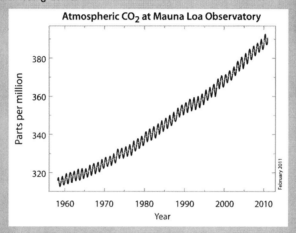

The saw tooth pattern reflects the presence of more dry land (and terrestrial vegetation) in the northern hemisphere. The greater amount of photosynthesis that occurs in the northern hemisphere extracts more CO_2 than is released globally, thereby causing the concentration curve to fall from late spring into autumn, after which much of the northern vegetation goes dormant. Photosynthesis in the southern hemisphere being more modest in amount than in the northern hemisphere thereby extracting less carbon dioxide than that released globally with the resulting rise in the curve from late fall into spring.

The atmosphere contains several important heat trapping gasses—the most important being water vapor, methane, and carbon dioxide—but the concentration of the third one most reliably predicts future climate because it is tightly correlated with the Earth's temperature in the past: the higher the CO_2, the higher the temperature with temperature lagging CO_2. The current CO_2 concentration is 25% higher than its highest concentration in the last million years, and when it was that ancient high, the Earth's temperature was much warmer than today.

Over the past century the atmospheric CO_2 concentration has increased 30 percent, rising from 300 parts per million (ppm) in 1910 to 390 ppm in 2010, with the rate of change over the century increasing from less than 1 ppm per year at midcentury to 2 ppm per year now. If we stopped the acceleration at 2 ppm per year, the concentration would be 570 ppm in 2100, and 480 ppm, if we reduced the rate to 1 ppm per year. With CO_2 concentration between 480 ppm and 570 ppm in 2100, the additional temperature increase over the next 90 years would be at least several degrees and could be more than 10°F. This change would increase the average surface temperature from 57°F to between 60°F and 67°F. Even a several degree increase is sufficient to cause major melting of the Antarctic and Greenland ice sheets, thereby raising sea levels 10 feet in perhaps a century and over 200 feet when they melt completely. A rise of 10 feet will inundate most coastal cities and eliminate the substantial fraction of global agriculture that takes place on major deltas like those of the Ganges, Mississippi, and Nile rivers. This coastal flooding will be bad for the people living there and agricultural yields; however, other climatic changes, including a significant increase in the frequency of weather extremes (exceptional rain fall, drought severity, class 4 and 5 hurricanes) and unpredictable changes in weather patterns (timing and duration of warm and cold periods and of wet and dry seasons, and timing of first and last frost), will likely stress global civilization even more.

Economic systems are human creations without universal fundamental principles. The Keeling Curve, the heat-trapping gas CO_2, and the climate and bioshpere's responses to heat-trapping gases represent biophysical reality grounded in the principles of nature. Humanity's wellbeing is inextricably linked to the rules of the natural sciences. A durable economic system cannot, in the long run, be in fundamental conflict with biophysical principles; however, our current global economic system and the beliefs that undergird it are.

likely result in another 1° to 2°F rise in the coming century. We have bought disaster, and with more heat-trapping gasses to come, we are financing an ever increasing down-payment on catastrophe.

The next morning I met Ferut to continue our discussion of the builder bids and interviews. My subconscious had had a busy night. Strehle was young and had a small operation; everything depended upon him. What if he got hurt? Did he have the highly qualified and competent colleagues that Smith appeared to have who might step in? At the same time, he and I appeared to be compatible and were both intense workaholics. I believed we'd do well together.

Ferut also sensed that Strehle was the person for Trail Magic, but we did due diligence. We visited the home of Brian Carter, the principal of Eastwood Elementary School, who had originally recommended Strehle to my wife. Impressed with the workmanship and the Reddi-Wall foundation, Ferut and I left the house knowing that Strehle had the job. I called to tell him. His response was level, without emotion. He would meet us for lunch and then walk the site.

As we toured the property, both Ferut and Strehle seized upon the shape of the pond. I had imagined it to be oval so as to make it as big and deep as possible. They immediately responded to the aesthetic appeal of a clump of tall trees on the eastern side that we could retain if the pond were kidney shaped. Creating a peninsula of elm, maple, popular, and spruce trees was exactly right. The view across the pond through the trees and down the property gave relief and character to the land while providing a physical boundary between the human managed and the more natural landscapes.

The Home and Garden Show was in Cleveland this week, and Strehle had a booth to network with suppliers and promote All Seasons Builders. I met him there Sunday morning. He introduced me to vendors and colleagues with whom he did business. I wandered around, trying to focus on big-ticket choices Mary and I would have to make. Strehle and I examined the diversity of plastic and wood decking materials and spent some time looking at raised seam metal roofs. All too quickly I had to depart for my flight home. I tossed my backpack into the overhead compartment and settled into my seat, feeling good. Trail magic had kicked in once again.

Chapter 5:
Oberlin Mud

The fall and early winter had been intense. Teaching one large section of introductory biology along with designing our house would have kept me fully engaged, but two sections of the course pushed me over the top. It was all I could do just to keep up with the design process. If I didn't have a more flexible teaching assignment in the spring, it would be impossible to disengage from 33 years at Rensselaer while preparing our house to sell, packing up, interacting with Joe Ferut on detailed design, and helping prepare the site for construction.

I'd proposed to our new department chair that I forego the intro course in the spring and teach instead only environmental biology, an elective course I had created, but had been unable to teach for several years. She agreed, provided that at least 10 students enrolled.

Environmental biology was an upper-level course in which I could control the agenda. Initially, 22 students signed up, but six dropped out in early January when I emailed them the course syllabus detailing the requirements: three books to read, a dozen short papers and a term paper to write, an oral report, and mandatory class attendance. After the first two classes, another five dropped. Twenty-two students had dwindled to 11, but all were dedicated, which would ensure an enjoyable final course for me. Teaching just this course also meant that I could work the schedule to give students full contact time while allowing me flexibility for my other major tasks.

Once Don Watson sent Trail Magic's schematic design to Ferut, my involvement in the bidding and design process became intermittent. I focused my efforts on teaching and cleaning up affairs at Rensselaer, including the 33 years worth of paperwork in my office. At home we prepared the house for appraisal. We had purchased our house 23 years earlier from the university with a buy-back, sell-back agreement that allowed the university to reclaim the house with one year's notice, or for us to sell it back to the university with three months' notice. In either scenario, an independent appraiser would establish the price. We needed only to prepare the house for two inspections, one by the university property management personnel, and another by the appraiser. We were ready in mid-March.

Rensselaer's property management people were pleased with the condition of our house. We'd replaced the roof in 2000, painted the exterior a few years later, installed a new furnace and hot water heater the previous summer, and had replenished the driveway with fresh gravel. The MAI (Member Appraiser Institute) assessor came several days later. I answered his questions and slipped in details that I thought would add value to the house. Interestingly, when I mentioned that our Vermont Casting fireplace insert provided half of the home's heat, he asked if we could remove it, thus making the fireplace functional.

Because I had saved the damper and all the related pieces, I responded, "Yes, but why would anyone want to do that?"

"A functional fireplace adds $2,000 to the value of the house, but a woodstove adds nothing," he replied. He then commented, "People like fireplaces." The insert, installed in 1991, had long ago paid for itself and had saved us hundreds of dollars and reduced our ecological footprint every year since. I just smiled, delighted to have the increased value.

It would take several weeks for the MAI appraiser to find comparable Troy properties that had recently sold. We had conservatively estimated the value of our house between $200,000 and $220,000, not expecting to recover much of the $30,000 we'd spent on recent maintenance, or any of the $25,000 spent on improvements. And for planning purposes in Oberlin, we didn't want to expect more than we might get. We were delighted, therefore, with an appraisal of $260,000. With real estate prices in Troy beginning to decline, we were lucky to be selling. At the same time, construction and material prices in Oberlin were still at their peak, so we were pleased to have the unanticipated dollars.

On New Year's Day, I exchanged emails with Watson to discuss our next steps. He summarized the forthcoming sequence of events. "There is a briar patch of questions ahead, delights, traps and falls along the way, but we have the necessary clearing tools at hand."

Watson had been down this road many times, but once again, Mary and I were venturing into the unknown. I expressed to Watson our appreciation for all he had done over the past six months. "The hand-off to Joe [Ferut] is a sad occasion," I wrote. "From our first meeting at the Athenian Diner in New Haven, to our picture-perfect gathering under the trees of the Winsted green, to the intensity of the past week's finalizing of the schematic design, you have been a masterful and patient teacher, guiding us through the process of translating vague ideas and notions into a pleasing reality of efficiency and beauty. You've been kind, gentle, and respectful, yet firm and disciplined, as you've tolerated our naïve and off-the-mark wanderings, always keeping us focused on the path just ahead. We believe the process has engendered a most satisfying relationship that has permitted us to work well together. We are most thankful to you for making this house designing process relatively easy and so satisfying and creative. We know you are vested in our 'dream' and still with us, but Joe must now take the lead. We are sad."

Watson replied, "Morning, not mourning. We shall all proceed to see the sun rise on your abode."

During January and the first half of February, Watson, Ferut, and I exchanged numerous emails to finalize Ferut's contract and to secure a builder. Once we had decided upon Mike Strehle, I wrote letters of thanks to the builders who had made unsuccessful bids.

Strehle, like Watson, was fast. The same day that he landed the job, he sent me a detailed list of questions. He needed answers so he could prepare a fixed-sum contract. This was an important document, I knew, but I didn't fully appreciate just how important. I had never been party to a contract in which

Sidebar 6: Ecological Footprint

The ecological footprint of a group of people is the total area of land and aquatic ecosystems required to provide their resources and to assimilate the wastes the group generates in a particular location at a specific time using current technologies. That is, to live sustainably, a group of people must use only the productivity of available ecosystems as well as not overwhelm the capacity of those ecosystems to assimilate the wastes they generate. The largest component, or about half the human ecological footprint, is the area required to sequester heat trapping gases released by human activities, primarily CO_2.

Currently, humanity uses about 40% more productivity and assimilative capacity than the Earth supplies. Stated another way, we currently need 1.4 Earths to live the way we do, but sustainably. If each of the 7 billion people on Earth lived as the average U.S. person does, we'd require at least 4 Earths.

almost every detail mattered. Once signed, even the smallest change could result in a dollar adjustment, up or down.

As a research scientist, I had administered many grants, but no contracts. A grant is open to change, even a major one, if problems arise or if new possibilities emerge. The overriding goal is to advance the field. For me, Trail Magic was a gigantic experiment. At some level, I believed, everyone working with us would have the same objective—to do what it took to get it right. My six months with Watson had fulfilled this expectation. We had signed a contract and did whatever it took to achieve a desired design without breaking the budget. In the culture of academic science research, this is what I had experienced.

It took me almost two weeks to answer all of Strehle's questions. (It would have taken much longer if we hadn't created a detailed owner's program.) On February 20, I sent my response: three-and-a-half, single-spaced pages with 11 categories: pond, roof, siding, windows and exterior doors, rear walkout patio, deck, solar domestic hot water, woodstove, flooring and trim, cabinetry, and driveway. For some items, like the woodstove, we could be quite specific, because we knew what we wanted:

Woodstove: Hearth Stone (www.hearthstonestoves.com), model: Tribute, 36,000 BTUs, heats 1,300 ft sq, hearth size: 29" W, 32" D, stove size: 18" D, 24" W and H. Hearth size is minimum required in U.S. Consider making hearth bigger by ~8" in depth and ~6" in width (close to Canadian code) to prevent damage to wood floor. (Will have to be sure it fits space available.) Stove has optional outside air adaptor we'll want. Not interested in domestic hot water by stove. Hearth material and back wall material open to Joe's and Mike's suggestions.

In other cases, we could only give a very general response:

Windows: Can we get quotes for highest quality and highest R/u values Alpen (fiberglass), Sunrise (vinyl), and Loewen windows (wood) to get comparisons on wood, vinyl, and fiber glass and "green" qualities of each?

Roof: Metal (steel), standing seam with color of Sandstone, Ash Gray, or Sierra Tan (LEED & Energy Star approved colors).

Driveway: For cost, gravel driveway is probably least expensive. Also consider Uni Eco-Stone permeable interlocking concrete pavement (www.uni-groupusa.org).

Strehle could get an exact price on items like the woodstove and its installation—we knew what we wanted—but not on items like windows, the roof, or the driveway because we didn't completely understand our choices, nor know the dollar or environmental lifecycle costs. It would take another two months of conversations, information-gathering, and interactions among everyone to workout the details of the contract.

On April 18, 2008, we gathered in Ferut's conference room to review and sign the contract. Despite our time and efforts, things were still missing: a woodbin near the woodstove, an on-demand hot water system, floor drains in the full bathrooms and pantry, fold-down beds in the south bedroom and study, and wires in the walls for speakers in the great room and study. Ferut and Strehle had to explain some of the terminology to us—ceiling drywall with stomped texture, IPEX or CPVC water supply lines, CMU's retaining blocks. And myriad details were left for the future, especially those items on allowance: HVAC system, plumbing fixtures, lighting fixtures, flooring, cabinets, and countertops.

Even more problematic were the specifications for construction (e.g., 18" x 8" continuous footings, exterior 4" footer tile drain buried in 2" stone with 2' straw screening, 12" TJI floor joists) as well as the brands selected (e.g., Therma-Tru fiberglass exterior doors, A.O. Smith hot water heater, Nutone CV350 vacuum, Kemper Select Cabinetry, and Schlage door knobs). How does one know if construction specifications are correct, or if the brands are of sufficient quality? Signing a contract for a house is an act of trust.

The new price for the house was $305,900: $14,400 or 5 percent over Strehle's initial estimate. Although we'd added and deleted items, the adjustment seemed reasonable. We had kept expensive items such as a raised seam metal roof, precolored Hardiplank siding, and a central vacuum system. We'd also added a few similarly high-end features—Loewen windows, pavers for the patio, and oak for the stairs, window sills, and interior doors.

Although the house was front and center, I also needed a plan for the barn. I was keen to use lumber from our oak trees.

By March, Doren Portman had removed the oak branches reachable from his bucket, and had tied ropes high on the two trunks, but weather conditions hadn't been right for dropping the trees. I chatted about the barn with some recent Oberlin graduates who were involved with innovative environmental work in town: three were razing and rebuilding a city block to LEED standards for a business and mixed-income housing development, another was converting diesel engines to burn biodiesel, and the third was running an energy-efficiency program to exchange 10,000 incandescent bulbs for compact fluorescents. I was inspired by their enthusiasm. The group thought a community barn-building weekend would be fun. Strehle was game to be the "builder boss" for the event. Nick Zachos, the young green builder who had been interested earlier in bidding on the house, also liked the idea.

It was in early April when I next traveled to Oberlin—this time for a two-week stay. Arriving at dusk after my nine hour drive, I was elated—ecstatic really—to see that Portman had felled the oaks.

During dinner that night with David Benzing, I asked him about my idea to cut down several dozen mature ash trees on the site. He agreed. The trees would likely succumb to the emerald ash borer that had arrived in Ohio and Lorain County. With that, I began to think seriously about lumbering more than just the two oaks and the other trees that required clearing for the house and pond.

The weekend was beautiful, sunny and in the 50s. I cut down three black walnuts on the house site, preparing two for Scott to mill, and cutting the smallest into firewood. On the pond site, I continued what I had started in the fall, clearing trees that were too small for lumber, but good for firewood. By Monday, I had piles of branches in need of chipping. Portman, with his helper, Dean, showed up, and we set to the task. Other friends of Portman's, Doug and John, helped clean up the oak branches and tree tops, taking them for firewood. That night, our daughter Virginia drove in from North Carolina, on her way to Arkansas. While Oberlin was not on a direct route, she wanted to help.

Our neighbors had a large red maple that was dying and leaning toward our building site. I offered to take it down. They agreed, and on Tuesday morning, with Portman's guidance and his chainsaw with a 28" bar, Virginia felled the tree. Seeing the beautiful pattern of colors and rings in the stump of the maple, I had a crazy idea: make tabletops from cross sections of it and the oak trunks.

Portman was game. Dean made an almost perfect 3-inch slice from the maple. The two oaks, over three feet in diameter, were far more difficult to cut cleanly through, but after several tries, Dean made five reasonable slices.

Portman, sensing I didn't have a clue about what to do next, explained the procedure he used, one that would prevent the wood from drying too fast and splitting badly: treat the wood with a 50-50 mixture of turpentine and boiled linseed oil in the beginning, and then gradually decrease the amount of turpentine to zero. He offered to bring several gallons of turpentine and linseed oil the next day. I mixed the solution and painted it on, turning each piece in order to treat the other side after the application had dried. We applied the mixture religiously for eight days, and then continued the treatment for about two months in Troy until the wood was unable to absorb any more linseed oil. My plan was to make tables for Watson, Ferut, and Strehle and tables from each tree for us. Little did I appreciate then the time, effort, and cost involved.

Ferut had requested an exact location of each tree north of the house site for his detailed site plan. Virginia, who routinely maps vegetation, was delighted with the assignment and provided not only the location, but also the species of each tree. Virginia and I felled the rest of the trees on the house and barn sites and worked with Doren and Dean to chip the limbs that resulted. Doug and John continued to clean up oak branches. Scott came by and selected a milling location on the eastern side of the property, away from house construction. Over the next few days we helped Scott set up his Lucas mill and prepared a drying place for the rough-cut lumber with a base of old railroad ties and 4x4 pressure treated timbers. Before the rains came on Friday, he had begun milling the black walnut logs.

Mary arrived on Thursday. The next day we met with Ferut and his firm's colleagues, Lee Goodman and Kim Annabel, to talk about detailed design

Sidebar 7:
Emerald Ash Borer

The emerald ash borer beetle arrived in North America in 2002, and by 2008, had spread through most of the north-eastern U.S. and all but a few Ohio counties. Adult beetles, metallic green and about a half inch long, lay eggs in ash tree bark in spring. Feeding larvae kill the tree by girdling it.

In 2008, when we lumbered our ash trees, we found no signs of ash borer infestations. In 2010, David Benzing showed me an ash tree on his property that within the year had been infected and is dying. Many of the large ash trees in Oberlin are currently dead or dying.

plans and to start making choices for colors and styles. I never realized how simple it was to move into a house someone else had built and tweak it to fit your needs and desires. The schematic design process with Watson had been time consuming and intense, but not particularly difficult. Making detailed design plans, however, forces the soul to meet the soil—it's down to a demanding set of brass tacks. Vague, preconceived notions of what is best must meet reality, and decisions have to be made.

Ferut had revisited all of Watson's plans, affirming what worked and adjusting what didn't. He had to resolve with our and Strehle's input many questions regarding envelope, vapor barrier, wall and roof sections, mechanical and electric systems, elevations and swales, placement and angle of barn relative to house, steps to deck and front door, roof styles over dormer and stairs, window sizes and positions, windows in doors, roof over deck-entry door, location of door into work room, and pond size and location. Watson stayed with us to provide a sounding board and timely advice. The final blueprints were finished on April 30, yet despite everyone's due diligence, it was impossible to create more than "working" prints. A plethora of questions, decisions, and changes still lay ahead.

It had been a good two weeks in Oberlin. The trees on the house and barn sites were down and cleaned up for milling or cut into firewood. Mary, Virginia, and I had cleared trees and brush from the pond site. Scott had begun making boards. The detailed design plans were nearing completion. We had, however, abandoned the idea of using our trees for the barn. A community built, post and beam barn made from on-site wood would have been wonderful, but I was overwhelmed. I hadn't found anyone who knew enough about using fresh cut lumber, nor did we have the time or energy at this point.

On the way home I calculated the number and sizes of boards we'd need for the stairway bookcases, for study and barn loft flooring, for kitchen and front porch beams, and for floor and door trim. I emailed a detailed cut list to Scott as soon as I got home.

When the new chair of biology at Rensselaer asked if I wanted to give a retirement seminar, I jumped at the chance; I had little interest in a department-level retirement luncheon, the usual affair. On Earth Day, April 22, I gave my talk. This was the first such event for a retiring faculty member in my department, and perhaps even in the university.

The seminar gathered together university people, friends, and colleagues from organizations across the capital district area (Albany, Schenectady, and Troy) with whom I had collaborated. I was pleasantly surprised to see an almost-full auditorium, and to greet such a wonderful mix of people from the community and university. I commented candidly on my 33 years at Rensselaer—community service, teaching, research, and the monumental environmental and ethical challenges before the university and the world. It brought closure to the third quarter of my life; the final quarter lay ahead in Oberlin.

Over the next few days I graded term papers and submitted grades for my last course at Rensselaer. Early Saturday morning, I loaded onto our truck 1,100 pounds of cobble stones whose tops had been worn smooth by a hundred years of wagon wheels rolling on 8th Street in Troy that I had salvaged years earlier and that we'd use for our hearth.

Scott had milled the black walnut logs, but hadn't started on the maple or oak. Strehle had dismantled my changing and storage shed and readied the pond site for excavation. All day Sunday I cut limbs and trunks into firewood and placed branches and brush in neat piles in anticipation of breaking ground for the pond.

On Monday, the excavator, Cameron Buchs, arrived with bulldozer, excavator, and dump truck. He and Strehle were busy making a giant mess with Oberlin clay. As the glaciers of the last ice age retreated from what was to become Ohio and the northeastern United States, all manner of material embedded in the ice during its slow grinding advance south was released to settle as glacial till. Lakes, flowing water, and biological activity further mixed and refined the glacial deposits in Oberlin that contain ten ton erratics, but mostly clay—finely ground rocks and silt-sized sediments. Clay soils, when dry, are hard and on the surface can be worn to a fine dust that penetrates into every imaginable place; when wet, they form a putty-like, plastic material that adheres to everything. And it takes considerable water and rubbing to remove Oberlin mud from clothing and skin.

Spring is wet in Oberlin, and this year was no exception. I jumped out of my truck and walked briskly onto the wet clay deposits Buchs had disturbed. In a flash, I was flat on my back in the mud. I righted myself and proceeded more slowly. My boots became heavier as each step picked up another layer of mud. Soon, they were encased in ten pounds of viscous muck. I hate Oberlin mud. Buchs and Strehle, however, were having the time of their lives, like two kids with big toys. Strehle would race to dump the clay-laden truck as quickly as possible; Buchs filled the truck with abandon. Of course, time is money, and idle equipment doesn't cover its keep.

It rained intermittently, but the pair kept digging, hauling, dumping, and spreading. By Thursday, one end of the pond had a foot of water, and some Canadian geese flew in to sample the habitat. They didn't much like the place and departed; however, a few frogs set up shop, courted, and chanced the next generation on the pond to be.

I continued to cut, split, and stack firewood, and fretted over the size of the pond. John Petersen and David Benzing had encouraged me to make it as big and deep as possible. The plans called for 12 feet deep, but the exact size was less precisely defined when we changed it from an oval to a kidney shape. We needed fill for the house and barn sites, and in the area where the derelict houses once stood. The pond would have aesthetic and practical value—providing beauty as well as a handy source of fresh fish. I encouraged Strehle to make it bigger. Buchs, a jokester, said he'd dig until my money ran out. Strehle was concerned about Buchs's bill and where he'd deposit all the diggings. I'm not sure if the pond got any bigger, but Strehle figured out where to put all the earth. And the pond is the uniting feature of the landscape providing us with lessons in ecosystem assembly as we attempt aquaculture.

By Friday, Buchs had finished the pond. Piles of clay were everywhere with no apparent pattern, but I'm sure there was one. Heading back to Troy, I simplified the lumber-cut list. We'd make six beams from the oak logs, plus boards of the same width and thickness from the rest of the logs for book-shelves, trim, and flooring. But by early June it became clear that Scott wouldn't finish milling our logs any time soon. I looked for other ways to accomplish this task, but no good leads emerged. My grand idea of lumbering the oaks first for the barn and then for beams and boards had run amuck.

Don Watson emailed me. "The house that you and Mary visited in Bethany, Connecticut, just received its LEED rating, at silver level. I know. It should have done better. The owner wanted full-force showers (thus no low-flow plumbing fixtures). Rainwater collection not connected, although we designed for it. The 4,200 SF size for two people got dinged which knocked off 12 points!" Mary and I had, and would, make mistakes, but not these.

As the detailed design plans were shaping up in early March, I emailed the LEED provider I had contacted in January. The situation had changed. The pilot program I was following had ended. I read the new LEED for Homes guidebook. The point number and distribution had changed some, but not by enough to concern us at this early stage.

Our LEED Team was:

Architecture and residential building design: Donald Watson, FAIA; Joseph Ferut
Mechanical or energy engineering: Donald Watson, FAIA; Joseph Ferut; consultant—David Borton (PhD in physics with expertise in solar energy and passive solar houses)
Building science or performance testing: Michael Strehle; Donald Watson, FAIA; consultant—David Borton
Green building or sustainable design: Donald Watson, FAIA; consultant—David Borton
Civil engineering, landscape architecture, habitat restoration, or land-use planning: Carl McDaniel (PhD in biology); consultant—David Benzing (PhD in botany)

I became the team leader because neither Strehle nor Ferut had the time, nor did we have the money. If we had paid them for their time, the price of doing LEED would have risen from about $2,000 to perhaps $10,000.

I made copies of the new LEED guidelines and sent them to Strehle and Ferut. Watson and Borton had copies available online. Over the next six weeks, I worked through the forms, talking with the others several times to review and discuss the application materials. In mid-May, we submitted our preliminary application. On May 21, the provider emailed, "Your preliminary LEED for Homes project review has been completed. Based on the review you may complete your registration with USGBC. My preliminary score is about 15 points less than your submittal. All that will get straightened out when

Sidebar 8: Value of Botanical Knowledge

David Benzing's deep understanding of botanical natural history (plant species and their life cycles, habitats, origins, physiologies, and ecological relations) are invaluable for assessing the health of a piece of land. In addition, this knowledge is needed to restore impoverished as well as unstable landscapes. When Benzing came to Oberlin in 1965, colleges and universities supported biologists of the natural historian persuasion who treated nature in a holistic way. Today the masters are retiring with no replacements. The caretakers of this knowledge, like those of integrated agriculture practiced by the traditional family farm, are becoming rare.

you do a full HERS model with the photovoltaic included." (The HERS number is a pre-construction assessment of a house's energy efficiency.)

We finalized the required forms and sent them to the provider with a check for $250. In the first week of June we received the step-by-step process for proceeding with our LEED application. The green rater with whom I had spoken in March was no longer involved with LEED projects, so the provider sent me the names of three current raters in Ohio. One was in Eastlake, not far from Oberlin. I called him four times, but he never called back. The rater in Yellow Springs was too busy to take us on. The rater in Cincinnati responded immediately and knew her stuff, but her fee was $1,000 plus $800 for the two trips to Oberlin for on-site inspections. This would push our LEED costs to over $3,000.

Ferut knew of a LEED home project in Cleveland and tracked down the architect's number. I called him and learned that his project's green rater was conducting his first LEED project. I called the rater's office. His fees were $200 for energy modeling and $600 for inspections. The provider agreed to him being our rater. Relieved and delighted, I arranged to meet him in a local restaurant on June 19. He was a matter-of-fact engineer type; I liked that. We discussed the project and our goal to be climate neutral. We reviewed the detailed design plans and other materials he had requested. He would have the energy modeling to us in a few weeks.

I had done, with the help our team, the best I could with the check list used by LEED to establish the number of earned points. The list we submitted with our application indicated that we would earn 95 points, with another 31 still in question. For LEED platinum, we needed 85 points instead of the standard 90 because our house was almost 600 square feet smaller than a standard home with five rooms that met LEED criteria for a bedroom.

Three of our possible points were for innovative design features—factors not covered in standard categories. Our provider had concurred with two of them: one for recycling 60 percent (or 150 tons) of waste from the derelict houses, and another for lumbering on-site trees for beams, flooring, book-shelves, and trim. I filled out the forms and emailed them to the provider. He expressed enthusiasm for the Trail Magic project that matched ours when he emailed, "Great, Carl. Now, let's build one heck of a LEED home."

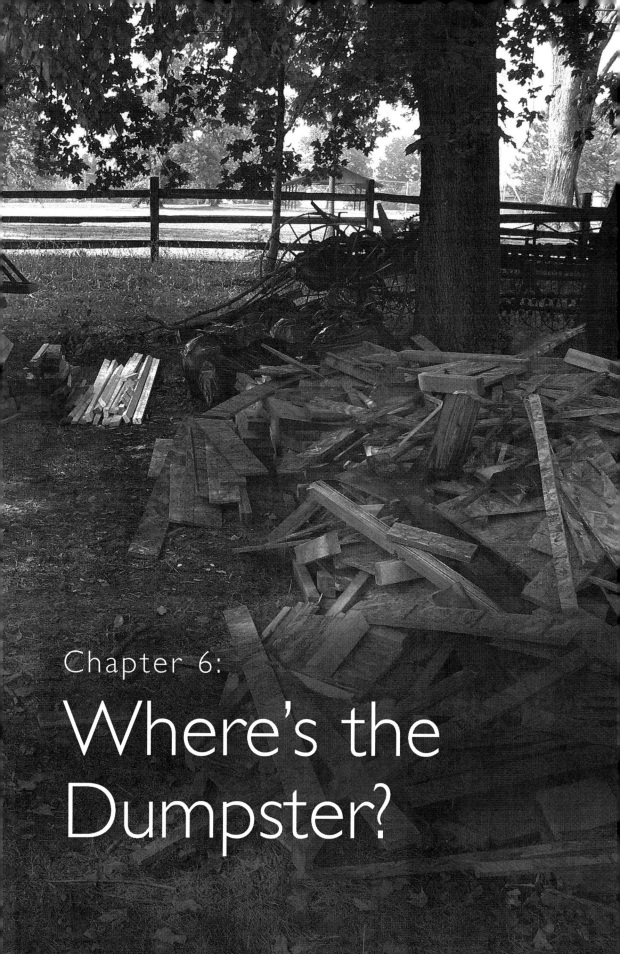

Chapter 6:
Where's the Dumpster?

Our plans for Memorial Day weekend included planting grass around the pond, especially the south bank, which had sufficient slope to seriously erode. David Benzing offered us six bales of straw, which would get us started.

Arriving at Trail Magic, we walked across the dry clay in sunshine to examine Strehle's work. The base of the foundation was complete—footers, footer drains, and gravel. Nine layers of overlapping Reddi-Wall polystyrene blocks foretold what was to come. We walked from the sun patio site into the ground floor through the framed door opening. It seemed so small. In passing, I commented to Strehle, "Can't imagine how everything will fit in that space."

"It will," was all he said.

Mary and I off-loaded the straw, along with flag stones and patio blocks from Troy. We drove to a nearby Tractor Supply center to buy grass seed, and then swung by a local farm for more bales of straw. Back at Trail Magic, we ate lunch on the giant oak stump overlooking the pond, initiating a tradition—lunch-on-the-stump, and then shifted the straw and grass seed to the side of the pond out of the way.

Oberlin College was celebrating its commencement and reunion weekend. We'd been invited to a reception Friday at the president's house, where we talked with Ray Anderson, founder and visionary of Interface Corporation, the half-billion-dollar carpet company that in 1997 took on the challenge of "harvesting yesterday's carpets, recycling old petrochemicals into new materials, converting sunlight into [all the] energy [we use], and [having] zero scrap going into landfills and zero emissions into the ecosystem [by 2020]." David Orr and Anderson were friends. Before Marvin Krislov had assumed Oberlin's presidency in 2007, we had tried unsuccessfully to have Anderson meet with Oberlin's former president and trustees. Now he was here, interacting with Krislov. Progress!

Saturday was one of those perfect spring days: new, deep-green leaves dancing in the breeze against a clear blue sky whose sun warmed the body and stirred emotions. We spread seed and covered it with straw. Just as we finished lunch, I remembered that Rev. Nancy Roth, an Episcopal priest and Oberlin graduate, was having a book signing for her latest book, *Grounded in Love: Ecology, Faith, and Action*, inspired by David Orr's visionary ideas and the Lewis Center. Roth was a founding member and dedicated supporter of EnviroAlums, the college's environmental alumni group.

Back at the pond, we continued seeding until almost dark. We then went to a graduation picnic dinner for Kristin Brazuinas, the Light Bulb Lady who had run the exchange of 10,000 fluorescent bulbs for incandescent ones. Early next morning, we headed back to campus to help run a children's ecological activity at the Lewis Center for Environmental Studies. Twenty-nine, 4 to 12 year olds, children of alumni on campus for their class reunions, streamed into the building with six chaperones. Mary took the youngest for ecological games and songs; I conducted an ecosystem exercise in which the older children constructed a deciduous forest food web and were introduced to nutrient cycling and energy flow. An Oberlin student gave each group a tour of the living-machine, a series of tanks filled with a host of microbes, invertebrates, and plants that purified the Lewis Center's waste water that was then reused to flush toilets and irrigate the landscape.

Returning to Trail Magic, we continued to plant and spread straw. That afternoon, we attended an environmental panel at the Lewis Center. Half-a-dozen students gave alumni and guests, including the chair of Oberlin's board of trustees, a sample of the numerous student environmental initiatives that were happening on campus, including SEED House (Student Experiment in Ecological Design), a duplex taken over by eight students that would be a front-page story in the *New York Times* on graduation day the next day.

On Memorial Day, Mary began cleaning up the east meadow, which was cluttered with remnants of brush piles that had been buried with tree stumps in a hole just south of the pond—a small act of carbon sequestration. On the west side of the pond, I stacked logs that Cameron Buchs had pushed over the bank and partially buried in clay when digging the pond. I labored with a shovel to break up huge chunks of dried clay to fill bulldozer tracks. How puny a shovel is in the hands of a small aging male compared to the machine that had left the mess. With no choice, I persisted. After a long time, I planted the remaining grass seed and spread the last bits of straw.

Sidebar 9: Birth of the Oberlin Project

The day Marvin Krislov assumed the presidency of Oberlin College in July 2007, he met with David Orr for several hours and did so again the next day. Six months later, Orr assumed a half time position as Special Assistant to the President of Oberlin College. With support from the new administration, Orr led the effort that over the next two years honed a vision for the Oberlin region.

In Orr's words, "On the immediate horizon is a large enterprise called The Oberlin Project—a collaboration between the College and the City to create the first integrated model of sustainability. The goal is to combine the various elements of sustainability—farming, forestry, urban development, green jobs, green building, solar energy, education, public policy, and finance—into a model of post, cheap-fossil-fuel prosperity. In a hyper-connected world in which small events anywhere can cause havoc everywhere, The Oberlin Project is intended as a kind of firebreak and model of resilience. But more importantly, it is a celebration of possibilities and of ecological imagination that defies the darkness some see gathering ahead.

We and all generations to come for a long while will live with the consequences of our fossil-fuel excesses: climate destabilization, leveled mountains, toxic wastes, acid seas, and ruined ecologies at a scale that beggars imagination. The time of healing—what economist David Korten calls 'The Great Turning'—is beginning. That turning—what our descendents will hopefully recognize as humankind's 'finest hour,' will be a mosaic of small events, trends, creativity, grace under fire, fierce commotions, civic courage, and what Paul Hawken calls 'blessed unrest'."

Many circumstances coalesced to make the time right for The Oberlin Project. Oberlin City had elected not to purchase coal produced electricity after the current contract expired in favor of electricity produced from non-fossil fuel sources. The college had signed the American College & University Presidents' Climate Commitment to become climate neutral that intensified, among other things, its efforts to replace its coal fired steam plant with another that burned non-fossil fuels. And, the City and College signed an agreement making them the 18th Climate Positive Development Program, a joint project of the Clinton Foundation Climate Initiative and the USGBC.

Mary had assembled several substantial piles of sticks and small branches that I tossed onto the truck. Driving up the meadow, we admired our accomplishments—straw covered pond banks ready to sprout green with the next rain and a tidied meadow. I then drove Mary to the airport; her school year was not quite finished.

It was misty and cool the next morning when Ferut came to see Strehle's progress and discuss the project. Ground floor walls were up, and Strehle had scheduled the Reddi-Wall concrete pour for the next day. We went through Ferut's three-page to-do list: permits, inspections, exterior doors, storm doors, flooring, metal roof, plumbing, cistern, woodstove hearth, bookcases, shower hardware, faucets, dual flush toilets, colors, cabinets, light fixtures—and then the work schedule. Strehle projected completing rough framing by early July, drywall by early September, and occupancy on November 1. The contract finish date had been October 1, but the late start and wet spring had slowed Strehle by about a month. I was disappointed.

Wednesday was again perfect. I weighed and laid out the cobblestone hearth so Strehle could see what we had in mind and know its weight to properly reinforce the floor. I spent the day cutting down thick poison ivy vines that had climbed the trees—some up to 50 feet—and collecting rocks that had been unearthed by digging the pond and foundation. I piled them around trees out of the way for use later. Many were beautifully colored granite—pink, green-black, brown, speckled black and white—while most of the rest were gray or brown sandstone. (We used them for the rock garden that borders the sun patio.)

The pump truck arrived about noon and parked as close as possible to the northwest corner of the foundation. The driver stepped out and freed up a four-section boom that lay on the truck and then strapped on a belt that held a controller box with a joy stick, dials, and gages. Stepping away from the truck, he adjusted dials and moved the joy stick. The 12-foot long sections of the boom rose and unfolded, with a 10-foot flexible trunk attached to the last section.

Not long afterward, the cement truck arrived. The driver positioned it so that the chute could deliver cement into the back of the pump truck. After last-minute checks and adjustments, the pour began. Strehle held the pipe while the pour boss manipulated controls to position the outlet several inches above the Reddi-Wall. Cement flowed into the 6-inch openings at the top of the polystyrene wall. Strehle's dad and Aaron, Strehle's helper, followed Strehle to ensure that the cement had completely filled the vertical and horizontal tubes, and to clean up spilt cement. I was impressed not only with the process, but also by the teamwork throughout the three-hour pour. Strehle was pleased—no blowouts or other complications.

I left for Troy the next day, arriving home at 8 p.m. I unloaded the truck and rubbed linseed oil into the oak cross section that I had prepared for Watson. Back in April, when we had brought the cross sections back to Troy, I'd used an electric plane to remove the chainsaw marks and even up the irregularities. It took many hours, and in the process I removed 90 pounds of wood from the six cross sections. We continued to apply linseed oil until the wood would absorb no more, the timing of which depends on section thickness. By mid May, the thinnest section was saturated. I scrapped it clean of residue, sanded it smooth, and rubbed it until the linseed oil finish glistened. We had a family gathering in Connecticut in late May, and I invited Watson to join us. I gave him his reddish-gold, 40-pound medallion of rings and rays. He received our token of appreciation with a twinkle in his eye and a promise to hang it on his wall. (The other 5 cross sections still wait in the barn for transformation into table tops that will go on stands made by George Ficke from the same trees.)

The packing process was now getting serious. Mary had 40 years of teaching materials to sort through, and I had 16 file cabinet drawers, a dozen boxes, and a wall of bookshelves overflowing with 50 years of science books. Needless to say, we were faced with the obligatory challenge and task to slim down our professional acquisitions.

Mary's teaching colleagues threw her a wonderful retirement party, attended by over a hundred colleagues, friends, and relatives. Two days later, I was again off to Oberlin, carrying another load of patio blocks and our Agway garden cart—invaluable for hauling things when it was too muddy for the truck, or inaccessible by vehicle.

I drove directly to the property to witness Strele's accomplishments over the past two weeks. I was greeted by a neat, five-foot high pyramid of gravel halfway down the driveway that contrasted with lumpy, irregular piles of dirt everywhere. A few had sprouts of grass—the topsoil piles—while the vast majority was as barren as the Dakota Badlands. Two distinct mounds of earth ran north from the foundation to the street, marking newly laid water and sewer pipes. A heavy duty extension cord ran from a temporary electrical junction box in the northeast corner of the front yard up to the open first floor. Stacks of recently delivered lumber rested awkwardly on the rough, dry-clay slope leading up from the driveway to a narrow gangplank that provided access to the first floor across the 10 foot gap between the front yard and foundation. Floor joists, covered with oriented strand board (OSB), concealed the ground floor with its recently poured concrete slab. Partial wall sections jutted awkwardly up from the floor on the east and the eastern ends of the north and south sides. I could see a lush band of green grass on the west and south banks of the pond, and, behind several piles of dirt, five huge oak logs piled next to one of the two oak stumps.

The next morning, while walking around the pond, I discovered that one of the firewood piles had been knocked over. Strehle must have hit it with his backhoe when he put in the pipe to drain runoff water from neighboring properties into the pond. I spent the next two days dealing with firewood. Putting the Agway Cart to use, I moved the jumbled pieces to a more out-of-the way location. I cut up all the logs I had piled on the west side of the pond, and using a hand maul, split them into firewood size. We now had three stacks, each containing more than a cord. If our house performed like the Bortons' house, we'd be able to heat Trail Magic for three years without cutting another log.

Danielle Young, executive director of the alumni association at the college, came on Tuesday for "lunch on the stump." She wanted to see the house. I asked if she would have a problem using the gangplank. "No," she said, so we walked up to examine the progress and imagine what was to come.

On the way out, the height and down slope of the gangplank spooked her. She tried three times, but could only take one or two steps down the plank. What to do? She walked into the house, closed her eyes, and mustered her courage. When she was halfway down, I asked, "Do you want a hand?"

With confidence she responded, "I'm OK," and she was. I was glad that Strehle had been in his truck eating lunch and talking on the phone and didn't see the event. We were early in creating our owner-builder relationship, and it might not have raised his confidence in having me on-site.

By Friday, when I flew to California for an Alumni Council Executive Board meeting, the exterior framing was going gangbusters. North, east, and south walls were up, as were half of the 16" TJI roof trusses. From the open end, I could see the skeleton with two dozen braces of various lengths at multiple angles holding it together.

I returned late Tuesday. Wednesday morning, an electrician consulting with Strehle noted that the kitchen window frame appeared too low. Without comment, Strehle checked his construction blueprint and measured the height of the window opening. Sure enough, the opening was almost four inches too low, thereby putting the window below the sink countertop. According to the plans, however, the kitchen window opening was correct. I called Ferut. Strehle was right. Ferut's people had put the wrong size window in the kitchen. Ferut had already ordered windows from Loewen, but perhaps we could change this. An hour later Ferut called with the bad news. "The kitchen window is being made. We'll have to reorder a new window. It's my mistake. I'll eat the cost." It was a $1,300 window.

Strehle did some quick measurements. He could place the window at the top of the opening, making it an inch higher than the other windows on that side of the house—but too little for the eye to notice. The sink counter would then overlap the window casement by a bit more than two inches, making the window flush with the counter. Strehle asked, "Is this OK with you?" I wasn't sure how it would look, but trusting Strehle, I responded, "Sure, we're all in this together. I don't want to waste Joe's money."

I drove to Troy the next day—Mary's last day of school. While I was away, her sister and brother-in-law came for a 24-hour blitz to assist Mary in packing her classroom. Boxes filled our sunroom, stacked four and five high. Mary had emptied the attic closets and moved the boxes to the first floor. I had started sorting and cleaning my office and had a good start on the basement. However, the heavy lifting of sorting through 40 years of living together and raising two children had barely begun.

On Sunday, June 29, we packed the fixings for a scallop-crab stir fry dinner with the Benzings, and set out for Oberlin. We drove in and out of torrential downpours until the sun came out when we neared Oberlin. Driving down our street, we were surprised to see Strehle's truck leaving the site. We chased him down and teased him about having nothing better to do on a Sunday. He gave us a knowing smile, and we chatted briefly. On returning to the site, we saw a car parked in the driveway. It was Doren Portman with his wife, Jo Ann, who was usually housebound with various ailments, sitting in their car. We offered to give her a tour, but she declined, seemingly pleased just to see the transformations to her home of many years. No sooner had the Portmans left, Scout showed up. He wanted a tour, as did Mary—she was anxious to see first-hand what had happened since Memorial Day. A fully framed house stood before us.

We spent five hours on Monday at Ferut's office reviewing a shopping list of topics and choices. Outside doors: style, color, hinges, handles, windows, storm doors? Bathroom: floor tile—manufacturer, recycled, texture, color;

shower tile—floor, walls, styles, colors, patterns; sinks—styles, materials, colors? Deck: synthetic verse wood, types of wood? Woodstove: stove color, wall tile, woodbin size and material? Wall colors: entryway, master bedroom, great room, kitchen, bathrooms, family room, guest bedrooms?

This was all new to Mary and me. Environmental and dollar considerations entered into every conversation. Ferut's people held our hands, researching a product when they hadn't used it before or didn't have good environmental information. Frequently, a product did not clearly indicate the environmental impact, or the manufacturer had not considered it at all. Despite our best intentions, we had to make too many choices without adequate information. All too often, we were unable to make appropriate comparisons.

The next morning we were on-site before eight for our job of picking up OSB and I-joist scraps and moving them to an area in the front yard where we sorted waste for reuse, recycling, or the landfill. Over the past two months, our three major roles in the actual building of the house had emerged: waste managers, janitors, and Mike's gofers.

We could earn three LEED certification points if our landfill waste was less than 0.5 pounds per square foot of conditioned space. Strehle maintained a clean site and never had a dumpster. He had a bin for scrap metal. He reused any scrap lumber longer than a foot, pulverized unused concrete for the driveway base, and plastic lumber wrap to keep things dry, and provided waste sheet rock to farmers for "liming" their fields as well as other things to have a modest waste stream. Strehle was primed to push the limit on waste reduction and had clearly stated his position early on: "I want those three points!"

I purchased a scale and put it in Strehle's truck—along with paper and pen—to record the weight of all waste and its fate. We instructed every supplier and subcontractor to leave all waste on-site for us to weigh and then reuse, recycle, or landfill. At our staging area, we placed Strehle's metal bin and a large plastic trashcan for lunch waste and other non-recyclables. We had buckets for glass and plastic. We recycled cardboard at the college or with the city after first using large pieces to protect concrete and wood floors.

Scrap lumber became our first major recycling challenge. Despite Strehle's building techniques for reducing lumber use, we still had 4,441 pounds of scrap wood and wood composites. We sent to the Oberlin landfill 170 pounds of pressure-treated, painted, or wood composites for which we could find no use. About a third of the framing and flooring scrap wood, or 1,322 pounds, we gave to friends or kept at Trail Magic for woodstove kindling and children's play blocks. Kurtz Brothers in Cleveland recycled 2,354 pounds of OSB and TJI beams into yard mulch. We transformed scrap from laminated support beams weighing 352 pounds into a workbench and heavy-duty shelves. We kept long pieces of painted lumber, weighing 135 pounds, for garden and landscape stakes. Larger pieces of scrap—pressure-treated lumber weighing 80 pounds—we saved for outdoor uses, and we spread 28 pounds of sanding dust across the back yard.

The second largest category of waste was sheetrock (3,660 pounds) and plaster (250 pounds). We broke this up and rototilled it into the side and back yards as soil addendum that neutralized acidic soil. This huge amount surprised Watson; it represented a waste of 27 percent (3,660 lbs of 13,470 lbs delivered). The substantial amount of sheet rock waste does, however, conform to an efficiency-driven market economy. If an item is inexpensive compared to labor and other costs incurred to use or reuse it, sizable amounts can, and often will be, wasted.

Other categories of reused or recycled waste were: HardiePlank siding (780 pounds broken-up for driveway base), cardboard (756 pounds recycled), metal (181 pounds recycled), and plastic (66 pounds recycled). Only the metal resulted in cash flow—Strehle earned $82.

Oberlin's landfill received 511 pounds of plastic, paper, insulation, contaminated cardboard, short pieces of banding straps, food waste, small pieces of pressure-treated wood, and other general waste not easily recycled or reused. For calculating LEED points, we used the number of square feet of conditioned space (in our case 2,496 ft² that includes the low storage loft and the basement). Diverted waste does not include metal, plastic, or cardboard that is routinely recycled, but must be recycled to earn points. Our total waste reduction was 95 percent (8,961 lbs ÷ 9,472 lbs), and we sent 0.2 lbs/ft² to the landfill (511 lbs ÷ 2,496 ft²). This was 60 percent less than the 0.5 lbs/ft² required to earn three LEED points!

Mary and I hauled and organized scrap OSB, I joists, and beams all morning. After lunch, I brought three more Agway Cart loads of scrap wood for Mary to organize and stack. I then swept water out of the ground floor; installers would lay tar paper on the roof the next day, finally allowing the house to begin drying out.

At this point, with Mary and me spending so much time in Oberlin, we were taking advantage of an arrangement made in April with Nathan Engstrom, who had become a friend. Although staying with the Benzings was a great arrangement, it meant that we had a 20 minute drive to Oberlin. Engstrom's house, just two blocks from our property, had a separate entrance to a bedroom and half bath—a perfect arrangement for us. He graciously agreed to have us stay with him during Oberlin visits until we moved to town.

Mary and Engstrom prepared dinner that night, which we shared with Strehle, Scout, and other friends. On the job, Strehle was intense, especially when focused on achieving a particular task. However, he changed hats effortlessly, easily joining the party with people he had only seen or heard about. It was eight when he excused himself and the party dispersed. Out of the blue, Scout announced to Mary and me, "I am going to show you the apartment that you are going to live in until your house is finished."

I was taken off guard. We hadn't yet decided when we'd be moving to Oberlin, but we had to settle in by early September; I'd be teaching a one-credit environmental studies course in the fall. I had asked Scout and others to look out for an inexpensive apartment convenient to Trail Magic, but it wasn't on our must-do list, and I wasn't yet ready.

With some hesitation, Mary and I followed Scout to his office. He drove us one block past Trail Magic and then north on the next street, pulling into the last driveway. At the end was a two-story white building with garage doors at the ground level, and two windows on the second floor—the classic garage apartment. A half-full dumpster sat in front. Scout explained that refurbishment of new windows, carpeting, toilet, and kitchen appliances was underway, and that the apartment would be ready for occupancy by early August. He escorted us up a wide staircase through a door into a modest kitchen with a separate eating area. Down a short hall were the bathroom and two small bedrooms, and to the right of the kitchen was a living room. The monthly rent was $600, plus utilities. It was perfect, but my response was flat. Scout's sudden presentation had surprised Mary, too. We told him that we'd think it over and get back to him.

We were on-site early the next day to finalize choices for bathroom faucets and shower and tub fixtures before embarking on a 10-day family vacation to St. Louis and Arkansas. I felt bad about my response to Scout's surprise. Mary and I agreed that he had found the perfect apartment—a 5-minute bike ride from Trail Magic; just the right size, with a guest room, space for bikes, and private yard; and the town's sole grocery store across the street. I called him with our enthusiastic response. I asked if he could get the rent lowered. He did—to $550—but with three months rent and a deposit paid up front. We agreed. Scout was right. It was where we'd stay until moving to Trail Magic.

Back in Oberlin, we met with the HVAC subcontractor, taking two hours to review the ventilation system. I gave him the spiel I gave to every subcontractor about our goal of a climate-neutral home. He assured me that the fan on the air handler was very efficient, and that between floors, the temperatures would differ by no more than 2°F. He didn't know if the energy recovery ventilation system was programmable as we had requested, but he'd find out and it wasn't.

Later, while the head electrician was marking locations of switches, plugs, lights, ceiling fans, speaker wires, cable, and phone jacks, I asked him about the Watts drawn by each ground fault interrupter (GFI). He hadn't thought about GFI-draw or about the phantom load that all electrical equipment uses on standby: GFIs, garage door openers, computers and TVs, ceiling fans, internet modems, and wireless routers, to name a few. He was surprised when I told him that studies estimated phantom load as accounting for 15 percent of home electrical use. As far as GFIs went, code required that he install them, but he could link several plugs to one GFI.

The next day, July 16, after stopping at a lumber store to obtain details for ordering bamboo flooring, we headed to Troy. Hot water was on my mind; Strehle needed a decision for the on-demand hot water system. He had given us a choice of a system with two 30 amp circuits that could provide a 60°F temperature increase at a flow rate of 2 gallons per minute, or one with three 30 amp circuits that could provide a 70°F temperature increase at a flow rate of 2.5 gallons per minute. I asked David Borton for his opinion. Estimating that the entering water temperature would range between 40°F and 65°F, and with a shower flow rate of 1.5 gallons per minute, we agreed that the two circuit system would be fine, except for in winter when two people wanted showers at the same time. We didn't see a problem; one could wait.

In Troy, our 2.86 kW PV system had generated all the electricity we used. Our water, however, was heated with gas. In my calculations for electricity use in Oberlin, I had failed to consider hot water. Borton did a quick calculation based on our use of 7 therms of natural gas per month for hot water in Troy—the annual use of 84 therms equaled 2,400 kWh! My heart sank. Our total estimated energy production for Trail Magic was only 3,350 kWh. I felt a little better when we accounted for tank heat loss and solar input from our evacuated tube, solar hot water system. The energy needed for hot water decreased to 1,000 kWh. This was still huge, and a deal breaker for climate neutrality; we had estimated our use—without hot water—at 2,800 kWh.

Borton quipped, "It's no big deal. What's five or six hundred kWh? It's less than one nice dinner out for you and Mary." He was right, but I wanted Trail Magic to run on sunshine, without question.

We had made a list of bare essentials that we'd need for the apartment in Oberlin. The plan was to drive both our car and the truck loaded with apartment furnishings. We'd stay for a few days to set up the apartment and work on-site, and then drive the car home. We'd continue packing the house and then drive a moving truck and the car back in time for a dinner and orientation program for new faculty on August 20. Before the drywall went up, we'd return to Troy, finish packing, close on the house, and return with another moving truck in early September in time for my first class.

Over the next week, Mary packed her doll collection and began sorting through two floor-to-ceiling dining room hutches overflowing with innumerable family treasures, gifts, and sets of dishes and serving platters. She applied a simple sorting rule. If we had used it within the year, pack it. If we hadn't needed it in five years, find it a new home. Give other items some thought before packing them. But, as you can imagine, this was easy to say, but hard to implement. I continued purging in the basement. Soon it was time to pack the truck with items for our apartment and venture west once again.

> ### Sidebar 10: Positive Energy and Climate Positive Homes
>
> A positive energy home uses on-site sunshine to provide more energy than is used for its operation. A climate positive home operates with no overall use of fossil fuels while having a net removal of CO_2 from the atmosphere. Both types of homes diminish climate change but the climate positive home uses only local solar energy. This distinction highlights the importance of directly using local sunshine because it shortens energy supply lines and increases resilience to infrastructure disruptions.
>
> Positive energy and climate positive homes are, however, only beginning steps for abating climate change. In Sidebar 1, I considered my wife's and my personal energy use in 2007 of 380 million BTUs, with house operating energy at 180 million BTUs. These 380 BTUs do not include another 320 million BTUs which are my wife's and my share of the energy used to create and maintain the country's infrastructure, police and military forces, educational and healthcare systems, and more; all of which need to be provided without adding heat trapping gases to the atmosphere, if we are to curtail climate destabilization.

We arrived on July 29. The two-story barn we had Strehle build boldly announced its existence, encased with white Tyvek DripWrap. The barn and house had metal roofs. Exterior doors were on the house, inside walls and temporary stairs to the study were installed. The plumbing and electrical teams had run the water and drain pipes and electrical wiring. We were impressed with Strehle's progress!

The next three days were much as before. We managed waste and cleaned up on-site, met with Ferut and various suppliers, ate lunch with Strehle to ask questions and make choices, and had dinners with the Benzings and at

Engstrom's. On Friday, when a new refrigerator and stove arrived at the apartment, we hosted a dinner for Scout. We celebrated his finding the apartment
and his efforts in helping us make connections in Oberlin. But, more important, we toasted his leadership in having the city kick its coal addiction and
Oberlin's challenge to become climate neutral.

We were up at 6:30 a.m. on Saturday for an early start to Troy. Stopping at
Trail Magic to give Strelhe input before leaving, we saw things to do, and the
good weather allured us. Before we knew it, it was noon. We loved being there
and didn't want to leave. Four hours into our drive, I realized that I was
exhausted, physically and emotionally. This was my 18th trip to Oberlin in not
much more than a year. I had always enjoyed the drive, but now it was too
much. Could we finish packing before August 19, and then move everything
in two trucks? Our close friends, Howard and Margaret Stoner, might be up for
the adventure, and Howard loves to drive. We called and asked for their help.

The pressure was on. I arranged to pick up two 26-foot Penske trucks on
Saturday, August 16; hired two men to assist us in loading the trucks on the
17th; and scheduled the house closing for the 18th. We let our close friends and
colleagues know that we would welcome their help in packing and cleaning
up the house. We had two weeks.

My crude calculation indicated that at least 40 percent of our possessions
needed new homes. Simply put, our Troy house had 4,000 square feet of space
for stuff, while Trail Magic would have 2,500 square feet. Our children took
what they wanted. The best furniture that we couldn't use went to the Troy
United Ministries furniture program, and a local auctioneer filled a pick-up
truck with unneeded furniture and other items. Mary delivered 15 carloads to
the Salvation Army and Goodwill Industries. We donated a snow blower and
rotary mower attachment to Capital District Community Gardens. Some 400
books found a new home at the public library. We happily treated friends and
people who dropped by to innumerable items, including lumber, kindling, a
computer table, house plants, a grill, and more.

We started early and finished late. Friends came to pack during the day and,
just as we were ready to quit, others would come with dinner and the motivation to keep us going. We were exhausted, but hopeful. Down to just three
days, we still had much to accomplish. I coveted a dumpster in the worst way.
Sunday came. Fresh volunteers joined in, and by dark, the house was mostly
empty and two trucks almost full.

On Monday, with a few unbelievably dedicated friends, we cleaned the
house and stuffed the remaining items into the trucks. At 11 p.m., I placed the
last bag of trash on the curb. We didn't, after all, need a dumpster. Over the
two months of packing, we disposed of 32 bags, or 640 lbs, in the Troy landfill. We locked the doors on an immaculately clean house, and crashed at the
Bortons' home.

Howard and I started our trucks at 6:30 a.m. and rolled across the Hudson
River, with Margaret and Mary soon to follow carrying a banquet for our lunch
later that day. Like real truckers, Howard and I pulled next to 18-wheelers to
take on 68 gallons of diesel fuel, paying the most I've ever paid to fill up:

$304. Mary loved watching the big yellow trucks weave amongst the green, rolling hills of southern New York. We pushed hard and beat the Cleveland rush-hour traffic, parking the trucks in front of the barn a little before 5 p.m.

Howard and I were up before 7 a.m. to prepare signage in the barn to facilitate an orderly unpacking and organizing of boxes so that we could find necessary items in the months to come. A week earlier I had emailed Portman, Scout, and others asking for help. A dozen people came, and, before noon, everything was in the barn. A neighbor brought a vegetarian lunch that we enjoyed under the shade of the maple tree next to the barn. It had been a hellish two weeks, but thanks to the generosity of friends, old and new, everything had progressed without a snag.

We returned the trucks to the rental company in the early afternoon. I met with our LEED green rater for his pre-drywall inspection. He spent about an hour scrutinizing everything, and asked a few questions. Enthusiastic and positive, he didn't see any problems, but would get back to me if he did. I invited him to the pre-drywall open house the following Sunday, and then headed to campus for the reception and dinner for new faculty members. Perhaps it was my coming down from the emotional intensity of the previous weeks, but this was surreal. Here I was, 66 years old, having spent the last 33 as a faculty member, attending a welcome and orientation evening as a new faculty member.

Chapter 7:
Deadline

Mike Strehle is a supreme master of "just in time" execution and getting people to cooperate with him. The lumber for the barn arrived on July 15; the next day Strehle and Aaron began framing. Two weeks later the barn was up, protected with Tyvek DrainWrap. Loewen windows were in place, and the roof contractors had screwed down the raised-seam steel roof. On the morning of August 19, as we caravanned across New York State, installation of the two garage doors and construction of the sliding door for the tractor entrance were taking place.

The next day, after we had stored all our belongings in the barn, Strehle hung the tractor door and secured a lock on the person door entrance. All the while, he was orchestrating finishing touches inside the house so that subcontractors could spray the closed-cell foam and damp cellulose insulation prior to our open house on Sunday, August 24. We'd invited 40 guests to come and see the guts of Trail Magic before they were hidden behind sheetrock boards which would arrive the next day.

In real time, Strehle was choreographing the integrated movement of innumerable pieces into the structural elements that formed the functional systems of Trail Magic. The creation of a house follows a pliable set of assembly rules which, when executed with precision, is as enthralling as any well-presented, free-form dance in which the next move depends upon what had just happened.

In late June, Strehle had moved all the oak, ash, and maple logs out of the way to the eastside meadow while I sought someone in the area to mill our trees for use in the house. I found people who could cut the logs and dry the boards, but no one seemed that interested or had the capacity to do everything—cut trees, buck the trunks, pick up the logs, and deliver finished boards in a timely fashion. Then we had a trail magic event.

Ferut had selected Douglas fir for the interior open-riser stairs to match the casements of the Loewen windows. Strehle ordered the boards from his supplier, but when they arrived, they were too rough and required sanding. A man named George Ficke, located about an hour southeast of Oberlin, could do the sanding. We learned that the Douglas fir boards were unusable for open-riser stairs, but Ficke had the capacity to process our logs.

I called Ficke and told him about the oak logs and ash trees that we were thinking about lumbering. He was interested in seeing what we had.

A week later I met Ficke and his foreman at Trail Magic. Ficke's affable nature was immediately obvious. He was curious about the house, so I gave him a tour. He and Strehle immediately engaged in "builder" talk. By the depth and pattern of their conversation, I knew they were two masters, each sizing up the other. Ficke was a stocky six feet tall with a charming smile that was a key part of his relaxed, confident demeanor. He was complimentary of Strehle's work and liked what we were doing. Strehle was his even, matter-of-fact self, but appeared appreciative of the good words.

We walked to the meadow to look at the pile of logs while I discussed our desire to use on-site lumber for beams, bookcases, and flooring. Ficke said he could do whatever we wanted, but reminded us that after cutting, wood takes time to dry, especially thick beams; those can take years to air dry and months in a kiln. He estimated a cost of $4,000 to $5,000 to process our pile. We walked down the meadow to the flood plain and then up the western side of the property, pointing out ash trees worth lumbering.

Clueless to the value of the trees, I asked Ficke, "How much will we get for our trees, and what will flooring cost?"

He responded, "Not very much. On the stump, about 10 percent of the finished product. Ash flooring is going for about $4 per board foot. Your share would be between 35 and 40 cents. But what you'll actually get depends on the market at the time." He thought we had several thousand dollars worth of ash, but he'd have to come back with his timber expert, Moses, to get a more precise estimate.

Ficke had started his career as a carpenter-cabinet maker, and after building houses for a number of years, established a highly specialized and lucrative form of cabinetry, creating the wood interiors for custom aircraft, especially those employed in the international transportation of medical patients. His avocation was aviation history, and he collected signed, first-edition books by aviators and other memorabilia. In his collection is one of 11 known checks signed by Wilber Wright, and a draft of the book *We* by Charles Lindberg. (I later learned that he owned several medical transport aircraft and flew them on missions around the world.)

I asked him if he had a business card. He didn't. He did business by word-of-mouth. I didn't know what to make of Ficke or his business. I liked him and felt good about what he could do for us. Clearly, he was not your ordinary wood mill operator.

Four days later, Ficke, Moses, and I walked the land to size-up the job of selectively cutting the ash with as little disturbance as possible. Moses concurred that we had plenty of ash trees to make cutting them financially worthwhile. Within the month, he would arrange for someone to fell the trees I marked. The next day I put a white circle with a red X on perhaps 35 trees, mostly ash, but two cherries and several black walnuts that were either dying or growing too close to the 80-foot-high, three-foot-in-diameter ash trees. We had several dozen other trees of lumbering size—mostly red oaks and sugar maples—but we only wanted to remove the ash that were likely to succumb to the emerald ash borer.

I had had the wild idea of using the wood from the 100-year-old oak trees for something at Trail Magic. Now, after a year of false starts, that wild idea gained traction. The several dozen ash trees, along with two oaks, two cherries, one maple, and a few black walnuts, provided us with our own wood to use at our discretion—flooring, bookcases, shelves, beams, counters, trim, and a custom made, dining room table. Ficke was willing to exchange his hardwood flooring for our wood (and thus replace the bamboo flooring we were about to buy). But first, Ficke suggested, we should consider flooring with mixed species. He invited us to see a floor with 65 species that he had created for a friend and colleague called Doc.

Three days later we were in Doc's house looking at an eclectic display of colors and grains among floor boards of different widths. The floor, initially shocking with such contrasts, was actually beautiful. The floor, as well as the kitchen cabinets, stairs, railings, and balusters in Doc's house were elegant, the work of a true craftsman with an upscale artistic flair. An uneasy feeling swept over me—the one I get when I step out of my comfort zone of the practical into the world of the elite where cost is of no concern.

We sat at Doc's dining room table and talked flooring. Mary and I weren't bold enough to embrace dozens of species in our floor, but the idea of three—ash, maple, and oak—had appeal, as did the differing board widths that Doc had in her floor. We picked two: 3" and 4½". Knowing the beauty of black walnut, we asked if he had black walnut flooring available for our stair landings. He did. We asked about price. Again, he said it was hard to know in advance. "Do we need a contract?" I asked.

"Sure," Ficke responded, and reached for a piece of paper. He wrote the list and we signed it:

> About 900 sq. ft. mix of ash, oak, maple main floor house
> App 1200 sq. ft. mixed (like Doc's) barn bal house
> App 100 sq. ft. of walnut natural two landings
> App $8000.00; $4000.00 on delivery of 1st item
> Balance will depend on trade offs of lumber harvested

This was a laid-back arrangement, kind of like when we shook hands with Doren Portman. Without knowing much about Ficke, I trusted him and, of course, he had to trust us. This is the way I believe arrangements ought to be. People discuss the overall parameters, arriving at an agreement, with exact details to be mutually worked out as the process unfolds—the KISS approach (Keep It Simple Stupid). I know that all people are not equally trustworthy and, all too often, disagreements emerge. We trusted that Ficke would be like Portman.

I kept Strehle abreast of our arrangements with Ficke, because they would radically alter Strehle's agenda. Over the course of four months, we had gone from bamboo flooring and oak for doors, trim, and baseboard, with Strehle doing everything; to bamboo flooring and oak doors, with Strehle doing trim and baseboard at a later time with site wood; to bamboo flooring and Strehle doing doors, trim, and baseboard in pine. Strehle didn't want to leave anything for later, especially if it involved him coming back. Now, we were throwing him an unpredictable knuckleball.

We absolutely loved the idea of using local wood for our flooring. It had to be better environmentally than gluing bamboo pieces together and shipping such a heavy product halfway around the globe. We were also pleased to support the local economy and Ficke's workers—it affirmed our desire to embrace local industry. The economics for us, however, were another matter. Bamboo flooring cost $3.85/ft² plus Strehle's installation cost of just over a dollar. Raw Ohio hardwood flooring was about $4.00/ft² with Strehle's installation and the contracted sanding and finishing costing $4.00/ft² more.

Nevertheless, we decided to replace the bamboo flooring with native Ohio hardwood on the first floor and on the two landings. And we would delay installing flooring in the second floor study and loft until Ficke could cut, dry, and mill our wood sometime in the spring.

Strehle didn't say anything when I told him our plan; however, I knew he wanted to complete the entire job while he was in the heat of it. Earlier we had backed away from using our wood, but this time Ficke had given us an opportunity we really wanted—beautiful hardwood floors from site and other local wood. We had to do it!

Taking this opportunity impacted Strehle in two major ways. First, the study and loft would go unfinished—floor, trim, and baseboard—until spring while we waited for the flooring made from our trees. This meant Strehle couldn't finish the house and would have to take time from another job later. Second and more problematic, he was dependent upon Ficke to get him the mixed hardwood boards for the first floor in a timely fashion. He knew nothing about Ficke, and making a finished floor from raw boards produced by a local mill had unknowns that store-bought, prefinished, bamboo flooring didn't.

In early August we decided to schedule a community-wide open house for later in the fall. I had been impressed with the huge turnout at Peter Crowley's open house six months earlier—Ferut reported that 800 people had come. Believing that Trail Magic would be far greener than Crowley's house because it was passive solar and likely climate neutral, I didn't see why we wouldn't attract an equally impressive crowd.

The open house would be a big event that required Don Watson's presence, and I really wanted him to see his creation. Because Strehle was confident about finishing the house by November, we picked November 8. If things unfolded as planned, we'd have moved in, and Ferut and I would have plenty of time to arrange for Watson to speak at Oberlin College and at Kent State, where Ferut taught in the architecture program.

Mary and I had an excellent working relationship with Strehle, and upon our move to Oberlin, quickly fell into a routine. We rode our bikes from the garage apartment, usually before 8 a.m., to carry on with our jobs of waste management and clean up, and to take care of any other tasks. Strehle was on-site at 6 a.m. and hit the ground running. He was no-nonsense, focused, intense, fast-working, and expected your full engagement. One day, Aaron was standing idle after completing a task. Strehle walked by and without breaking stride said, "Find something useful to do."

Sheet rockers generally get a bad rap. But I was impressed with our workers' efficiency and had informative conversations with several. But they did leave a mess. For two weeks, Mary and I swept up scraps and organized large pieces, thinking they could be used. I don't know if our salvage efforts made any difference, but a massive 3,660 pounds were waste.

Because it would take another three weeks to tape, plaster, and sand the sheetrock, Strehle turned his attention to outside tasks. He finished the Hardi-board siding, installed on the front porch ceiling the Douglas fir wainscot that I had polyurethaned, cut and assembled the 6x6 timbers for the front walk and porch, and filled the foundation of the porch with old chunks of concrete and asphalt dumped on the property many years earlier.

He overwhelmed us with final decisions: interior paint colors, faucets for bathroom sinks, make and color of dual flush toilets, bathtub, tile for the bathroom floors and master bathroom shower, towel racks and toilet paper holders, hardware for interior and exterior doors, material for sun patio surface, all appliances, fold-down beds and mattresses, light fixtures, speakers to mount in the great room, shelving and clothes racks for closets, and shelving and countertop for the pantry. Every day we added at least one decision item to our list. We had discussed many of them earlier, but now Mike needed final choices.

For a long time I had been bothered by putting a small, under-the-counter refrigerator in the downstairs kitchenette because small refrigerators are energy inefficient. The best available had an annual use over 100 kWh, and none were Energy Star rated. In early September, as we sat with Strehle on the front porch timbers, I complained once again. A bit tired of my whining, he smiled and said, "Just give your guests a cooler."

The next day I greeted Strehle with, "I have an idea. I thought about your cooler suggestion last night. Let's build an under-the-counter ice box. When guests come, we'll take freezer packs from the freezer and put them in the ice box." He didn't say so, but I suspect he regretted his quip; after all, "let's build" meant "Mike build." And, of course, it was a change order that would cost much more than a small refrigerator. However, it would use little energy and last as long as the house.

In fall 2005, we elected to install a PV system on our house in Troy, expecting to stay there awhile. When we decided a year later to move, I was disappointed because I thought the agreement I had signed stated that New York State, because of subsidies, had a lien on the system for five years. After we purchased the Portman land, I reread our agreement. Our only obligation was to provide the installers, Mike Stangl and Kevin Rose, with our annual kWh production numbers for two years. I asked Stangl to confirm our obligations. His query to New York State affirmed my assessment that the system was ours. I was overjoyed! We could move the system from Troy to Oberlin for several thousand dollars; purchasing a system new would cost $25,000. On August 9, just six days after recording our two year production numbers, Rose and his crew disassembled our system.

Stangl and Rose had always treated us well because I advocated what they were doing. A few years earlier, I had written a short article about energy and our experience with the PV system, "Positive energy: A true understanding of energy use comes only with hands-on experience," for Oberlin's alumni magazine. They, others, and I handed it out to hundreds of people at talks, solar tour open houses, and energy fairs. Since 2005, Stangl and Rose's business had grown from part time to full time, and by the summer of 2008, they were overwhelmed. Despite their backlog of jobs, they fit us in.

Rose explained how the panels and inverter were wired and offered to secure for us at cost the necessary materials for reassembly. Not knowing who would reassemble the system in Oberlin, I video recorded key parts of the disassembly process. Several days later, Rose brought me 22 used panel boxes from another job in which to transport our panels to Ohio, along with the required hardware to reassemble the system. He also offered to be on call, if needed.

In Oberlin, Ferut and Strehle recommended that Strehle and his electrician reassemble the system because the local electrician who was experienced in PV work was expensive. I went against their recommendation, however; I wanted to support the electrician in the community who advocated PV.

The reassembly got off to a rocky start. On a raised seam roof, the PV panels mount on aluminum rails that attach to the seams via specially designed S5 clamps. The clamps are U shaped, with two ridges at the inside top of the U. With the open part of the U facing down, the clamp slips over the raised seam, and two headless bolts in the clamp screw against the seam to tightly fasten it to the roof.

In preparation for mounting the panels, I took a scrap section of our Firestone UC-4 roof to ensure we knew how to attach the clamps. To my surprise, the U didn't fit over the raised seam of our roof. Had Rose given us the wrong clamp? I called him to ask if we had the right clamps; he thought so, but would check. I spent an hour on the Firestone and S5 clamp web sites, but neither provided any useful information.

Two days later, I finally reached Mark, who had installed the roof. Yes, we had the right S5 clamp, but to make one fit the UC-4 roof, the seam had to be crimped. Mark told me his roofers had attached the snow guard rails to our roof with S5 clamps, so I climbed up and looked. Sure enough, the seams were crimped, but in the process it looked like the coatings on the metal might have been gouged making it possible for the roof to rust. To see if I could make a clamp fit without crimping the seam, I filed off the two ridges at the top of the U on an S5 clamp. It slipped over nicely. But were the ridges necessary for the clamp to hold? Strehle thought that we needed at least one ridge. I called David Borton for the physics. Yes, we needed one. Because it would take about half an hour to hand file off one ridge on each clamp, Strelhe tried his crimpers on a seam. He could crimp the seam and slip a clamp over without marring the finish. Problem solved.

We were adding two new panels to our system to use the full capacity of our DC to AC inverter and, to fit the roof, we required three rows of eight panels instead of two rows of 11 panels that we'd had in Troy. Because of the different pattern, we had sufficient length of rail from the old system, but we had to cut and splice them. Ensuring that we knew how to splice rails and attach panels, I assembled a pair of spliced rails with S5 clamps and panels and showed Strehle. Mary and I then began to take a final inventory of all the clamps, screws, bolts, ground clamps, and splice connectors to confirm that we had what we needed.

As we finished lunch, Kim Annabel from Ferut's office called. She was still working on the woodstove problem that arose on Monday. Because Strehle and Ferut weren't familiar with woodstove installation, Strehle had installed a three-foot-high, standard 2x4 wood-stud, sheetrock wall to separate the stove from the piano. But the narrow width of the stairwell wall in the great room, where the woodstove and piano were, only allowed five inches between the stove and the separation wall. Code required a 16" separation if the wall was combustible. Strehle discovered the code violation and asked me to work with Ferut on a solution.

I called Ferut to get his recommendation for materials for a non-combustible wall. He called the stove manufacturer, Hearthstone. They referred him to the dealer, who referred him to their installer, who referred him back to Hearthstone. Frustrated, I called Watson. Always calm and never critical of others, Watson this time welled up with emotions of irritation: "I can't believe that no one there knows what to use! Marble, stone, or tile on rock board with steel studs." Unfamiliar with rock board, I asked about it. "It's cement board with non-combustible backings," he explained. Ferut decided tile was the easiest to use and cost effective; Watson agreed.

That problem solved, I continued helping Mary with the inventory of rail mounting hardware. We discovered that we only had 25 of the required 56 stainless steel bolt-nut-washer assemblies to connect rails to L brackets, but everything else was in good order. After dinner at Strehle's house and seeing the knock-down plaster finish on his ceilings—what he recommended—we went shopping for paint for the OSB walls in the workroom and for the balance of steel bolts, nuts, and washers we needed to attach the panels.

I was at Trail Magic at 8 a.m. the next morning. Strehle was on the roof measuring. I set up my computer in the pantry and asked him if he wanted to watch the disassembly video.

"I don't have time," he said.

"Mike," I replied, "I didn't make the video for my health. I'll show you the most informative five minutes."

Afterwards, I reviewed Rose's design for electrically connecting two serial strings of 12 panels in three rows with Strehle. He studied the diagram for a minute and said, "I'm not going to do it that way." Surprised, I responded, "Well, how are you going to do it?" His sequence of steps was an improvement over the previous plan and affirmed again how quickly Strehle's brain solves spatial problems. (I did feel better about all my planning and videoing when he commented that the video did show him how to secure the ground wire tautly from panel to panel by tightening the ground clamp before the final laying down of a panel between rails.)

The electricians arrived at 9 a.m. to mount and wire the inverter and meters. Meanwhile, my first job was to assemble the rails while Strehle attached 5S clamps with L brackets to the raised seams. By eleven, Strehle had attached two rails to the roof. Aaron took up a panel to see if it fit between the rails. It was tight, but slid in. Strehle asked an electrician to test it; the sky was crystal-clear—the electrons jumped.

After lunch, we tested all the panels. Then the assembly routine began. Aaron carried panels to Strehle on the roof while I attached and greased the ground wire connector on each panel. Although we had a few new connectors, most of them had been left on the panels and required removal, cleaning, and reattachment in the proper place before being greased.

I hit a few connectors that were difficult to remove and was in the barn when I heard Strehle yell from the roof, "Carl! Where are you? I need panels." I stepped out, looked at Mike on the roof and replied, "Coming. Had a few corroded connectors," and went back into the barn thinking, "I'm just part of the crew," as I hustled to get a panel to Aaron.

Mike wired and anchored 16 panels, and I had positioned all the ground connectors before we quit late that afternoon. I was on-site early the next day to help Mike with the remaining eight panels, but they were up: he had actually mounted them the evening before. The electricians returned and ran the ground wire and the wires from the two strings of panels through the conduit to the workroom, and then connected the panel wires to the inverter. The next morning they wired the system to the grid and ran it for 30 minutes. On Monday morning the Oberlin city inspector checked the installation and turned on the system. The meter began running backwards.

I was immensely satisfied with the whole reassembly process. Strehle was a master at doing what he had never done. With a little help from his workers, he had mounted and wired a 24-panel system in one 12-hour day. The city of Oberlin also won my admiration. In Troy, it had taken a month for the power company to inspect and turn on our PV system. Oberlin did it in one business day!

Saturday, September 20, was memorable. Over the past week, Stehle had spread numerous piles of subsoil and topsoil in preparation for Cameron Buchs to rough grade the disturbed areas around the house and barn. The two men that George Ficke had hired to fell our trees arrived. The crisp morning air and deep blue sky buoyed my confidence in what we were about to embark upon. I watched them as they downed trees and then trimmed branches and bucked logs from slain giants. I marveled at their skill and efficiency. I returned later to see them fell our biggest ash—four feet in diameter—parallel to several others they had dropped. At 4:30 they packed their tools, having taken down some 40 trees. Buchs and Strehle worked the bulldozer and backhoe until dark to finish the grading.

The landscaping around the house and barn looked fantastic compared to the ever-changing visual disarray it had been for the past five months. The bottom two acres, however, were another story. The eastern meadow was impassable, cluttered with half a dozen tree tops and trunks. In the bottom land floodplain, two dozen slain trees lay singly or in piles of crisscrossed trunks with branches reaching 15 to 20 feet into the air. A dozen more corpses lay scattered across the western side savanna and prairie. Despite the horrible sight, most of our large trees remained. Skyward, the canopy had changed little except for the southeastern bottom land floodplain. There, the muted green of clustered mature trees had been replaced with blue sky broken by sparse, thinly leafed branches of young trees, mostly sugar maples, now relieved from the dominance of giants that had for decades constrained their growth.

On Sunday, I gassed-up my chain saw and headed to the eastern meadow to clear branches and open access to the downed trees. We worked until dark. I chain sawed while Mary carried and neatly stacked branches for chipping at a later date.

The class I was teaching at the college met on Monday afternoons. While I was busy with the course, Mary had discovered a beautiful piece of scrap granite left by a recently relocated stone company that we might be able to use for the top of the three-foot wall that separated the woodstove from the piano and wood bin.

On Tuesday morning, Trail Magic was humming with subcontractors: sheetrock tapers; solar hot-water installers; two men attaching wire mesh on the outside ground-floor Ready-Wall in preparation for stuccoing; and a concrete crew framing-up sidewalks. Mary and I carried on in the meadow all morning and into the afternoon, and then drove to the lumber store to pick colors for the cultured marble, bathroom sinks. We stopped to see if the stone company where Mary had dropped off the granite on Monday could cut and polish it for the woodstove wall—yes, they could.

Back at Trail Magic I chain sawed for an hour, finally opening a path to the floodplain below the field. Leaving my saw, I walked into the floodplain and climbed over the tangled mess of more than a dozen trees. In one place, five tree trunks with diameters of 18" to 30" crisscrossed in a pile ten feet high.

Originally, Ficke indicated that he would arrange for felling the trees and transporting logs to the sawmill. I would clean up the treetops for firewood. But then he asked if Strehle and I could get the logs to the road where a lumber truck could easily load them.

As I sat atop the five crisscrossed tree trunks, I knew that maneuvering the entangled logs to the road would be impossible without help. This was a lumbering operation, not an outing to gather firewood. I called Ficke, and after a few comments on the cleared branches in the meadow and the tangled mess in the floodplain, I stated simply, "George, you've sent a boy to do a man's job." He expressed confidence in me and then replied, "I wanted to keep the cost down, but I appreciate the situation and will make some calls and try to get you help."

The Amish crew leader who had been at the site on Saturday had offered to send me logging tongs; they arrived Wednesday. Portman loaned us even bigger tongs. All day Wednesday I worked to expose tree trunks. At 5 p.m., Strehle fired up his backhoe, and we began dragging logs to a spot near the street and next to the driveway. We moved a dozen logs to the road that evening.

On Thursday evening we hauled logs again. New equipment improved our efficiency. Portman had brought a logging chain that was much easier to use than tongs. I was awed when Mike pulled a huge ash log—two and a half feet in diameter and 25 feet long—out of the trees below the pond and hauled it up the field.

As I turned to find the next log, Mary saw a man walking briskly toward us and headed up the meadow to greet him. With intent in his stride and arms swinging, he was a man on a mission. Jogging to catch up with Mary, I recognized him as a neighbor whose property abutted ours. "What are you doing?" he exclaimed. "I can't believe an environmentalist is cutting down trees!"

"Have you heard of the emerald ash borer?" I asked.

"The emerald what?" he replied. "You cut down trees on my property! They were well into my land."

Wow! This would be interesting. I was confident about the western boundary; Scout had shown me a farmer's two large rocks and the iron stake marking the southwest corner of our middle parcel, and 10 feet to the west, another iron stake marking the thin, 10 feet by 840 feet western parcel. From this second iron marker, the property line extended due north and was clearly indicated by intermittent, rotten fence posts and sagging barbed wire. The few ash trees we had removed on the western side of the property were at least a dozen feet inside the fence line, but I could have been wrong.

I apologized and told him about the emerald ash borer killing ash trees and how we planned to use the lumber in our house. Still upset, he asked, "We had our property surveyed. Have you?"

"No," I said, excusing myself to get the next log ready for Mike.

While Strehle hauled out the log, I returned to explain further. The neighbor and Mary were chatting, and the passion had abated. He apologized for being so straightforward. I commented, "If someone had cut down our trees, I'd for sure be irate." We shook hands and agreed to confirm the property line. The next evening he came over while we were dragging more logs to the road. He apologized again for his behavior. I pointed out the iron stakes, which seemed to satisfy him. I told him that we would cut the limbs and branches into firewood and I'd bring him a load for his fireplace. He offered to pay. I refused.

George Ficke had had no luck in getting us help for our entangled trunks and in moving logs to the road. He suggested that we ask Cameron Buchs to move the logs with his heavy equipment. Over the next two weeks, when I could free myself from other tasks, I cleared access to most of the remaining trunks; some, however, were buried or otherwise inaccessible. We needed to wait for Buchs's equipment.

I knew that this was not what a 66-year-old academic ought to be doing. I worked for a few hours at a time, and only when alert. I studied the lay of the trunks and the positions of limbs, predicting what would happen when I made a particular cut. Whenever possible, I positioned a log or large branch between me and the log or branch I was cutting. More than once, I seriously questioned the sanity of engaging in this treacherous work and devoting innumerable hours just for the sake of using site wood at Trail Magic.

Buchs arrived at 8:30 a.m. on Saturday, October 11 with his heavy-duty backhoe, but after sizing up the job, decided that his Bobcat skidder was better suited to the task. The Bobcat is smaller than a pickup truck, but built like a bulldog. The driver sits in a well-protected cage with controls and a joy stick to maneuver the attachment on the front, in our case a forklift. A huge weight mounts on the back to counter balance the load in front. Caterpillar treads, gearing, and brakes enable the driver to turn on a dime. When Buchs climbed into the cab and began hauling logs, man and machine fused into a single ferocious organism.

With tongs or chains, Strehle had been limited to one log at a time. The Bobcat could carry two to four modest-sized logs (8 to 16 feet long, 1 to 2 feet in diameter), or one big log (12 to 30 feet long, 2 to 3 feet in diameter). I'd direct Buchs to a log, and with the skill of a brain surgeon removing a tumor, he'd push, pull, lift, and rotate a log until he could slip the forklift tongs underneath the load and carry it at top speed to the road. It quickly became a contest between the old guy with a chain saw and the man machine, log devouring monster. I had about 5 minutes from when the satiated beast roared up the field until empty tonged, it screeched down the hill on the south side of the pond ready to be fed. I had to find and clear, if necessary, an access path to the next meal. For two and a half hours I kept the beast constantly on the move, and then Mary appeared with pizza for lunch. We had cleared all the logs along the eastern meadow and in the savannah and prairie, and had begun to work in the floodplain.

The trunks in the swampy area of the floodplain were the most challenging—the ones I didn't believe we could retrieve until I witnessed the marvels of the man machine beast. Although standing water no longer remained, the area was a potential quagmire that Buchs wished to avoid. We broke out a logging chain and two heavy-duty chains we could hook together to make a single chain about 25 feet long. While Buchs hauled a log to the road, I'd maneuver the logging chain around another trunk and attach it to the long chain. When Buchs returned, I'd connect the loose end of the long chain to the Bobcat, and he'd pull the trunk free and out of the swamp. If the trunk were too long, I'd buck it.

By 5 p.m., we had retrieved all but about a dozen trunks. Those dozen, however, were entangled in and buried under treetops and limbs. I labored until dark to clear access. Sunday morning we pulled the rest of the trunks from the floodplain, even discovering a good-sized one buried under four other trees. Two days later, on October 14, the fifth truck load of logs was heading south where they would become boards. The driver told me that each truck load was about 2,500 board feet, for a total of 12,500 board feet. A board foot is equivalent to a board one inch thick, one foot long, and one foot wide. We later learned that our logs, when cut, had yielded 14,310 board feet of useable green lumber, sufficient to do 35 living room floors, 15 by 20 feet.

Sidebar 11: Lumber from Trail Magic Trees

Total wood harvested was 16,759 board feet of which 2,449 board feet were cants or centers that were worthless, thus yielding 14,310 board feet of usable green wood. The following table provides a breakdown of the usable lumber and grade given in board feet.

Type of Wood	Select	#1 Common	#2 Common	Total
Ash	4,351	3,845	1,923	10,119
Red Oak	1,427	528	241	2,196
Black Walnut	428	327	371	1,126
Red Maple	337	86	41	464
Cherry	284	34	87	405

Shrinkage during drying was ~7%, or 1,001 board feet, leaving 13,309 board feet of dried lumber. Volume lost in cutting, planing, and molding was ~22%, or 2,928 board feet, leaving 10,381 board feet of useable lumber. Projects at Trail Magic used 7,640 board feet. Most of the remainder became flooring and stairs in the Vermilion Valley Vineyards, a new local winery designed by Joseph Ferut and Associates in which David Benzing is one of three owners.

In late September, Ficke delivered local oak, ash, and maple flooring boards that he had milled for us from dried boards he had in stock. On October 6, Strehle started to lay the floor. He'd estimated three days to install the raw boards, with finishing work coming later. But Ficke's boards frustrated him. Flooring that's milled by a small operation has irregularities and defects not found in mass-produced flooring, especially when different species are milled at different times. Some of Ficke's boards had small variations in width, and others had knots or excessively rough areas, rendering them unusable. With two widths and half a dozen species—ash, maple, and several species of oak—creating an interesting, pleasing pattern took time. With his modus operandi stymied, Strehle was not pleased by the five days it took to lay the floor.

Strehle's irritation, however, welled up from deeper pools than Ficke's boards. Trail Magic's open house was less than a month away. Although mostly unspoken, we all accepted that the house would be ready for occupancy then. Mary and I had been working consistently long days and most weekends since we had moved to Oberlin. Strehle, as his references had stated, was a workaholic. He was always on the move, pushing hard to complete whatever he was doing. At the same time he was calm, adjusting smoothly to whatever happened. Mary and I routinely had lunch with Strehle on-site and often had him to our apartment for dinner. Lunches had their relaxed moments, but they were brief, and our conversations were mostly job related. In contrast, our dinners together were relaxed, leisurely affairs. However, as September waned, Strehle's intensity notched up.

Mary and I were naïve, not only about the endless list of tasks to accomplish in the next month, but also about their interdependencies. Strehle wasn't. He asked the sheetrock contractor to expeditiously finish plastering and sanding. Appreciating our deadline, the owner asked his crew to work on Saturday, and even came himself to plaster. This made it possible for Strehle to prime the walls and ceilings a few days sooner, thereby allowing him to complete the flooring at an earlier date. When laying the floor consumed more days than planned, all was pushed back. He couldn't install kitchen cabinets until the floor was laid. Door frames and base boards had to wait until contractors sanded and polyurethaned the floors. Sinks and faucets, of course, needed countertops, but countertops first needed cabinets. Strehle knew that he had to keep in line these many temporally related interdependent strings of events, or the deadline would be history. He managed his team well—even Mary and me, the volunteer home-owner crew.

The last two weeks in September we devoted to waste management. After a final sorting of wood waste, Mary took two truck loads of scrap OSB and TJI joists—1,980 pounds—to Kurtz Brothers in Cleveland for recycling into yard mulch. It took an entire weekend to haul 3,660 pounds of sheetrock waste from the house and spread it over the landscape. Mary spent hours cleaning unused plaster from dozens of discarded plastic bags and spreading it in the front yard.

In October, our efforts turned to the land. We spent days dragging logs to the road and picking up rocks before planting grass in the front yard and winter wheat on the remaining acre of disturbed land. We then spread 100 bales of straw over the seeded areas to hold the ground and keep the seeds moist. Strehle often needed us to fetch something for him—nails, screws, paint, zip ties, drain pipes, drawer knobs, and cabinet handles—or to make a decision that often involved a trip to one of his suppliers.

On October 7, we hosted our first dinner at Trail Magic for Strehle and Scout—stir fried chicken that we'd made at the apartment. We set table on a picnic bench in the master bedroom that Strehle was painting green, and sat around it in lawn chairs. After dinner Strehle continued painting while Mary and I spent two hours cleaning up the mess in the great room that Strehle and Aaron had made putting down flooring.

This became our nightly routine for the next month. Strehle was just over 30 years old, and his body resilient—one 14-hour day of physical labor after another wasn't a problem. For Mary and me, with our 66- and 62-year-old bodies, this routine might have been considered cruel and unusual punishment if we hadn't volunteered. I often wondered how we kept going. Daily or twice daily doses of ibuprofen helped. At the same time, I felt better and better as continuous physical exercise conditioned my body, and I got stronger.

November 1 came. The house wasn't yet ready for inspection, but we were going to make the November 8, open house deadline. A few weeks earlier, we had compiled information and data on all aspects of Trail Magic and gave it to Kelly Viancourt, then editor of the college's alumni magazine. With creative genius, she put together an attractive four-page brochure. We printed 800 copies for the open house and for publicity purposes. Ferut and Strehle passed them on to professional associates and friends, while Mary and I used them at the college and in the town to promote the event. We all utilized whatever contacts we had to attract media attention.

Just past noon on Thursday, November 6, I picked up Don Watson from the airport. I was on an emotional high when I drove him down the driveway past Trail Magic's split rail fence. Watson had seen his ideas become reality many times, but I somehow imagined this time would be unique, special. After introductions, we walked to the sun patio, pleasantly warmed by the afternoon sun, to eat lunch. As we settled into talking and eating, we heard a car drive in. David Borton had arrived from Troy. Everybody was here. After lunch we offered to give a tour. Watson politely excused himself to commune with the spirits of Trail Magic alone. Borton took the tour.

Watson, the consummate professional, contemplated and took pictures, but didn't say much; it was hard to know his thoughts. Borton, on the other hand, was delighted with Trail Magic, his vicariously created passive solar house. He thought it fantastic and was anxious to see performance; he believed it would be twice as energy efficient as his home.

Watson was speaking at the college that afternoon, a talk titled "Sustainability Begins at Home: A Century of Green Design." Watson masterfully articulated the convoluted path by which the principles undergirding Trail Magic's design had been discovered. Afterwards, Ferut, Strehle, Mary and I joined him on stage to discuss Trail Magic.

Ferut's wife joined us for a celebratory dinner, which like the gathering a year earlier on the Winsted green, was a sublime moment. We had, indeed, harmonized and made sweet music.

All day Friday, while the rest of us continued with tasks at Trail Magic, Ferut and Watson were at Kent State where Watson talked and met with students and faculty.

On Saturday morning, we bustled around preparing for our noon start. Watson created and placed several dozen signs explaining the various attributes and design features that gave Trail Magic not only efficient performance, but also provided comfort, health, and aesthetic beauty. Expecting several hundred people, we hung signs directing guests to the workroom entry door on the ground floor, where Watson would greet guests and hand them a brochure.

The weather had turned cloudy and cold, but fortunately it didn't rain. People trickled in from noon to one, but then the house was pleasantly full.

Our visitors, after seeing the PV meters and the energy recovery ventilation system in the workroom on the ground floor, then entered the family room, where Buck Webster, the man who'd installed the pond loop for the heat pump, explained the loop and heat pump as well as the solar and instant hot water systems. His wife helped him and kept a tally of visitors.

In the north bedroom I set up a continuously playing, six-minute Power Point presentation on the building of Trail Magic. The south bedroom had Strehle's display of Redi-Wall construction. People then headed upstairs, where Ferut and Strehle were in the great room answering questions. Borton, Mary, and I floated to wherever we were needed.

The last guest left at 4:30. Exhausted, but delighted with the curiosity and questions from many of the 350 visitors, we talked and relaxed in the great room for an hour before dinner.

It was the fall meeting of the college's Alumni Council Executive Board, whose members had been following our move and house-building adventure. Danielle Young asked if we'd host a catered dinner for two dozen people. A little before 6:00, she arrived with the food, disposable plates and cups, and plastic utensils. Before dinner we gave tours that were greatly enhanced by Watson's signage. At mealtime, we discovered that the caterer had failed to include serving utensils. Having none in our kitchen, Mary placed two plastic cups in each serving pan. We ate, told stories, and laughed. The party broke up about 9:00. I drove Watson to an airport hotel so that he could sleep soundly before departing on a 7 a.m. flight to New York City for an afternoon event.

No one in his or her right mind would have planned all that we had: months of intense work followed without a break by a whirlwind weekend of events and visitors. It was, however, an incredibly satisfying way to honor what together we had accomplished. At the same time, I knew the celebrated accomplishments were but a promise. The challenge that we accepted in seeking to create a positive energy, climate positive home introduced us to the Oberlin community with an obligation to determine whether we had attained these objectives.

Chapter 8:
The Big Decisions

The four small window holes on the north and west walls of the kitchen were a curiosity to workers and visitors alike. Before installing the windows a guest's first question was, "What's the purpose of the small holes?" I took the Socratic approach and responded, "Look at the height and location of the holes. What purpose do you think they serve?"

More often than not, the visitor wouldn't see the relationship between the holes and the location of future counter tops, and I'd have to tell them, "They provide daylight to the counter tops." After a few weeks I simplified my response, "Gun ports." That got their attention!

In early August, Mike Strehle filled the 8 square holes with custom-made Loewen windows. Immediately, I knew the size was wrong. Don Watson's design called for "8"W×8"H site-built custom units," that is, windows with a pane that size. Somewhere during the translation of schematic design plans to window order, "site-built custom units" became "fixed 8"×8" custom," thereby making a window unit with a glass area of 16 square inches not 64, because the 2" wide Loewen wood frame surrounded the glass. As a result, it reduced the window area and therefore the light from the window by 75 percent. Although all of us involved reviewed the construction plans, saw the window order and the window holes many times, no one caught the mistake.

Among the innumerable decisions we made in the process of designing and building Trail Magic, this was a minor mistake. If I hadn't pointed it out, no one would have known. After all, the counters were daylighted, just not as well as they might have been. I've often wondered why people make poor choices or obvious mistakes in building their houses. Now I know—they make myriad decisions in a brief time period, often in rushed circumstances, and without adequate information; however, the truly important revelation is not that mistakes are made, but rather, how few there are.

We can count on one hand the really important decisions when seeking to create an appropriate house for the 21st century. The top two? Size and envelope. For several hundred years, the trend in the United States has been toward an ever-increasing house size. A one-room log cabin with 100 square feet sufficed a few hundred years ago. A six-room, 1,200 square foot home was the norm in the middle of the 20th century.

But with ever-increasing wealth and access to resources, the norm has more than doubled, and 5,000 square foot houses are not rare today. By real estate and Ohio property tax code definitions, Trail Magic has 1,309 square feet of standard living space with seven rooms—lavish in size 200 years ago; modest in size today. It is more than adequate for two people and would be quite comfortable for a family of four.

Although I always shunned having a big house and knew that our 2,300 square foot home in Troy was bigger than necessary, especially when our two children left, the full implications of size came only with designing Trail Magic. In principle, I knew that the energy and materials to make a house, and then to operate it, are proportional to size—the smaller the house, the smaller its ecological footprint. And, if we were really going to build a house for the 21st century that helped mitigate climate change and reduce resource use, it had to be modest in size. It was, however, only when our culturally inculcated wants met the brass tacks of our "green" aspirations, that making our house smaller gained sufficient traction for us to act.

Don Watson's experience with the house in Bethany, Connecticut, that grew from 1,800 to 4,200 square feet, is illustrative of the stranglehold that our culture exerts. Intellectually, we understand that smaller is better for humanity's future, but it takes pressure and encouragement to emotionally "get it" and then act. If it hadn't been for Watson's constant reminders of, and adherence to, the fundamental principle that "size matters," I suspect we'd have a bigger house and more debt, neither of which we need.

Getting the envelope right is a completely different matter. Unlike size, selecting an envelope with the appropriate properties to dramatically reduce heating and cooling energy use is a physics problem. As I came to find out, deciding upon an envelope in a world of new materials and changing techniques is fraught with complexity.

The energy crisis of the early 1970s was a wake-up call to the importance of energy and my introduction to what is now called "the envelope"—the floor, wall, and roof that surround the living space. In our first house in Troy, we heated with fuel oil. In 1975, I added 6" of fiber glass insulation to the existing 6" of vermiculite insulation in our attic floor, and we turned our thermostat down to 65°F. In 1979, we put an airtight woodstove in our semi-finished basement where we and our two small children spent much of our time. We adjusted the thermostat to 60°F.

The Bortons built their passive solar house in 1981. I didn't pay much attention at the time, as I was totally consumed with family and my academic career. After several years, however, it became clear that David and Harriet had done something really important. In 1985, we moved from that well-built, relatively tight, 1950s custom house to a 1930s center hall colonial that was drafty and not as well insulated. Energy audits and conservation measures became common in the 1980s. Our audit identified many ways to conserve water and energy resources, especially for heating.

I grasped the importance of an envelope that kept heat in during the winter and out in summer. I did not, however, understand the details or the science. When we decided to build our energy efficient house in Oberlin, Borton became an envelope consultant. He described his house's envelope: wall—all cracks in the outside framing wall sealed, double wall of 2×4s separated by several inches to give a 10" thick cavity filled with two layers of fiberglass insulation separated by a 1" Styrofoam board, and most important, a vapor barrier on the inside; roof—all cracks in roof framing boards sealed, 16" of fiberglass insulation separated by a 1" airspace from the roof itself, and a vapor barrier on the inside.

Borton recalled the time he showed up at the building site; the builder was putting in place the roof-ceiling drywall, but had not installed the vapor barrier. "I was lucky to have come then," he mused. "Without the vapor barrier, moisture might have condensed in the roof insulation, leading to roof rot. We'd not have known we had a problem until the roof needed major repairs." Apparently, Borton had told the architect that he wanted a vapor barrier in the wall and roof, but because the builder didn't routinely use them or understand their importance in super insulated houses, it slipped by.

Thus, I learned that in northern climates you need a vapor barrier and that it must be on the warm side of the wall. If the barrier is on the cold, outside wall, moisture from the house enters the wall but cannot escape. In cold weather, the temperature in the wall drops. When the water vapor in the wall reaches the dew point, it condenses. Liquid water in the insulation makes it less effective and facilitates wood rotting. Even without a vapor barrier, if the house has a high moisture level, water vapor can build up in the wall and condense at cold temperatures.

Borton was also keen on keeping the vapor barrier intact without penetrations. He suggested that we add 2×2 stud extenders after the barrier so that plumbing and wiring were on the room side and did not breach the vapor barrier. Watson, Ferut, and Strehle had us consider a variety of wall and roof types: SIPs, ICFs, insulated double 2×4 wall, and straw bale. Among perhaps a dozen common insulating materials, we considered seriously just the five suggested by Ferut: cellulose, polystyrene (Reddi-Wall, an ICF), straw, and closed and open cell polyurethane foams.

Throughout January and February we evaluated envelope types. Although Watson and Strehle believed SIPs worthy of in-depth consideration, Ferut was not enthusiastic because a colleague's roof SIPs leaked, thus resulting in having to replace the entire roof. Three, wall envelope types rose to the top of our list to consider—double wall, Reddi-Wall, and straw bale. After we visited houses representing each wall type, we eliminated straw bale.

Mary and I came to like Reddi-Wall because Strehle was enthusiastic about its performance and the information on its advantages was convincing. We saw two of his Reddi-Wall houses, one entirely Reddi-Wall and the other with a Reddi-Wall basement only and conventional stick construction elsewhere. Reddi-Wall makes an extremely solid, very tight wall with considerable thermal mass and has an R value of at least 26. In addition, no moisture entered the Reddi-Wall because polystyrene is impermeable to water: location of the dew point was a mute question. We considered making the entire house Redi-Wall, but three factors persuaded us against it. Once poured, windows and door locations would be difficult to change because of the rebar and concrete. Second, Ferut wanted walls to be R-45, meaning another R-19 had to come from additional insulation. Third, we wanted any competent builder to be able to replicate our above ground wall envelope, but Reddi-Wall, like straw bale construction, required special knowledge and training.

Ferut and Watson had both suggested a prefabricated concrete wall called Superior Wall for the ground floor, a walkout basement. Designed to accommodate additional insulation, it made R45 possible. I had seen Superior Wall in the Crowley house, but was more impressed with Reddi-Wall. A compromise emerged: we decided to use Reddi-Wall for the ground floor like Strehle had done for the basements in several other houses. To increase the R value, Strehle suggested furring out 2.5" with an interior stud wall and insulating with 2.5" of cellulose, thereby achieving R35. This satisfied Ferut because much of the ground floor was below grade, making a higher R value unnecessary. And by furring out, wiring and pipes did not penetrate the Reddi-Wall.

We would then build the rest of the house with a double wall, similar to what Ferut had done for the Crowley house: seal all cracks in the sheathing OSB, have a 1" air barrier of closed cell foam, and then have 10" of damp spray cellulose before the sheetrock. We selected closed cell foam over open cell foam because it does not take up water unlike open cell foam. This meant that we'd have an excellent air barrier, but because moisture does not move through closed cell foam, the foam would also be a vapor barrier that was on the outside.

We had a problem! David Borton was emphatic about placing the vapor barrier on the inside. And Don Watson had written in his nationally recognized guidelines for house construction in northern climates that the vapor barrier should be on the warm side of the wall. I asked each of them if positioning the vapor barrier on the outside would lead to moisture problems.

Conversations and emails went back and forth for a month until it became clear to me that we were experimenting with many variables. Watson argued that we didn't want to trap moisture in the wall with a vapor barrier on both sides, and if the damp spray cellulose was dry when we erected the dry wall, then we should use a vapor retarder of caulked drywall and interior paint. If we were uncertain that the cellulose was sufficiently dry, then we needed to consider a different insulation, such as icynene spray foam.

Ferut consulted with his envelope expert and reported, "He doesn't like the idea unless we really nail the dew point location in the foam." Borton agreed that the damp-spray cellulose should be dry before erecting the dry wall, and that the dew point had to occur in the closed-cell foam. His calculation indicated that it was in the inch of closed-cell-foam; however, his understanding of the physics involved, and the lack of empirical data, led him to believe there was a small chance that moisture from the house or other variables might make it wrong to place the vapor barrier on the outside.

Strehle did not use a vapor barrier in the houses he built, but rather, caulked and taped to seal his houses tightly. He believed that little moisture would diffuse into the walls once the initial construction materials dried, because the vast majority of moisture moves with air, and that in a very tight house, minimal air moves through the wall or ceiling.

To my amazement, the answers of our advisors were not the same or definitive. Apparently, the use of closed cell spray foam and other materials to seal the outside of the envelope to prevent air leaks was a relatively new technique in making high performance buildings. No one had conducted the empirical research to know under what circumstances a vapor barrier on the cold side worked. What to do? We could abandon closed-cell foam, caulk and seal well, and insulate with only damp spray cellulose. We could use icynene spray foam instead of cellulose, or we could go with Ferut's recommendation and believe Borton's calculation that the location of the dew point was in the foam. We pondered the three perspectives and decided to embrace the envelope that Ferut suggested, hoping it was the right choice!

The importance of size and envelope are relatively easy to quantify. The importance of the third major decision—orienting the house with the long axis east-west to facilitate passive solar features of heating and lighting—is more difficult to quantify. In many places that have cool or cold winters, most of the energy for heating can come from the sun by putting the proper amount of window area in the right locations. Even in the northeastern U.S., with far less winter sunshine than western and southern states, a large fraction of the energy to heat the house, perhaps more than half, can be passive solar. Unfortunately, it is difficult to precisely measure the solar heat provided to a house; however, solar heating of greenhouses and imprecise measurements for passive solar houses establish that sunlight contributes significant energy for heating.

The empirical data collected over the past century have established the rules builders and architects use to calculate the appropriate limits for window area, as well as window locations, to optimize heating in the winter while averting overheating in the summer. Other features like roof overhang, shading roofs and trellises, adjustable window shades, and added thermal mass in the house are used to fine tune passive solar heating to the climate in which the house is built. Trail Magic reflects Watson's skill and knowledge of these features, honed by 50 years of passive solar design.

We estimate Trail Magic's passive solar heat to be 15 million BTUs and its daylighing at 5 million BTUs. The cost of these passive solar features is essentially nothing (see Chapter 9 and Appendix D). Orienting the long axis of the house east-west also facilitates using sunlight to generate electricity and to heat water via roof panels. We opted for both of these active solar features.

Trail Magic's 3.12 kW PV system provides annually about 11 million BTUs, while its evacuated tube solar hot water system delivers about 9 million BTUs annually, although only 0.1 million BTUs end up in the hot water used. These active devices are expensive in comparison to passive features. In addition, active solar BTUs are even more costly because the active devices do not last as long as the house; however, a BTU of electricity is far more useful than a BTU of heat.

Based on two year's data, Trail Magic's actively supplied operating energy was 28 million BTUs annually (PV electricity ~8 million BTUs, solar hot water ~ 0.1 million BTUs, woodstove ~20 million BTUs). Assuming it is an average house, this is a quarter of the annual 110 million BTUs purchased to operate the average U.S. house, or a savings of 82 million BTUs.

If Trail Magic were the size we initially wanted (60 percent larger), then the operating energy budget would, perhaps, increase from 28 to 45 million BTUs. The reduced house size thus accounts for perhaps 17 million of the 82 million BTUs saved with envelope design and house orientation responsible for the rest. Assuming a 100-year life for Trail Magic, the energy savings from its smaller size, its proper orientation, and its tight, high R value envelope would be 8,200 million BTUs (82 million BTUs/year $\dot{x}$ 100 years). These 8,200 million BTUs are equivalent to the total annual energy that supports the average person in the U.S. for 24 years. Stated in another way, Mary and I have offset our portion of the U.S. energy budget for 12 years by building Trail Magic instead of a conventional home. Yes, this is a rough approximation and the payback is over 100 years, but it illustrates the immense importance of the big three: size, envelope, and orientation.

After the big three, water use is next in importance. Many factors influence the amount of water a home uses. Families with infant children or teenagers have greater water needs than older couples. People living in areas with limited amounts of fresh water are required to adopt technologies and behaviors that conserve water. Oberlin receives annually 36 inches of precipitation (water), with more than two inches every month, thereby making water relatively plentiful year round.

We selected our site in the city of Oberlin so that we could use city water and sewer. To reduce household water use, we purchased both water-efficient washing machine and dishwasher, and we installed low-flow bathroom faucets and showerheads, and low-use dual flush toilets (over 25% of household water is used for flushing toilets). We also collect rain water from barn and house roofs in a 1,875-gallon cistern to avoid using potable water for watering the garden, landscape, or other outdoor uses.

Equally important to reducing overall water use is conservation of hot water because people use substantial amounts of energy to heat water for domestic use. We elected to combine an evacuated-tube, solar-hot-water system with an electric, on-demand, hot-water heater. An 80-gallon preheat tank stores solar heated water that feeds the on-demand system. We believed this combined system would be an excellent choice with a reasonable payback time, because most of the energy to heat water would be solar. Unfortunately, as I discuss in Chapter 9, this type of solar hot water heating is not economically or environmentally cost effective in Oberlin-like climates.

In making choices, we employed systems thinking to resolve conflicts that arose from the individual perspectives of architecture, beauty and aesthetics, building standards and codes, economics, energy and resource use, and environmentally appropriate construction. Design and material decisions rarely have one optimal choice, but rather a preferred choice within the context of the particular project. Our overriding criterion was the lifecycle cost which we measured environmentally and economically, except in trivial choices like handles for kitchen cabinets or bathroom vanities where we only considered quality and dollar cost.

Our analysis, when electing to have a raised-seam steel roof instead of the standard asphalt shingle roof, is typical of our rationale. Strehle could have put a 25-year, asphalt roof on the house for about $5,500, compared to a steel roof for about $17,000. An asphalt roof requires replacement about every 25 years, and is likely to require maintenance between re-roofings, while a steel roof should last for 100 years and be mostly maintenance free. A petroleum product, we must dump an asphalt roof at the end of its life in a landfill. A metal roof is made with about 70 percent recycled steel and it can be reprocessed.

So, while the short-term economic costs favored a traditional roof, the lifecycle economic costs leveled the playing field a bit; replacing the asphalt roof three times raised its "comparable" price to about $22,000. For all of these reasons, we settled on installing a steel roof.

We selected prefinished fiber-cement Hardi-Plank siding and trim because of its durability, fire resistance, and low maintenance, although conventional wood or vinyl sidings would have been considerably less expensive ($22,500 verses $14,800 for vinyl siding). We chose double and triple pane, low-E, argon filled Loewen windows with warm edge spacers for their exquisite construction and durability despite the price premium ($25,300 versus $15,900 for fiberglass or vinyl windows with similar energy performance). Environmentally and economically, we believed the lifecycle costs of these two choices were equal to or less than the other selections, but precise comparisons are difficult, if not impossible.

We decided to color the cement slab on the ground floor instead of installing another type of flooring over the cement because it was attractive, functional, and far less expensive. On the first and second floors, however, we had local and on-site hardwood trees milled for flooring instead of imported bamboo flooring; although, it was 60% more expensive ($8,800 versus $5,500). Even though LEED and others consider bamboo a "green" product, it comes from halfway around the globe and is made with questionably suitable glues and other chemicals. The combination of local ash, maple, and oak boards of two different widths in the first floor flooring is exquisite, and our ash boards of three widths on the second floor are equally attractive. In this decision, beauty and aesthetics, energy and resource use, and environmentally appropriate construction won out over economic considerations.

We made innumerable other choices of far lesser significance in the context of what was available, what was expedient, and the environmental and cost information we could muster at the time. Were we to do it again, some decisions would be different, but the overall pattern and outcome would likely be the same. By focusing on the three big decisions and honoring to the extent possible our overriding metric of lifecycle cost for all decisions, we trust that we have created a house for the 21st century. Of course, the proof is in the pudding. Like the grand experiment on Earth—one planet, one experiment—Trail Magic is for us a once-in-a-lifetime investigation that will continue running long after we have passed on.

Chapter 9:

I felt like I had died and gone to heaven. From sunrise to sunset we were bathed in natural light that even on cloudy days was enough to allow reading in almost every room. In November, sunshine filled the entire great room. By winter's solstice, as the sun hung low in the southern sky, rays reached across the great room and into the kitchen. On sunny days, the inside temperature rose into the 70s without lighting a fire in the woodstove or activating the heat pump, even though temperatures were well below freezing outside.

Large-as-life views through the picture windows brought nature close. Two substantial oaks and a gnarled but magnificent osage orange on the north side of the pond dominated the scene of field and woods that gently slopped over the 500 hundred feet to the wooded Plum Creek flood plain. At dawn and dusk, deer grazed in the meadow and around the pond. Common gray squirrels gathered acorns and maple seeds when not chasing each other around tree trunks or leaping from tree to tree. A dozen or more bird species flitted among the branches and pecked seeds on the ground. A pair of eagles routinely feasted on a deer carcass hidden in the trees southwest of the pond. Ducks and Canadian geese visited the pond. Occasionally, a great blue heron walked the shoreline in search of frogs and fish. We were cocooned, but still part of the world surrounding us.

Delighted, we eased into a more sane existence. However, despite our efforts and Strehles's best intentions, many small tasks remained—install door stops, ceiling fans, braces for the chimney pipe, and a board with hooks for coats, and replace incorrect LED lights (light emitting diode), a defective toilet seat, and the horrible sounding doorbell. Of course, nobody moves into a new house without a list of minor to-dos; but the decision to use our wood for flooring, the pantry counter and shelves, closet shelves, stairway bookcases, and kitchen and front porch beams meant that we had only transited to upscale house-camping from a sparsely furnished garage apartment. With no bookcases or shelves to fill, all our books and innumerable unpacked boxes remained in the barn. We slowly moved things into the house, but our approach was to think and plan first. We used the furniture we had. Virgin walls were a new experience; we wanted to hang each picture once.

Even though walls were bare, the pantry devoid of shelves, and the roof over the front porch held up by makeshift supports, we welcomed friends and strangers to see what we touted as an energy-efficient, environmentally appropriate house designed for the post-fossil-fuel world of the 21st century. But was it? My new obsession became collecting data and doing experiments to establish if performance matched prediction. Would the winter sun really heat the house when it was zero outside with a 40-mile-per-hour wind? Would the small woodstove keep the house warm? How much wood would we need to heat the house? Would the evacuated tube solar hot water system provide most of the energy to heat water as we were told, and I had assumed? And, being all electric, the biggest question was: Would we generate annually all the electricity used?

When the Oberlin city inspector activated the PV system on September 22, its production meter still displayed the kWh made in Troy: 5,167 kWh.

On the same day, the Oberlin Municipal Light and Power System (OMLPS) meter read 169 kWh, the electricity Strehle had used to date. On November 12, a few days after we moved into the house, the PV meter read 5,622, while the OMLPS meter was 99,910. The PV system had provided all the electricity that Strehle had used (365 kWh) and ran the meter backwards an additional 90 kWh. As satisfying as this was, the real question remained: What would the two meters read a year from now—November 12, 2009?

Over the summer I had made a quick calculation indicating that the Oberlin PV system would make 3,350 kWh, based on our production in Troy and about 6 percent less sunshine in Oberlin. In Troy, we had generated all the energy we used except that for hot water and heating. Believing the plug load of 2,050 kWh in Troy would be larger than ours in Oberlin, I projected 1,800 kWh for Trail Magic's plug load. I estimated heating and cooling at 500 kWh, air circulation at 200 kWh, and hot water at 750 kWh, for a total similar to that of production. This prediction, however, was fraught with unknowns, making success uncertain.

Our approach would be to use only what we needed and to know how much electricity each device used so that we could avoid waste. I had purchased a Kill-a-Watt meter in Troy to do the same. The item in question is plugged into the Kill-a-Watt meter, and the meter plugged into an outlet. I measured the Watt flow at Trail Magic for everything that had a plug: internet connection, 14 Watts; laptop computer, 20 Watts running and 1 Watt on standby; wireless router, 2 Watts; laser printer on standby, 1 Watt; TV, 75 Watts on and 1 Watt on standby; phone charger, 1 Watt when charging and no measurable reading otherwise; kitchen radio-CD player, 1 to 4 Watts depending on volume; stereo system and CD player, 30 to 100 Watts depending on volume. This knowledge affected our behavior. We can clearly hear the kitchen radio-CD player in the great room, so we routinely use the kitchen radio instead of the stereo that uses 10 to 50 times more electricity. When the computer, printer, internet connection, and router are on but not in use, 18 Watts are flowing. This doesn't seem like much electricity, but 18 Watts 24/7 for a year is 160 kWh or 5 percent of our projected PV production. We have them on only when we are using them.

> **Sidebar 12:**
> **Plug Load, Baseline Operating Energy, and Phantom Load**
>
> The plug load is the electrical draw of all devices that are "plugged" into the electrical system of a house except for items like the furnace, AC unit, and hot water heater. The baseline operating energy for an all electric house is that part of the plug load that is never turned off (e.g., refrigerator, freezer), as well as the furnace in winter and AC unit in summer. Within the baseline operating energy is the phantom load or the electrical draw of equipment on standby (garage door openers, TVs, computers, internet routers, ceiling fans) or devices performing functions like microwave and stove clocks. When residents are at work, or on vacation, the electricity used is the baseline operating energy. If the house is not all electric, then gas or oil used would also be part of the baseline operating energy.

Refrigeration is a substantial part of plug load. We wanted a freezer for garden produce and bulk purchases. I had read that a refrigerator without a freezer is more efficient than a similar sized refrigerator with a freezer. Thus, we decided to purchase a refrigerator with no freezer and a modest sized chest freezer. When I measured the energy used over three several day periods, the refrigerator had a projected annual use of 150 kWh and the freezer 230 kWh. This 380 kWh for 18 cubic feet of refrigerator space and 13 cubic feet of freezer space was good news because we had used annually over 400 kWh for 21 cubic feet in an Energy Star refrigerator in Troy that included a freezer compartment.

Although compact fluorescent bulbs had substantially reduced our electricity use for lighting in Troy, LED bulbs cut Watts per lumen by another 70%. That is, the amount of light from a 100 Watt incandescent bulb equals that of a 30 Watt compact fluorescent bulb or a 10 Watt LED bulb. LED bulbs were just becoming available, and to save electricity we put two, 12 Watt, dimmable LED bulbs in the entry way and one in the pantry. They are bright and provide the equivalent of a 120 Watt incandescent bulb. With a predicted lifespan of 50,000 hours and with usage of but a few hours a week, someone will replace them in the middle of the next century. At $75 each, however, they were expensive.

To continue our experiment with LED bulbs, I purchased seven lower Wattage bulbs online. Each of our stairways is well lighted with two 2.3 Watt LED bulbs, one directed up from the landing between floors, the other down. Because LED technology is advancing rapidly and prices are coming down, we are waiting a few years to finish the fixed lighting in the kitchen and great room, as well as to change out the rest of our frequently used, compact fluorescent bulbs with LEDs.

With all the lights in the house turned on, we flow 500 Watts from 30 compact florescent bulbs (306 Watts), 8 tube florescent bulbs (112 Watts), 10 LED bulbs (52 Watts), and one incandescent bulb (30 Watts)—or the equivalent of five, 100 Watt incandescent bulbs. We normally turn lights on only when necessary. When we go out at night, we turn on two, 2 Watt LED bulbs that cast light in the kitchen and great room. During the day, even on cloudy days, we rarely need to turn on a light because the house is so well daylighted.

It is impossible to know with any precision how much electricity we save because of excellent daylighting, but it is most likely hundreds of kWh. We can, however, crudely estimate the combined effects of house design, bulb choice, and our behavior on the amount of energy we use for lighting. According to the U.S. Department of Energy, the average US house annually uses 110 million BTUs of energy, of which 11 percent is for lighting. This would be 3,500 kWh for lighting. The average house has 2.5 people, so we would be expected to use annually 2,800 kWh. If we had all of our lights on for one hour each day, we'd annually use 183 kWh, but our use is less, likely under 100 kWh, for an annual savings of 2,700 kWh (9 million BTUs), or $270 at $0.10/kWh. In terms of carbon dioxide reduction, it would be 5,400 pounds at 2 pounds/kWh in Ohio.

Although our children and their families had been through Oberlin to see the property, they had not seen the house. They all came for a week at Christmas: Stuart's family of five and Virginia with her partner. Every room, except the great room and kitchen, became a bedroom—two rooms are furnished as bedrooms, two rooms have a Murphy-like fold down bed, and we can put a bed in the ground floor family room. The great room was the center of all activities, including meals together. Although we call it the great room, it is only 12 by 22 feet, or 264 square feet; however, the woodstove hearth comes out 5 feet from the wall, reducing usable space to about 200 square feet. We coveted a larger room!

In January, I turned my attention to finishing our LEED application. The previous May, our LEED team had met several times to go over the various forms and submit them to the provider. In June, we asked the provider to clarify some items in the LEED for Homes Project checklist, mostly concerning definitions and unclear specifications.

With Ferut and Strehle versed on LEED requirements, Mary and I focused on getting the three LEED points for excellent waste management. In August, the green rater's pre-drywall inspection uncovered no problems. Throughout the fall I reviewed and updated the LEED checklist.

Trail Magic was Strehle and Ferut's first LEED project, and my first time building much of anything. To save money, I had taken on the responsibility of team leader. Concerned about receiving every possible point we had earned, I wanted perfection in preparing our final LEED checklist. To avoid problems, I prepared for the provider and green rater detailed documentation for each category and subcategory, indicating what we did or didn't do, along with our explanations and the points earned. In early January, I emailed it to Borton, Ferut, Strehle, and Watson for corrections and suggestions. After his comments and suggestions, Watson wrote, "All in all, a splendid effort that LEED, among others, should dance and shout around."

Normally, the USGBC requires 90 points for LEED platinum, but because Trail Magic was small for a five-bedroom house, we needed only 85. Our tally was 94 points earned with 5 more points in question. We had reached platinum level with some to spare!

On January 14, I emailed the provider and green rater the 15 pages of documentation for their comments and suggestions before polishing our checklist in preparation for the green rater's final inspection. I was shocked by the reply from the provider the next day. They could not certify our project under the LEED for Homes program because we had failed to meet a few prerequisites. How could that be?

Apparently, we had incorrectly interpreted the LEED for Homes Rating System manual. Because of the way in which the manual presented the prerequisites and because nowhere in the manual was it explicitly written that certification would be denied without every prerequisite met, we believed that the program required prerequisites in a particular category only if you sought points in that category. Anybody who has been specifically trained in the LEED process wouldn't think such an interpretation possible. But I was so overwhelmed at the time that I believed we had some choices, and neither Ferut nor Strehle caught my mistake. In fact, it appeared that they had come to the same interpretation on their own.

This misunderstanding was solidified in our minds because some of the requirements weren't best practice or even appropriate in our case. One requirement—to install in all bathrooms a fan that exhausted to the outside—we didn't meet. We had decided that an exhaust fan in the half bath was inappropriate; it served no need that a window couldn't serve, and it put a hole in the envelope, allowing unnecessary air movement through the wall. In previous houses, we'd had kitchen fans that exhausted directly to the outside, but they were ineffective at clearing smoke and smell when something burned or when moisture occurred from canning. Instead, we'd open doors and windows. Therefore, we decided that adding another hole in the envelope for a kitchen exhaust fan was not best practice. Achieving a tight house was our top priority.

Neither did we use metal ducts for return air in the ventilation system. Strehle and Ferut believed that using wall plenums (the space between wall studs) for return air instead of metal ducts presented no health or safety concerns as long as we kept the plenum ducts clean and dry during and after construction. Plus, we had a very simple, compact ventilation system with just six return ducts.

Both of these prerequisite failures should have been obvious to the green rater when he'd made his pre-drywall inspection the previous August. That he didn't tell us otherwise affirmed how we'd interpreted the LEED for Homes manual. Because we believed we had flexibility in meeting prerequisites, we decided for energy efficiency and environmental lifecycle costs to forgo points in several categories.

Immediately upon having the provider reject our LEED application, I contacted the entire team. We decided to send a letter to the provider explaining our interpretation of prerequisites and requesting that our application go forward for LEED certification. First and foremost, we noted that the green rater hadn't told us of our prerequisite failures which were correctable then. Second, the presentation of prerequisites in the LEED for Homes manual led to our initial misinterpretation.

In response, the provider stated: 1) he could not forward our project to USGBC for certification under "special circumstances" and 2) neither providers nor the USGBC trained or certified green raters. With this absolute refusal, we appealed the provider's decision with the USGBC on February 4, 2009. A USGBC representative interviewed me on the phone for more than an hour on April 22. He told me that ours was the first appeal in the LEED for Homes program.

During the conversation I explained that the house had been inspected and tested for the Energy Star program and had earned the highest rating, Five Stars Plus. He had interviewed the provider and would interview the green rater and the Energy Star inspector before meeting with the LEED technical group and would get back to me with the decision as soon as possible.

Having heard nothing by July, I called the LEED representative and left a message. Several days later he sent me an email indicating a decision in a week. Over the next five months, I made several inquiries, but still silence. In early December 2009, we received the decision.

Dear Mr. McDaniel,

Thank you for contacting the U.S. Green Building Council, Inc. (USGBC) regarding your LEED for Homes project located at 495 E. College Street, Oberlin, Ohio. We greatly appreciate your commitment to educate others regarding sustainable building practices, and also your enthusiasm towards building a net zero home.

In response to your request for appeal, I regret to inform you that USGBC does not offer a process for appeal at this time. While USGBC does maintain a process for accepting and reviewing appeals, such processes are only available to project teams only after a completed application has been submitted (through a provider) and has been denied certification by USGBC to deny certification based on an extensive third party review of an application and all submitted documentation. At this time, your application for certification has not yet been submitted, and thus your current request for an appeal is premature.

You commented that you believe the LEED for Homes rating system is not clear regarding prerequisites. While the LEED for Homes ratings system is certainly complex, it, like all LEED rating systems, is comprised of a series of prerequisites and credits arranged by category. Within categories are contained both prerequisites and credits. Prerequisites constitute mandatory design and performance elements that must be achieved. The mandatory nature of these requirements is clearly and consistently communicated throughout the materials associated with the LEED for Homes program. USGBC will only award certification to the extent that a given project can demonstrate compliance with such requirements.

USGBC has instituted a "credit interpretation request" (CIR) process to permit project teams to ask for clarification of credits and prerequisites. The CIR process allows project teams to submit proposed alternative designs that satisfy the intent of a particular credit or prerequisite though deviate from the suggested method of achieving the same as identified in the LEED for Homes rating system or reference guide. CIRs may be submitted at any time following project registration and are reviewed by volunteer based USGBC Technical Advisory Groups. Your provider should be familiar with this process. Please note however, CIRs are seldom granted unless a project is physically or legally unable by legal mandate or other compelling unique circumstances to meet the prerequisites or credits as they are identified in the rating system.

It appears based on conversations you have had with USGBC homes staff, that there has been a fair amount of failed communication concerning your project between and among the project team, the provider and Green Rater. USGBC providers are well versed in LEED for Homes Rating System. Further, there are many other persons who are knowledgeable and qualified to advise you on how to satisfy credits and prerequisites, as well as comply with the program requirements and procedures. Should you choose to continue to proceed to seek LEED certification for your home, we recommend that you seek the counsel of an experienced practitioner to help guide you.

On behalf of the U.S. Green Building Council, I want to thank you for your dedication to furthering the green building movement.

Regards,
Susan E. Dorn
Legal Counsel, U.S. Green Building Council, Inc.

Despite our best intentions and persistent efforts, LEED platinum certification was placed out of our reach.

We debriefed the LEED experience in order to know how attempting LEED platinum certification had influenced what our team had done in designing and then building Trail Magic. Watson encapsulated our assessment, "LEED made no difference to me. What I did with your house was not influenced by LEED criteria. I'm an observer of LEED. A lot of what they say is helpful in raising the bar. It takes the bad to good. It does not take the good to excellent. Our goal was excellent. We knew how to achieve the good. We didn't have to be told." However, we all did agree that we were motivated, especially Strehle, Mary, and me, to push the envelope on waste reduction because of the real challenge by LEED to earn all three points.

What could have been a win-win situation became a lost opportunity. LEED could have had a positive energy, climate positive home to its credit, and Trail Magic could have received the imprimatur of LEED platinum. The media attention alone would have opened opportunities to promote efficiency in energy and resource use with off-the-shelf technologies in addition to highlighting replicable design choices, building procedures, and behavioral choices that can make both new and old homes positive energy and climate positive.

Over the first two years, I conducted many experiments and collected data that I thought would give insight into what we had and had not accomplished. My goal? To enable others to replicate our successes and avoid our failures.

I was excited about our solar hot water system, so was shocked one day when I saw that the water temperature in the storage tank dropped from 122°F to 95°F overnight, even though we hadn't used any hot water. Our "top-of-the-line" hot water tank was terrible.

I contacted the subcontractor, who agreed to add insulation to the tank. I measured the temperature drop in the storage tank over a dozen times, determining that the average temperature drop was 3°F per hour. After the added insulation, which was rated at R-21 and probably tripled the tank's initial insulation, the temperature drop rate deceased by 50 percent to 1.5°F per hour. Clearly, hot water tanks for homeowners are poorly insulated. Most of the energy used to heat the water escapes into the surrounding room.

Hot water at Trail Magic is heated in a combined evacuated tube hot water system that preheats water with sunlight and an electric on-demand heater. Copper in the evacuated tubes on the roof absorbs heat from sunlight that transfers to a glycol solution that is then pumped to a heat exchanger in the mechanical room where the heat in the glycol moves to water in an 80-gallon storage tank. When we require hot water, the solar heated water in the storage tank flows to the on-demand electric heater, where the water heats to the desired temperature, 111°F in our case. If the preheated water is over 111°F, the on-demand heater stays inactive.

We had selected the combined systems because we believed most of the energy to heat water would come from the sun. I could estimate the amount of energy provided by the sun if I knew 1) the amount of electricity used by the on-demand heater, 2) the electricity used to pump fluids in the solar hot water system, 3) the temperature of incoming water, and 4) the amount and temperature of hot water used. The subcontractor also wanted to know how his system performed. He agreed to install a water meter on the inflow pipe to the storage tank, if I acquired a meter to measure the electricity used by the on demand heater. I collected data for six months, from August 2009 to February 2010. The results were not what we expected. A mere 7 percent of the energy used to provide hot water comes from sunshine (28 kWh or $2.80). What had we failed to consider when designing the hot water system?

First, we designed and equipped Trail Magic to conserve hot water. Low flow shower heads provide 1.5 gallons/minute while bathroom faucets deliver 0.5 gallons/minute. The clothes washer is a front loading machine that uses 2 gallons of hot water per regular cycle when put on the cold water setting. The dishwasher uses 5 gallons of hot water per regular cycle. Mary and I take showers that consume between 4 and 8 gallons.

These design features and our demands have led to an annual hot water use of 3,000 gallons. This compares with the annual average hot water use of 8,000 gallons by U.S. couples over 60 years old.

Second, the pumping of fluids in the solar hot water system uses a substantial amount of electricity, 200 kWh annually. This compares to an annual use of 100 kWh by the on demand heater.

The decision to install this combination of hot water systems is even more embarrassing. A theoretical calculation indicated that the total amount of energy needed to heat 3,000 gallons of incoming water to 111°F is about 1.4 million BTUs, or $41 of electricity. Even if we used the average annual amount of hot water for our age group, or about three times more than we do, it would cost about $123 if heated solely by the on-demand heater. After two years we had the evacuated tube system removed and actual measurements indicate 360 kWh or $36 for heating the 3,000 gallons of hot water we use annually.

From the collected data and our analyses, we now know that the most energy efficient and cost-effective hot water system for us, and for many single-family homes in climates similar to that of Oberlin, is an on-demand heater fed from a large, uninsulated storage tank—an uninsulated tank reduces heating energy because cold, incoming water equilibrates to room temperature before going to the on-demand heater.

The features that curtailed our hot water use, along with dual flush toilets that use 0.8 and 1.6 gallons/flush, reduced our indoor water use to 26 gallons/day or about 9,500 gallons/year. This compares to the average annual use for two U.S. people of 50,000 gallons. This data for hot and total water use at Trail Magic indicates that modern technology and water-conserving behaviors can reduce water consumption by 80 percent.

Sidebar 13:
Water Conservation Reduces Energy Use and CO_2 Release

Rumi Shammin in Oberlin College's Environmental Studies Department calculated the energy to take a gallon of water from the Black River, make it potable, deliver it to a home, and return it to the Black River after treating it in Oberlin's wastewater plant at 86 BTUs or 25 Watts, resulting in the release of 0.013 lbs of CO_2.

Trail Magic uses 9,500 gallons per year or 40,500 gallons less than the average two-person home, thereby resulting in an annual savings of 3.5 million BTUs or 1,010 kWh, and a reduction in carbon dioxide release of 530 lbs.

Although I had resisted installing a central heating and cooling system, believing that the Borton model of relying on several baseboard electric heaters for supplemental heat was right for us, I was convinced by others, even the Bortons, to put in a central system. Strehle is an advocate of ground source heat pumps, and we ended up with a heat pump using the pond as a heat source and sink.

To heat in the winter, the heat pump takes heat from the pond and puts it in the house. To cool in the summer, the heat from the house transfers to the pond. Ground source heat pumps are very efficient, using 1 BTU of electrical energy to move 3 to 4 BTUs of heat energy. In contrast, a high-efficiency gas furnace will use 1 BTU of energy to provide 0.97 BTU of heat: 97% efficient.

I've always loved a wood fire. For almost three decades, Mary and I have used a woodstove for some of our heat. With a high-performance, passive solar house we expected our small, soapstone woodstove to provide all our heat. Even though Oberlin had an unusually cold winter, we used about a cord of wood the first winter. Our second winter was milder, but January and February 2010 were very cloudy—over 60 days without a day of full sunshine. Again, we used about a cord of wood. With two acres of trees on the property, an annual harvest of one cord is easily sustainable.

We had installed the pond source heat pump as a back up, especially for when we aged and might not be able to manage the woodstove. A theoretical calculation using the average degree heating days for the past four years indicated that it would take about 2,600 kWh annually for heating, assuming no solar heat gain. In February 2010, we ran the heat pump for 9 days and measured the kWh that we needed to maintain the house temperature at a constant 68°F. The data indicated that it would take about 2,100 kWh annually for heating, or $210 at $0.10/kWh. The lower value in this empirical assessment likely resulted because of modest passive solar heat gain over the nine day experimental period (six of the nine were totally cloudy while the other three were mostly cloudy).

Although it is extremely difficult to measure or calculate solar heat gain because of so many uncontrollable variables, we know it is substantial. Greenhouses become hot because of solar gain. Even on a sunny winter day, a car parked in the sun with closed windows will get toasty warm. We measured temperature gain on several winter days with the heat pump off and no fire in the woodstove. On January 16, 2009, at 10 a.m., the temperature was 62°F inside and -10°F outside. All day the sun sparkled in a crystal clear blue sky, and there was no noticeable wind. At 2 p.m. the temperature had risen to 68°F inside and 0°F outside, for a house temperature gain of 1.6°F/hour. We also measured heat loss at night with no internal heating. On January 23, 2009, at 9 p.m., the temperature inside was 70°F and 6°F outside. It was a calm night, and at 8 a.m. the next day the inside temperature was 62°F and 1°F outside, for a temperature loss of 0.7°F/hour. A second observation established that Trail Magic is so tight that wind has little effect on heat loss. On December 21, 2008, at 9 p.m., the temperature inside was 70°F and 0°F outside. A constant wind of 20 to 40 mph blew all night. At 8 a.m. the next day the inside temperature was 61°F and 5°F outside, for a house temperature loss of 0.8°F/hour. These data indicate that full sunshine provides sufficient energy not only to offset heat loss, but also to warm Trail Magic to a comfortable temperature when the temperature difference between inside and outside is about 65°F.

Our first summer at Trail Magic was cool, with few days that merited air conditioning. The second summer was hot. I ran a five day experiment to assess the annual kWh required to keep the house at a constant 75°F in summer; 910 kWh, or $91.00 at $0.10/kWh. We did not open windows for passive cooling during the experiment; however, the wind tower design feature suffices to keep the house cool except for a few afternoon hours on days over 90°F.

During our first two years at Trail Magic we've used the heat pump to determine that we could annually heat and cool with 3,010 kWh, or $301 at $0.10/kWh. Our actual annual cost was perhaps 100 kWh of PV electricity for heat pump cooling and heating and a gallon of gas for the chainsaw to cut a cord of firewood. And we do run the air circulator many days which uses 0.4 kWh per day, or annually perhaps 100 kWh.

The National Climatic Data Center ranked 174 cities according to their annual percentage of possible sunshine. At 90 percent, Yuma, Arizona, is first. Juneau, Alaska, at 30 percent, is last. Cleveland, Ohio, is in the bottom fifth, at 49 percent. Most of Oberlin's possible sunshine comes from March through October, so we fully expected the electric meter to run forward in the winter. Our OMLPS meter hit its record high reading of 350 in the second week of February 2009. Although this meter reading told us that we had used 440 more kWh than we had produced since occupying Trail Magic, our average daily use of 6.9 kWh meant that we were on track to produce more electricity than we used.

On November 12, 2009, the OMPLS meter read 98,997 kWh and the PV meter read 8,814 kWh. We had used 2,279 kWh and made 3,192 kWh. On-site sunshine had provided more than 100 percent of the operating energy. We hadn't used any fossil fuels, and 913 kWh had been sent to the grid.

Trail Magic is a positive energy and climate positive home!

This achievement is testimony to Watson's exquisite schematic design, to Ferut's superb detailed design plans, to Borton's practical knowledge of physics and solar energy, and to Ferut and Strehle's professional excellence in executing the building of Trail Magic. Our success demonstrates that people can build high-performance houses using off-the-shelf technologies and building practices available to everyone.

We had accomplished the first of two primary objectives. Our second was to demonstrate that making a home positive energy was affordable and similar in cost to standard construction (see Appendix D for details). Trail Magic cost $146 per square foot of conditioned space (heated), an amount not different from that for a quality, custom-made house in northern Ohio that purchases its operating energy. Trail Magic has many upscale features including a metal roof, a sun patio, Hardiplank siding, Loewen windows, a rainwater cistern,

Sidebar 14: Annual Operating Energy in Million BTUs for Average Household and Trail Magic

Energy Category[1]	Average Household	Trail Magic (all supplied by the sun)	% less (more) for Trail Magic
Heating	34.1	20 with wood	41
		7 with heat pump	79
Cooling	13.2	0.3	98
Water Heating	13.2	1.3	90
Lighting	12.1	0.3	98
Refrigeration	8.8	1.4	84
Total for below items:	28.6	4.2 (electronics, clothes	85
Electronics	7.7	washer and dryer, dish washer,	
Clothes washer & dryer and dishwasher	5.5	computers, other)	
Computers	1.1		
Other	14.3		
Purchased Energy	110	none	100[2]
Passively Acquired Energy	small	20 (heating, 15; lighting, 5)	(~100)[3]
Total Energy	110	48 with wood heat	56
		35 with heat pump heat	68

[1]For the electrical energy in the various categories, BTUs purchased by a household from the grid and those produced by Trail Magic's PV system have different amounts of embodied energy. That is, to get energy and change it to a grid Watt-hour is about 3 times the energy available in a grid Watt-hour, while the energy to produce a PV Watt-hour is from sunshine and essentially all of it is directly available for use. Therefore, although Trail Magic uses 25% of the electricity used by the average household in Oberlin (2,400 kWh [annual amount Trail Magic uses] vs 9,500 kWh [Oberlin average annual household use]), Trail Magic actually uses 6% of the energy used by the average Oberlin home for electricity (2,400 kWh × 3412 BTUs/kWh = 8 million BTUs vs [9,500 kWh × 4] × 3412 BTUs/kWh = 130 million BTUs). The carbon emissions from the production of the electricity generated by Trail Magic's PV system are only from the indirect energy used in producing, transporting, and installing the PV system that is embodied in each kWh, which is less than 10% of the total embodied carbon emissions associated with the production of an Oberlin-grid kWh. Trail Magic heats its water with renewable solar electricity while many Oberlin homes use natural gas, a non-renewable fossil fuel.

[2]Trail Magic's operating energy is 15 million BTUs with heat pump heat and 28 million BTUs with wood heat, if the BTUs of passive heating (15 million BTUs) and daylighting (5 million BTUs) are not considered. Woodstove heating is inefficient compared to ground source, heat pump heating (geothermal); however, it requires much less material and technology. This operating energy for most homes would be purchased energy. Trail Magic's operating energy, if purchased, would be 14% ([15 million BTUs ÷ 110 million BTUs] × 100) or 25% ([28 million BTUs ÷ 110 million BTUs] × 100) of the average home and 8% or 15% of the 180 million BTUs for the 2007 operating energy of our home in Troy, NY (see Sidebar 1). These comparisons establish that design features and off-the-shelf technologies combined with behaviors that conserve resources can reduce home operating energy use to 25% or less of that used by the average U.S. home, and all of this energy can be provided by the sun in northern U.S. climates.

[3]About half of Trail Magic's total annual operating energy of 35 million BTUs, or 48 million BTUs, is acquired passively from sunlight (20 million BTUs). The investment to acquire these 20 million BTUs is close to zero, because they result from design features—long axis oriented east-west, most windows placed on south side, and shading devices like roof overhangs and trellises. These 20 million BTUs save $400 per year (20 million BTUs × $20/million BTUs). No income tax is paid on these dollars, meaning another $100 is saved. Assuming the house lasts for 100 years, the lifetime savings provided by passive solar will be $50,000, a huge return on the small investment (see Appendix D: Cost Analysis for Trail Magic). In addition, over the same time period, passive solar heating and daylighting will prevent at least 130 tons of CO_2 from being released to the atmosphere compared to using natural gas.

and custom lumber for floors, shelves, bookcases, and beams that do not enhance its energy efficiency. If these features are omitted or replaced by ones that provide similar energy efficiencies, the cost per square foot becomes $110, the price for a development house. We have established, contrary to common belief, it not only costs nothing extra to build a house that runs on sunshine, but also to do so pays handsome dividends, because operating energy is free sunshine.

We have given many talks on Trail Magic to the local community, and even presented a short course on the project at Lorain County Community College. People are uniformly surprised and enthusiastic about our huge reductions in water and energy use, and are impressed that sunshine provides total operating energy. But, the conversation always turns to what can we do with existing houses. Although many people have made improvements in their homes by replacing incandescent bulbs with compact fluorescent bulbs, weather stripping doors, or adding insulation, we seldom see documentation or publicity stating the costs, savings, and environmental consequences.

Our good friends in Troy, Margaret and Howard Stoner, who live in a typical 1950s house, listened to Borton and me talk about climate change and read environmental books that we recommended. They observed how we had reduced our energy footprint with simple conservation measures—compact fluorescent bulbs, night setback thermostats, turning off lights—and by replacing old appliances, heating with wood, and installing PV systems. In 2006, the Stoners had heard enough and decided to do something.

The Stoner house is a conventionally constructed, 1,200 square foot, one-floor dwelling with a full basement that in 2005 used 127 million BTUs of natural gas and electricity for a cost of $2,450. The next year they began simple conservation efforts: installed electric strips so computers, TV, and other devices could be turned off easily and not use electricity while on stand by; and they turned off lights in unoccupied rooms. In 2007, they installed a programmable thermostat, put plastic covers on their windows in winter, installed compact fluorescent bulbs, started using a clothes line instead of an electric dryer, and had a thorough energy audit, including a blower-door test to assess air tightness. The next year Howard caulked every crack and air leak in the house that he could find, removed the attic exhaust fan in winter and insulated the ceiling hole, insulated his basement walls and the attic floor, and hired a company to insulate first-floor walls. Blower-door tests before and after these caulking and sealing measures showed a 60 percent increase in envelope tightness. The cost for these improvements was $5,500 minus $400 in subsidies. These measures reduced the Stoner's annual energy consumption from 127 million BTUs to 57 million BTUs, or a savings of $1,400. Because they don't pay taxes on this $1,400 that they would have had to earn, the actual savings is closer to $1,900. In three years the cost of the improvements will be paid back, and the Stoners will have an annual dividend of $1,900 at current energy prices for as long as they live there. If I offered you a guaranteed 33 percent return on a $5,000 investment, you'd think it was a scam, but it isn't. It is a personal, high-return investment you can make in your home today.

The Stoners also accepted the scientific consensus that human activities are a major factor in changing the climate. To reduce their carbon footprint even more, they installed an airtight wood stove to heat their house, an efficient gas-fired boiler for hot water and backup heating, and a 3.3 kW PV system. These items cost $45,200 minus $20,000 in subsidies and tax credits, making their cost $25,200. For the past two years, the PV system produced all the electricity that they used, and the only fossil fuel that they burned each year was 180 therms of gas equivalent to 18 million BTUs and 2,160 pounds of carbon dioxide. Because their PV system produced 3,400 kWh of electricity that were not generated by the power company, they prevented the release of 6,000 pounds of carbon dioxide, *thereby making their home climate positive and essentially positive energy* (they collect firewood off site).

The simple measures taken by the Stoners to weatherize their house, along with their easy-to-replicate conservation measures, establish that we can significantly reduce home energy use at a profit. The major changes they made demonstrate that a family does not have to build a new home or spend an extravagant amount of money to create a climate positive home.

As impressive as the numbers are for the Stoners' house and for Trail Magic, the data I've presented for Trail Magic are but the easily quantifiable part of the performance story. Although we know passive solar gain is substantial, it is not easy to assess. Borton has attempted to measure his house's passive gain for years without consistent results. Likewise, he can only estimate Trail Magic's passive gain. Interestingly, it is the design features that foster passive solar heating and daylighting that also significantly enhance the quality of life for those living in a passive solar house. And, similar to solar gain, we cannot precisely know how much the quality of life is enriched.

I am a scientist, an animal and plant developmental biologist by training. For several decades I grew plants, and conducted experiments in the university's greenhouse. Merely walking into the greenhouse made me feel good, and on numerous occasions, when I was feeling down, especially in the winter doldrums, I'd find an excuse to go there. The intensity of natural light, even on a cloudy day, along with the rich green of the plants, positively affected me. On occasion, I'd bring a paper to read or change my plans and find something to do in order to remain longer.

At the other extreme, I moved into what had been a janitor's storeroom for my office during the renovation of my laboratory that had three, large, south facing windows. Several fluorescent tube lights lit the closet. Within a few weeks I felt poorly, tired, and lacked my normal motivation. I spent as little time there as possible.

We evolved in a world of sunlight that at dawn ever so slowly increases in intensity until it brightly illuminates our world, only to change once again by ever-so-slowly decreasing in intensity as sunset becomes dusk, and dusk merges into night. Eons have honed our genes to prescribe physiologies acclimated to these changes and to daylight itself. Sunlight and its patterns of change are elements of our habitat—what we would choose if we had a choice.

A well-designed passive solar house enables its residents to return to the world of their origins. When we entertain guests, we often eat at sunset. The two windows high on the west wall brightly illuminate our kitchen and great room until the sun descends behind the barn and the rooms darken slowly. More often than not, we continue talking and eating until, all of a sudden, we realize it is dark. Apparently, the change in light intensity is so natural that we don't notice it.

In the morning, we rarely turn on a light. Our bedroom and the great room have south-facing picture windows that allow enough light to fix breakfast or complete other morning tasks. In the winter, we often enjoy the softness of candle light at breakfast and the gradual brightening of the house feels normal. On days both cloudy and sunny, the natural light and the views through the picture windows combine with our high ceilings to create an illusion of being in the natural world—a place not bounded, but open.

Sunny days are spectacular, visually and thermally. Even when temperatures are below freezing outside, the house warms degree by degree into the high 60s or low 70s by early afternoon. As the sun eases toward the horizon, the indoor temperature slowly settles back. We may or may not light a fire in the evening, depending on mood and the likelihood of another sunny day.

The great room is lighted from different directions depending upon the time of day, but always well and evenly. Direct sunlight creates definitive shadows which move across the room and define the space, like tree shadows on a savannah.

I don't believe these lighting conditions are conducive to seasonal affect disorder, but rather promote emotional and physical health. Thermally and visually, a passive solar house is a place of gradual change that enchants our senses that were honed long ago by evolutionary forces. In more than a poetic sense, we have come home.

Our thick walls and roof exclude urban noise, and the absence of internal mechanical sounds leads to persistent quiet when the windows are closed. This silence was likely more common in our hunter-gatherer habitats than in modern human settings. Neither Mary nor I mind the deep quiet in cold weather. Perhaps it is calming and healthful. Unfortunately, the thick envelope also excludes the sounds of wind and rain; but, warm weather nights with passive cooling are delightfully filled with choruses of birds, insects, frogs and toads. Of course, I do not claim that these particular connections to the biological world are unique to passive solar houses. However, with all windows shut during the five day experiment to assess cooling cost, we missed the night sounds.

Living at Trail Magic is also enriched by design features that evoke aesthetic feelings and emotional pleasure. Ferut and Watson are the people whose profession brings visual beauty to a structure, and Trail Magic, despite my proclivity for the practical, is aesthetically pleasing. I know that Ferut and Watson employed centuries of acquired principles to the task, but for the most part, they are hidden from me. I do know that the house is attractive and looks right, inside and out. Ferut created a railing system for the deck that meets safety requirements and is elegant in its simplicity; powder polished iron railings that undulate between wooden posts permit views of the pond, trees, and field that are sensually pleasing. The colors of the roof, siding, trim, and doors flow easily with each other, and with the landscape, but cleanly define elements of the house. The placement and size of the windows not only light the rooms well, but also effortlessly bring the inside and outside worlds together. Rooms feel much larger than they are, especially the kitchen-great-room complex and master bedroom.

Although Watson and Ferut and his associates deserve most of the credit for Trail Magic's beauty, the wood from our land in the hands of George Ficke truly brought a special, unique touch to our home. The mixed colors and grains of ash, maple, and red, white, and black oak on the first floor bring new meaning to the elegance of hardwood floors. The ash flooring on the second floor holds its own with a pleasing blend of light sap wood and various shades of brown heartwood, all accented with diverse patterns of grain.

The large ash beam that visually divides the kitchen from the great room features dark and light hues of grain that complement the floor, the rustic-alder kitchen cabinets, and the Douglas fir window casements. The inch-thick ash pantry shelves are overkill for storage space—canned goods and paper towels are rarely, if ever, so attractively stored. The white oak beams that now support the front porch roof are engaging and accent the front of the house with a finish of fine furniture.

The crowning jewel of Ficke's woodworking and Strehle's carpentry skills, however, are the stairway bookcases. Mary had found a picture of a stairway bookcase, and it became the best space-saving idea we brought to the design process. In spring 2009, when our wood was drying in the kiln, we considered many possible designs for the bookcase, but soon agreed. The casement boards and shelves would each be a combination of four species—ash, oak, maple, and black walnut. As we discussed the spacing of shelves and whether or not to make them adjustable, Ficke suggested black walnut for the facing edge of each casement board and shelf. "It will be spectacular!" he said. Instantly, we all knew he was right. The stairway bookcases are the most elegant, eye-catching feature in the house.

I write this chapter on performance from the desk in the dormer study feeling good about what we accomplished. I am also deeply humbled because I know well that it is not my or our doing. It is an ongoing culmination of the genius and hard work of many people over the centuries that made it possible for us to bring it all together, allowing Mary and me to live well in a home not estranged from the world in which humanity evolved.

Chapter 10:

Trail Magic and Oberlin—

Gesture and Challenge

The atrium of Oberlin College's Lewis Center for Environmental Studies was delightfully filled with sunlight as city and college officials gathered with others for a simple signing ceremony. The Clinton Foundation and USGBC had selected Oberlin College and the City of Oberlin to become the 18th city in their Climate Positive Development Program. This signing on March 4, 2010, of a memorandum of understanding by Oberlin City Manager Eric Norenberg and Oberlin College President Marvin Krislov, opened new vistas for this northern Ohio community.

Bob Berkebile, an internationally renowned Kansas City architect speaking for the USGBC, encapsulated the challenge:

> This is an agreement that rethinks the whole idea of community building, education, and research and development. It looks to be so ambitious. I think that it looks to change the Rust Belt into the Green Belt. Each of the projects in the Climate Positive Development Program is unique. Let me mention two of many for Oberlin.
>
> Oberlin, like all communities with an academic institution, has town-gown issues. Everything will change. This alignment of common purpose, of having to work together, will change this community in ways unimaginable and for the better. The ramifications will extend to Ohio. And, dare I say, to the world.
>
> Oberlin College has a long tradition of fostering radical change—opening higher education to blacks and then women in the early 19th century, civil rights in the middle of the last century. When my granddaughter graduates from Oberlin—she is four months old—she and the community will look back on what we have begun today as more important than all of the profoundly consequential transformations that have occurred here in Oberlin.

By signing, the college and city committed themselves to become climate positive. I wonder if anyone in the Lewis Center atrium that afternoon understood what climate positive entailed. I certainly didn't. I have claimed that Trail Magic is climate positive, but this refers only to operating energy. Mary and I are not climate positive for most of our activities: food, water, transportation, entertainment, health care, clothing, and other consumption that result in the release of heat trapping gases.

The scale of the challenge for us, and Oberlin, to be climate positive becomes apparent when we consider each person's total energy consumption. The U.S. annually uses 100 quads of energy measured in BTUs, or per-person, 350 million BTUs. Thus, Mary and I together are annually responsible for the use of 700 million BTUs.

By design and our behavior, Trail Magic has reduced our expected consumption of 110 million BTUs—the operating energy of the average U.S. home—to a small surplus of electrical energy. This leaves 590 million BTUs, of which about 80 percent comes from fossil fuels, or 470 million BTUs for which we are responsible and must account for without release of heat trapping gases, if we are to be climate positive.

How much PV would we have to add to offset 470 million BTUs? If we assume that our PV electricity replaces coal-generated electricity (80 percent of the electricity generated in Ohio is from coal), then we only need to replace one quarter of our 470 million BTUs or about 120 million BTUs, because it takes four units of coal energy to make one unit of electrical energy. To mine, process, and transport a unit of coal requires about 25 percent of the energy in the coal, while converting the heat from burning the coal to electricity takes another 50 percent of its energy, leaving one quarter of the original energy in the resulting electricity. To make Mary's and my 120 million BTUs, we need to produce about 35,000 kWh (120 million BTUs × 1 kWh/3412 BTUs), the annual output of a 35 kW PV system in northern Ohio (Trail Magic's 3.12 kW PV system annually produces 3,200 kWh or ~1,000 kWh per kW). At $6 per Watt, this PV system would cost about $210,000 and last for, perhaps, 30 years. The payback time for the embodied energy in the PV system might take 5 years, and then we'd be climate positive for the next 25 years or more. (Embodied energy is a measure of the energy to make, transport, and install the PV system.)

Using the same logic, we can estimate that Oberlin with 8,000 people (city and college) could become climate positive by installing 164,000 kW of PV for about $100 million.

It is unlikely that we, or Oberlin, will become climate positive by installing this much PV. Most likely, we'll take varied approaches, first reducing substantially our energy use, and then replacing or offsetting fossil fuels with energy sources that result in no net release of heat trapping gases.

We have a 6,000 square foot garden that is seven times larger than our Troy garden. Our garden there produced about 15 percent of our food, so we expect to have harvests in Oberlin equivalent to most of our food consumption once we substantially improve the texture and fertility of our heavy-clay, garden soil. Our pond will provide fish, and we're thinking about raising chickens.

In addition to two acres of woods, we have started planting trees to convert the front yard into a little forest and to replace the mature ash trees we lumbered in the flood plain and other places. Existing trees that die and dead branches that fall will provide wood for heating while our several hundred other trees continue sequestering carbon as they grow.

We have planted prairie grasses—big blue stem, Indian grass, switch grass—and perennial prairie flowers in the eastside yard and backyard, as well as clover and timothy grass around the pond and in the swales that drain water away from the house and barn. We are restoring the small prairie and larger savanna-like area below the pond. The deep rooted prairie and other vegetation will sequester carbon over the years as they improve the soil. We mow the eastern meadow, swales, and yard when necessary to mulch the garden for weed control and soil enrichment.

Local mechanics are keeping our 1995 Saturn wagon roadworthy until we purchase a small plug-in hybrid that we can charge from our PV panels. In anticipation of this carbon-free transportation for local driving, and to offset more coal-produced electricity, we have exchanged our solar hot water system with the company that installed it for a reduced price on a 2.10 kW PV system. With 5.22 kW of PV, we will produce annually about 5,500 kWh that will cover our current annual use of 2,500 kWh while leaving 3,000 kWh for local transportation and cooling the house as the climate warms, and eventually for heating if we no longer are able to manage the woodstove.

These actions are meaningful steps as we grapple with changing other behaviors to reduce our consumption while living a quality life. Local transportation can be carbon free by walking, bicycling, or driving a plug-in hybrid, but long distance transportation is our biggest contributor to climate change. Our children's families are in Arkansas and Florida, and we have relatives, friends, and colleagues in places distant from Oberlin whom we enjoy visiting from time to time. The challenge is to reduce long distance travel as much as possible. Until climate-neutral public and private transport are available, old time phone calls, email, and skype will suffice for some visits. And we will need to embrace low-carbon, local choices for recreation and vacation.

As retired persons, we purchase new clothes infrequently, having a closet full of choices that satisfy most occasions. For health care we only see our doctors for minor problems and annual check ups. Of course, this could change.

Will Mary and I become climate positive in regard to everything we do? I seriously doubt it. Of course, we could consider more PV or get together with others and fund a portion of a giant wind turbine to put us in the positive. In any event, we came to Oberlin to join others in an effort to create a more durable pattern of habitation.

What will the Oberlin community look like when we achieve the intent of the memorandum of understanding? In the 1990s, David Orr envisioned the Lewis Center as a prototype for what all colleges and the wider community needed to do. When under construction, the process respected human health and the environment in Oberlin and elsewhere by using recycled materials, wood from sustainably managed forests, organic compounds that do not readily evaporate into the air, and minimal toxic glues, paints, and adhesives. The Lewis Center uses about one third the energy of a traditional classroom-office building and is climate positive for operating energy because all its energy comes from PV systems on its roof and over an adjacent parking lot. Its spaces are welcoming and in high demand for special events, especially the atrium.

Outside, a quarter acre "forest" of native trees with 10 years growth is beginning to provide shade and habitat for insects and birds. An orchard of a few dozen apple and pear trees yields several bushels of fruit in the fall, while a raised bed garden provides fresh produce. A small pond creates habitat for native plants and animals, as well as a pleasant place to relax and commune with nature.

To the casual visitor passing by or walking through the Lewis Center, it looks like a newish building with a few unusual features, but its most remarkable ones are not evident. Trail Magic is similarly deceptive, as I suspect will be the case for Oberlin, when its citizens achieve their goal of becoming climate positive.

Sidebar 15:
The Oberlin Project and the Tenth Anniversary of the Lewis Center

In 2010, *Architect Magazine* asked 150 international green building experts to name the most important green buildings of the past 30 Years. Among the 121 buildings nominated, the Lewis Center ranked first. For ten years the Lewis Center has catalyzed hundreds of projects around the world that sought to replicate or exceed its accomplishments. On October 11-12, 2010, preeminent leaders in green architecture and ecological design convened in Oberlin with alumni, faculty members, staff, and students to celebrate the Lewis Center's influence and to formally launch The Oberlin Project.

The Lewis Center was a LEED platinum building before the USGBC had established its certification program and became an icon for ecological design almost immediately. As impressive as these and other accomplishments are, one might argue that the Lewis Center's most important contributions to the future are the philosophy it embodies and the lessons it teaches. Our buildings and how we live try to make the natural world fit us, while the Lewis Center attempts the opposite: we need to adopt ecological principles to be compatible with four billion years of evolution. This lesson of the Lewis Center has already inspired several generations of Oberlin undergraduates and many others to strive to live in accord with the principles of environmental sustainability.

The Lewis Center was in the vanguard of the current green building movement. Now, we need to bring into being durable communities. The Oberlin Project is Oberlin's attempt to create a model for holistically resolving the challenges of the 21st century. The Project has assembled ten teams to address particular elements including economics, greenbelt, energy, policy and finance, education, community, and revitalization of a core corridor encompassing Oberlin schools, downtown, and south Oberlin that will radiate out into the city and region.

The ultimate goal of the Project is to create a resilient community in which energy comes from renewable sources, and where local agriculture, forestry, and other industries provide a substantial portion of the region's needs. In addition, educational institutions—Joint Vocational School, Lorain County Community College, Oberlin City Schools, and Oberlin College—will work together to formulate curricula that produce citizens and workers whose skills and knowledge address first and foremost local needs, as well as those of a global society.

Although human activity is already increasing climate instability, most US citizens are not even familiar with the basic scientific evidence establishing that humanity's activities are forcing this instability. Despite the fact that the Swedish chemist Svante Arrhenius demonstrated in 1896 that the Earth's climate would change if we substantially increased the concentration of carbon dioxide in the atmosphere, it is the kind of complex abstraction related to a distant consequence that the human psyche did not evolve to intuitively grasp and act on. The eminent evolutionary biologist, Edward O. Wilson, gives insight into humanity's conundrum:

The relative indifference to the environment springs, I believe, from deep within human nature. The human brain evidently evolved to commit itself emotionally only to a small piece of geography, a limited band of kinsmen, and two or three generations into the future. To look neither far ahead nor far afield is elemental in a Darwinian sense. We are innately inclined to ignore any distant possibility not yet requiring examination. It is, people say, just good common sense. Why do they think in this short-sighted way? The reason is simple: it is a hard-wired part of our Paleolithic heritage. For hundreds of millennia, those who worked for short-term gain within a small circle of relatives and friends lived longer and left more offspring—even when their collective striving caused their chiefdoms and empires to crumble around them. The long view that might have saved them their distant descendants required a vision and extended altruism instinctively difficult to marshal.

Although it is uncommon to think far into the future and plan for it, this is exactly what Oberlin's citizens will have to do. We require a bold vision, as well as altruism for each other and for generations to come. This is what Bob Berkebile meant when he said, "Everything will change. This alignment of common purpose, of having to work together, will change this community in ways unimaginable and for the better."

More and more Oberlinians are changing behaviors and affecting the transition to a more resilient community. Among them are Cindy and Andy Frantz, who were the first residents in Oberlin to install PV panels on their roof in 2004, despite the absence of large enough subsidies and tax credits to have given them a reasonable payback time—years not decades. They have two children, keep chickens in their garage, have a garden, and in 2010 replaced their failing gas furnace with a ground source heat pump, again with modest economic incentives.

Cindy recognized her family was among the privileged, with the resources to reduce their carbon footprint, but knew others could barely pay their utility bills. She, in collaboration with Zion Community Development Corporation and Oberlin Community Services, created Providing Oberlin With Efficiency Responsibly (POWER) to improve the energy efficiency of houses for those financially unable to do it themselves. In its two years, POWER weatherized, changed out incandescent bulbs for compact fluorescent ones, installed night setback thermostats, and accomplished other energy efficiency measures in almost two dozen houses.

People in Oberlin, like early adopters in many other communities across the country and world, have demonstrated proof of concept for dramatically reducing the release of heat trapping gases. It is truly low hanging fruit to build and retrofit buildings to be climate positive in operating energy. We know how to produce much of our food locally, food that not only tastes better but is less energy intensive to grow and deliver than industrially produced food. We also know that the activities associated with local food enrich the community emotionally and economically. We have made cars that get 70 miles per gallon, and prototypes that do as well or better using electricity produced without fossil fuels. But even more relevant are the numerous examples of efficient, safe, and cost-effective public transportation that we can improve and replicate. It is the quality of life that resonates with a meaningful life, not the quantity of things we consume.

A cadre of kindred spirits is working in Oberlin—college and town—on a 20-year vision of a vibrant city region that will be a net producer of renewable energy and have farms, forests, and industries that feed and provide many, if not most, of the region's needs and wants locally. Perhaps it's a fantasy, but Oberlin is big enough to provide a relevant model and small enough to do something meaningful in a relatively short period of time. We came to Oberlin to join these visionaries. Trail Magic is our gesture to the larger challenges here and beyond.

Coda

You have seen through my eyes the emergence of Trail Magic. What were the perspectives of other key players? I wanted to discover their stories and give voice to their reflections. I interviewed Joe Ferut, Mike Strehle, and Don Watson and asked Mary to write her perspective after I had finished a complete draft of the book. They had not read, nor had I discussed with them, what I had written. I utilized interview transcripts and Mary's statement to produce the following narrative that provides nuance and new accounts of what transpired during the creation of Trail Magic.

In late December 2009, a little more than a year after we moved in, I met with Don Watson at his home in Connecticut to hear his reflections on Trail Magic. When I asked his opinion on the most important architectural things that we accomplished, he replied, "Well, we are still friends."

Not exactly the response I expected, but it rang true as I remembered the comment of a family member whose father had been a general contractor. Upon seeing the amicable relations between Strehle, Ferut, and us at the time of project completion, he remarked to me, "This isn't the usual situation my father encountered. At the end of a project, after the shouting stage, no one was talking to anyone. And they were definitely not friends. Something went right here."

The process we followed was what Watson called a "rollout strategy," meaning that his business plan was to spread the knowledge he had gained by collaborating with architects across the country and the world. Watson did the schematic design on our house, and then we found an architect in Ohio who, with our help, did the bidding process and the detailed construction drawings with input from Watson and the builder.

In the 1980s, Watson had been the architect and builder for houses in Connecticut, where he was able to control and accomplish everything himself. But situated 500 miles away from Oberlin, that wasn't possible in our case. "Everybody behaved," Watson said. "There could have been a breakdown at any point. Joe could have changed things without my permission. Mike could have fouled things up by not executing the plans professionally. As it turned out, everybody performed well."

One does not often achieve such a positive outcome, as both Watson and Ferut related. "For example," Watson explained, "an owner I've done the schematics for is now trying to build according to a builder who is giving him different information than I am. He got into a partnership with a builder who said, 'Here is my way of doing it.' The owner took the builder's way. I have to separate myself from the project."

Ferut put it in a broader context. "Something really important for me was how we did the project. If anybody knows the traditional roles among architects, clients, and contractors, it's usually adversarial. Typically, what happens is the architect in various ways puts the contractor in a bad light, especially in a house project where the architect does the design, but isn't involved in contract administration—the day to day overseeing. As the project gets going, the architect is less involved while the contractor and the owner are with each other a lot. And, for various reasons, the contractor disparages the architect. But what I saw through this process was that there was a very honest, open relationship. As one of my mentors told me, 'It was never about confrontation. It was about cooperation.' Not that we didn't have some hiccups, but a positive attitude was set. I haven't had a lot of projects that have gone this way."

When I first contacted Watson in June 2007, I believed that his 50 years of solar architecture knowledge, combined with our relationship as colleagues and friends, made him the ideal person to hold our hands as we entered the unknown world of house creation. As we proceeded to exchange ideas and to check each other out, it became obvious that we really needed him while he was doing us a big favor. This clarity of relationship engenders humility and fosters a cooperative, "let's-work-things-out" pattern of discourse. I am inclined to be this way, while Watson is unconditionally so. He is a mediator par excellence; however, when something doesn't work out, he accepts what happened and moves on.

Watson is a realist, tempered by his long experience in architecture, who knows that mistakes will occur, but he chooses not to dwell on them. "Look at the number of times the baton was passed. There were you, Joe, Mike, the subcontractors, and me. Every time something could have been dropped. I trust we made some mistakes and we will find them."

I asked if he saw any mistakes. He gently sidestepped the question. "No, no. I think everything is fine. In my practice I do custom homes. A custom home means you customize attention to every detail. What I have learned is that the house belongs to the architect only up to a certain point. Many architects would have told you how to live. There are famous stories about that. I would not have been a successful architect if Trail Magic had not become your house."

The affirmative attitude that Watson, Mary, and I initially established put a positive spin on the project that permeated the team. Ferut commented, "There was a really good symbiotic relationship among all the team members. In the beginning, when we all first met, there was that typical sort of tension, the honeymoon thing. But we got past that. And then there was real mutual respect. These sorts of projects have great student-teacher relationships in them; that was one of the nicest things that came out of this project: the relationships among clients, contractor, and architects. "

Strehle had the right personality to complement the team with his unflappable, "can-do" attitude. When I asked him how he got that kitchen window to work, he replied, "The window should have been four inches shorter. We realized too late, after we ordered the windows. I measured and determined I could make it work if I pushed the window all the way up in the opening. The countertop would then butt into the wood of the window frame. I looked at the window diagram. It would be close, but I wasn't 100 percent sure. If it didn't, we'd have figured out something else."

The baton had dropped somewhere between Watson's window schedule and placing the order with the manufacturer. When we discovered the error, Ferut realized it was his and offered to cover the cost. I didn't want anyone to pay $1,300 for a replacement window, so I told him that I was satisfied with Strehle's solution. I heard Strehle quietly say with a smile, "Joe owes me one," and went back to work. I think we all owed each other; the responses each of us had to this first major glitch solidified our emerging pattern of working as a team, with the common goal of making the best house possible.

Watson had signed a memorandum of understanding that specified what he would do for $6,000 that would get us to a schematic design. During the design process, he was open and responsive to all of our questions and concerns, and remained equally so once Ferut took over. I said to Watson, "I feel bad because, after you handed off the schematic design to Joe, we continued to use your time. That seemed unfair."

He responded, "No, no, no. I know that to get quality results, there is no upper limit. If you're an Olympic runner, you don't start taking it easy at lap three. It is a matter of practice that you give 110 percent, and you have to be ready for that. In some jobs what owners tend to think is, 'If I talk to the architect, I'm going to have to pay a fee.' I think you and I had a clear way of communicating without you paying a fee."

"Blackcap jelly," I said.

"Yes, but I hope I left the impression that you could talk with me at any time, in any form, without running into a fee discussion." He continued, "I learned this approach decades ago. Just do it for a fixed fee. It is the only way to quality."

I commented, "That seems unique to me. It concerned me to ask you to do more than you agreed to do."

"How about the doctor who doesn't take that position? Doesn't show up at the post-operation discussion? These are my babies," he explained.

When Watson began, I knew he was a master of passive solar design and an accomplished architect, but only after living in our new house through all seasons did I fully appreciate what he and Ferut had accomplished. Much of how they did it will be forever a mystery to me—I don't know enough to explain the nuanced interplay of light, heat, materials, colors, patterns, and spatial relationships that creates a sense of well-being and beauty. So much has to be integrated in the architect's mind, and then spatially expressed in the elements that make up the house, all while adhering to the clients' desires within the challenges of a budget. In Watson's words, here is Trail Magic's birth recounted in his home two years after he completed the schematic design:

> You and Mary were friends of mine, and you had a very reasonable program. It was clear from the start that you weren't building a mega-mansion. In fact, we had budget constraints from the beginning. The budget was a discipline that made the project more challenging, and you and I quickly said, "Let's try to build the most energy-efficient and environmentally responsible house possible—and within a budget."

Consider the design of the Honda Insight. Engineers spent 10 years making it energy efficient, but also economically appealing to customers. Trail Magic embodies ideas that developed over decades—ideas scribbled on paper, some dating to the early 1970s. We were working back then on energy-efficient, climate responsive houses. We actually built and tested them, so the ideas became conclusions. Whatever guidance I was offering to you was based on empirical evidence.

What were the challenges with the Trail Magic site? The site was ideal—it sloped to the south and was spacious. There were flood issues, and those—plus the distance from the road—helped determine the cross section. Our real discipline came from building a house that you could live in, and that would meet your unique requirement of having an area for guests who could be comfortable for extended periods of time.

From the beginning, we considered the notion of the "hot spot"— the sun spot—which moves through the day with the sun. When it is windy or cold, you seek out and are comfortable sitting in the sunny space. The notion of the hot spot will always be an important aspect of a home. In your house, the sun spot and fireplace hearth come together in one room, the living room. But we didn't design just for winter condition. With your house in Ohio, you and I were aware from the beginning of cooling and ventilation needs because of global warming.

I have always been interested in natural ventilation. In building a house, the basement can help with that, but it typically isn't used. In your case, we made the lower floor a living space with doors that open it completely to the upper floors. When the upper floor windows are open, cool air from the ground floor moves throughout the house via the stairwell. This acts as a wind tower.

Since the early 1980s, I've used basements for cooling with a vertical thermal zoning strategy. Most architects don't. Nor do builders. Why? I can't explain that fully. Much of it is driven by the economics of construction. In other words, if your budget were doubled, or if we were building a mega-mansion, we wouldn't have to be so careful to include natural ventilation methods. We could accomplish the same thing through mechanical and design devices that use energy. Most of the time, it's when builders and architects have the discipline of budget that they use these passive elements.

In your house, just as it is in my house, the lower floor is typically 10 degrees cooler in the summer because it is earth-bermed. In my house on a summer day, it is comfortable downstairs, whereas it is hot on the main floor. Zoning is one of the keys to the science of both your house and my older house.

Trail Magic has three vertical zones: lower floor equals cool; middle zone equals heated by sun; upper zone equals warmth, enough to induce ventilation in the summer, and also to be the warmest and coziest zone in winter. You also have the horizontal section, which follows the arch of the sun from east to west. That is why we have your dining room and deck on the west, the sunset area. You have a sunrise window, so you are aware of the sun as soon as it appears on the horizon. The sunset window, particularly in winter, is important. When you don't have that, you really miss something. In the typical engineered solar house, the focus is on the south and misses the full range of natural lighting that connects inside to outside.

In the earliest solar houses, architects and builders concentrated on winter heating only, and we overdid it. We underestimated the importance of ventilation and shading. Sun shading is impossible to figure out in a fixed way. Fixed sun shading will work sometimes, but not at other times, even with the sun in the same position. If it works from September through October, it is excluding desirable sun in March and April. Fixed shading is only a partial solution. In your house we combined shading from the roof overhang and shades inside, which are part of the design for temperature regulation in all seasons.

Something we didn't do in your house was to install radiant heating. The house I did in Bethany, Connecticut, just prior to yours, has radiant heating. But due to the high level of insulation and the passive gains, they hardly use it. We overdid it.

I've always said that every house should have a place where you can live without electricity. Your house will always have such a place. That was part of my design intent. You have three zones inside. You also have the deck and the south patio, which is intended as a micro zone for plant growth that would not otherwise happen in less favorable conditions.

We struggled with where to put your deck. By putting it off the first floor, which is where you walk out and have dinner in the summertime, you essentially double the size of the living room. That's important. The indoor-outdoor is always important. But we couldn't put the deck on the south side of the house, because it would shade the ground-floor south windows. So we put it on the west and combined it with under-deck wood storage.

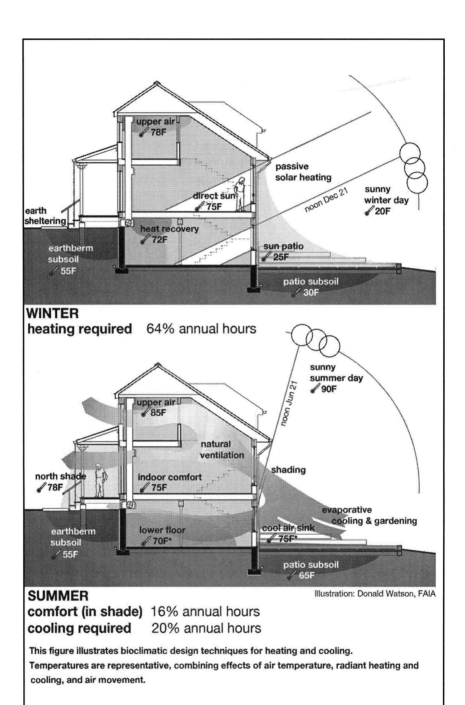

WINTER
heating required   64% annual hours

SUMMER
comfort (in shade) 16% annual hours
cooling required   20% annual hours

Illustration: Donald Watson, FAIA

This figure illustrates bioclimatic design techniques for heating and cooling.
Temperatures are representative, combining effects of air temperature, radiant heating and
cooling, and air movement.

Sidebar 16: Bioclimatic design features embodied in Trail Magic

The bioclimatic design features of Trail Magic are summarized in the figure on facing page and can be employed for a home anywhere. Bioclimatic design utilizes the "ambient energy" at the building location; that is, temperature effects of sun, earth, masonry, and air flow to achieve human comfort.

Part of the job is done by merely sitting there. In Oberlin, based on 30-year weather data, one can be comfortable in the shade for 16% of the time, during which no energy is required other than to find a place in the shade. All a house has to do is to act like a shading umbrella. Buildings that gain too much solar heat in spring, summer, and fall require "cooling" even when it is comfortable under the apple tree.

Cooling is typically required in Oberlin 20% of the time. But, just as the cooling breeze is all you need under a tree, so it is inside the house. If the house can be ventilated in a way that air flows across the room, it cools you by accelerating evaporation from your body.

Shade overhangs limit summer sun almost entirely from south-facing windows in the living area on the first floor of Trail Magic; however, summer sun does enter lower floor windows, but to date the ground floor temperature has remained in the 70s during the hottest days. If over heating accompanies global warming, operable shades can be installed to exclude unwanted sun.

In summer, you will feel cooler in the lower floor of a home like Trail Magic that has masonry foundations for two major reasons. We are comfortable as a result of the combination of air temperature and radiant "temperature." Radiant temperature is not read on a thermometer. If you touch a masonry wall and it is cool to the touch, then your body is radiating heat to it. The walls and floor of a lower floor in an earth-bermed home act as "heat sinks," absorbing heat that you radiate when surrounding surfaces are cooler than you. Some solar gain is desirable into such spaces to provide "solar drying." This is a building technique understood by traditional builders since colonial times. It helps to temper the air and provides a heat source for natural air drying.

The south patio can be cooled in summer by spraying water over the patio paving and on the rocks in the surrounding garden. For several hours, as the water evaporates, temperatures can be decreased considerably making it a pleasant place on hot summer evenings for coffee and desert.

Cold winter hours (and cool periods in early Spring and late Fall) represent 64% of the year in Oberlin. Passive solar gain is useful for much of this time, often all that is required. The passive gain from the south side of a home naturally flows upward, so that the warmest part of the house is the upper floor.

On cold but sunny winter days, the upper level of a house can be "too hot," in which case circulating the warm air to the lowest level helps to distribute the heat. In Trail Magic this is accomplished by the blower in the heating-cooling system that can be run independent of the heat pump. Alternatively, residents can activate the Energy Recovery Ventilator (ERV) to introduce fresh air while distributing passively gained heat evenly throughout the house.

Earthberming on the north, east, and west sides has a modest insulating effect. A subtle but important benefit is on the south sun patio. It is protected from the cold winter wind (generally from the Northeast) and can represent a "microclimate" that is 5°F to 10°F higher than the more exposed areas of the site. One can see this difference by earlier snow melt and by spring growth of plants and blossoming of flowers in the south patio garden. Best of all, one can enjoy sitting in the protected sun patio on sunny Spring and Fall days, when it is too cool or windy in other outdoor locations around the house.

Trail Magic's super insulation and low air infiltration enables passive solar heat gain to remain in the home well into the evening, often throughout the entire evening into the following day. The effect is to create a "stable" temperature in the home, reducing or eliminating the need for mechanically assisted heating to cycle on and off. Super insulation also helps keep the home cool in summer.

Although the bioclimatic techniques go far, there are hours when the passive techniques are not adequate to provide comfort. In summer, one can take the glass of ice tea to the shaded deck or under a tree. In winter, one throws a log on the wood stove and invites company in, or retreats to the upper level to write a book.

Donald Watson, FAIA

Joe was a part of getting the deck elevation right. When you stand on the ground and look at the number and height of stairs that you have to climb to reach an entryway, your psychological comfort is determined. If it is too high, you feel it's beyond your energy and effort.

In science jargon, this is based on the "perception of effort." By experience, we figure out how much effort it takes to go from here to there. We have done this for millennia; we will always choose the path of least effort. I've done houses where builders or owners have cranked up the entryway so high that my concept of being comfortable changes as I approach the house. Three feet is no problem. Five feet is too much. We made it easier to reach your deck by berming up the north and west sides. And we picked up six inches with a step down to the deck from the entry door. These actually play out as critical, in my opinion.

There are other ways we had to customize your house. We made it a long house with a lot of glass on the south for passive gain. The fact that we had the stairway in the middle made me struggle from the beginning on how to do the stair column that interrupted the lines, so there were compositional challenges.

There was a good deal of work in trying to resolve the roof lines. The task was to keep it both simple and elegant, so as not to have a fractured house. We wanted the house to look elegant in its simplicity. I think we achieved that on the north side, the entry side.

We also had to resolve the height of the windows, the height of the living room, and the height of the study on the second floor. We had to account for every inch. In order to make things easier, we could have added a foot, but that would have made the house too high. For its size, the living room is about as high as it can be without having a grand ballroom feeling.

The best thing about this house is your and Mary's dedication to it, and the fact that you are monitoring its performance and energy use. Architects can say anything—and usually do—without validating performance.

I believe Trail Magic is one of the most energy-efficient and lowest-impact houses in the United States. There are many "net energy" homes, but a lot are built with two or three times the money. Dollars for result, I don't know of any house that competes with Trail Magic.

It's actually hard to build a simple, elegant house. Things get complicated and not simple. Try to design a flower. Just try it.

You included some details that I wanted, such as the small windows in the kitchen. Those are purely aesthetic—very little energy will be saved. You put more into making the window than you'll ever save. They have little to do with function, but rather aesthetics—a splash of sun across the counter, a place to put colored glass and catch the light. The rain chain on the entry way porch is another aesthetic touch. [Carries water down a copper chain from the porch gutter to a bowl that empties into a flower box on the side of the porch.] Like little bells and wind chimes that tell you about the passing of time, of the weather.

Finally, this house isn't completed yet. Your garden has had only one season. Your landscape is just settling in. The landscape will stabilize and get productive. Yours is a food-producing, self-sustaining homestead. It is only going to get better with time. We are at the very beginning of this phase.

Once we hired Watson, we had little choice but to use his roll-out strategy and he had no problem with this approach. "This is actually a business strategy that I like to follow. First, I educate another architect, and then I see a house built in another region that is more or less following my ideas. In this case there is at least one builder, Mike, who can take this practice forward. And one architect, Joe, who can take the lessons further. Those are small wins."

We could have never predicted it, but as far as Ferut was concerned, it was not a small win.

The people I got to work with on this project were really wonderful. In my education back in the '70s, I probably read a book by Don Watson. When I realized who I was working with and realized the kind of care and intelligence that was brought to the project by Don, by yourself, by David Borton and his understanding of physics and solar design, and even by Mike Strehle, a young "Mr. Cool," I felt really wonderful. This was a pivotal project for me as an architect and a teacher.

For the last four or five years, I've tried to learn as much as I could about positive energy houses—well, not positive energy actually, because that's a new term this house propelled. I've attended Affordable Comfort and Passive House conferences and Northeast Sustainable Energy Association meetings where I've heard about R values, thermal bridging, tightness, and envelopes, and discussed it with different colleagues. Then this project came along. I really saw, through the people I worked with on Trail Magic, what could be done—how to actually create a positive energy house. I'm taking what I learned to my other projects and striving to improve upon what we accomplished with Trail Magic.

In my design studios at Kent State University, I take the production of this house into the studio, where it becomes a teaching tool. I work to have my students understand that if they want to do a green project, a sustainable project, the process itself has to be sustainable. It has to be holistic and front-loaded. Energy is always on the table. Environmental issues are always on the table. And that isn't what usually happens. If you don't use a cyclical, front-loaded, holistic process, you are using a linear process. If you don't bring energy to the table from the beginning, then you are backing energy into the project. And when you back something into a project, it doesn't work.

Trail Magic is a model. It is a really good house. If architects from the beginning are not looking systemically at the issues of firmness (durability), commodity (efficiency), and delight (beauty), then they never get to the issue of sustainability. It will not be a good building. Trail Magic embodies the primary essences of a really good building. It is grounded to its site. It acknowledges the sun.

I had a really good conversation with the dean of architecture at Kent. He told me that a client for whom he worked said that it was not only the energy efficiency of the building that the client liked, but also how wonderful he felt being in the building. We forget that buildings are meant for people. Trail Magic has been designed for responses to natural light and natural ventilation; strong passive strategies, yet also strategies that make people feel good. People feel beautiful in Trail Magic because they are in a building that creates a relationship with nature.

With Trail Magic, I learned how to think about a project differently. I had done projects that were "low energy"—double-walled houses, straw bale homes—but I didn't have it all together. For example, I thought we understood load in terms of heating and cooling on one particular house, but we missed the boat on plug load. We missed the boat on the users' impact on the building's performance. And we didn't focus on the sun. Those are really big things.

Now, when I start a project, I think about the things I missed and have a systems perspective. Now that I've learned about those things, I can't turn back. If I don't think about these sustainability methods, then I'll feel guilty. I look at it ethically now. I think an architect has to bring these things to the client. If the client doesn't want the project to be more sustainable—to make the house smaller; employ solar energy and passive cooling; make a tight, well-insulated envelope—there's not a lot you can do, but you have to explain why they should consider these options.

You were an educated client, but most people aren't. They look to the architect to give them a house that is truly sustainable. A lot of people think that a house is green simply by adding things like bamboo flooring. I had a discussion with a client recently about why putting a large kitchen window on the west side was inappropriate. She didn't listen, but I tried.

When I met Ferut in November 2007, he was in the midst of a vocational midlife crisis. After almost three decades as a standard architect, climate change and other environmental issues made him realize that conventional architecture, what he was doing, was a big part of the problem. He had teamed up with Mark Hoberecht, a NASA engineer by profession, and together they were advocating the passive straw bale house. Ferut was also keen on the high R, tight, double wall construction that he was doing for Peter Crowley. I felt comfortable with having Ferut take over from Watson, because he clearly understood the importance of energy efficiency and other aspects of green building. I thought he'd not only contribute to, but also learn from working on Trail Magic. I didn't appreciate that our initial months of interactions could have led to a very different outcome, as Ferut relates:

> The people I worked with on Trail Magic were wonderful—the best. And the project itself transformed my professional life. At the start, however, I didn't feel comfortable, because I didn't have all the answers. You were explaining to me how critical passive solar was and other things about solar and energy efficiency that I didn't fully appreciate. That bothered me. I wanted to know more.
>
> There is an old saying: "People support what they help create." When you came to me, you already had a design. We hadn't helped create the design, and I didn't know Don. I really didn't quite understand some things. Perhaps if I had understood the big mission statement, or if I had been brought into the fold and told, "Joe, this is why you are so important," I might have felt differently. Maybe you did say those things, but I didn't recognize it. It was an ego thing. That was the hardest thing for me. Without your attitude and Don's ability, this project couldn't have been.

If Ferut had been prickly or had had a bigger ego, we might not have ended up with the cooperative relationships that emerged. The physical distance between us would have been a major stumbling block if Ferut hadn't seen and been swayed by the positive aspects of the project. And Strehle's low-key personality and self-confidence also permitted us to get through the complex dynamics of making positive, cooperative relationships. But, as in most successful human interactions, tensions and frustrations existed. As Strehle relates, some aspects of the project that made it successful were new to him and stymied his efficiency.

> This house had the whole system in mind as we were designing and planning how to implement the job. We focused more on how the house worked instead of how it would look and feel inside. Most clients are concerned about their kitchen and countertops; in this project it was more about getting the house built right—its basic design and the systems that would make it very energy efficient.
>
> The team approach made this very different from most jobs. Many more people were involved. In other jobs, I work with the architect first; the owners come in later and usually go with our recommendations. With Trail Magic, there were several people involved, with lots of going back and forth, round and round, before a decision was made. You got everybody's opinion and then you'd come up with an

answer. By the time I got the answer, I'd be off thinking about something else.

We had a lot more communication; that was both positive and negative. Positive, because we came up with good ideas. Negative, because it took longer to get answers. If there had been fewer people involved, we could have come up with answers more quickly, but the answers might not have been as good. I do think that everything came out really well.

The project began very quickly. We started within two weeks from signing the contract. But a lot of decisions hadn't yet been made, and the design wasn't completely done. We had a foundation permit, but we didn't have all the permits because we didn't have all the information yet. Everything was rushed. We probably made some wrong decisions because things were happening so fast. That wasn't good.

My job was to build what was on the plans and give input as far as systems and how things were to be done. My main goal was to get the envelope right—seal it up with the proper amounts of insulation, reduce thermal bridging, and work with the double wall system to make sure that everything was done right while reducing the use of lumber as much as possible. Getting the envelope right was the most important thing—you can't go back and redo it. Framing the house was simple. You had two dormers, one on the front and one on the back. The back dormer was very simple. The front one took more thought, with roof lines and the thick walls and roofs coming together.

Early on, the elevations were a huge problem. I needed one reference point from which to work that I didn't have. We needed a surveyor. I spent five hours one day using a laser and calculations to figure it out. It was tight, almost didn't work. The sewer barely made it coming in at the basement floor. The barn was close to the house and at a different elevation. Very tricky.

Your ideas about lumbering the trees on-site kept changing. We'd have to stop and regroup based on your newest plan. You selected bamboo flooring, which we got real close to installing. But then you decided to use local wood for the flooring and to mill the ash trees for the beams, shelves, and the floors in the study and loft. Those changes affected the course of the job.

I did like working with the wood flooring and how we used three different species of wood with different widths. I liked the look of it and would do it again, but installing Ficke's flooring wasn't much fun.

Despite the routine problems, I liked our focus on energy and making this a positive energy house. We all had that goal. It was a challenge for me to get the envelope tighter than in any other house I had built, but I did. I took a lot away from this project. I learned a different style of building walls and roof sections. The biggest thing I learned was the importance of using south-facing windows for passive solar heating. In past jobs, I had been more focused on R values in the walls and air sealing, and was missing out on the passive solar gain. I'm incorporating passive solar heating in the house I'm currently building.

Ferut made an interesting comment when talking about the house in which he'd missed the boat on plug load and didn't employ passive solar heating. "The difference between your house and that house was that they gave us an owner design, while you gave us an architect design." Because Mary and I didn't know enough to design our house, we were open to Watson's suggestions. His schematic design emerged from our response to his question of how we lived. As a result, Watson had free reign to provide a design that worked for our particular pattern of living. And he had to do it under budget constraints, and with the goal of creating a house appropriate for the environmental challenges of the 21st century. Our ignorance benefited us; Watson didn't have to constrain his architectural experience and wisdom.

Ferut and Strehle executed Watson's initial design well with few glitches. The complaints we have about Trail Magic are minor; however, the design discussions on mechanical systems were not definitive, as Ferut relates.

I don't know if we overdid the mechanical systems. Granted, geothermal has a great efficiency ratio, but this house almost doesn't need a system. When we started to design Trail Magic, we had this notion of the German Passivhaus design, in which all that was needed was an Energy Recovery Ventilation device (ERV) with a ductless mini-split. Would it work? I was timid about it. We had a conventional engineer who didn't think a nonconventional system would work, no matter what it was.

Early on, I wondered if we even needed an ERV. I had conversations with Don about this. Was exhaust-only ventilation sufficient—install a fan and let it ventilate? Did we need heat pump loops in the pond? I think the question, "Would we have done it differently?" has a lot to do with the current state of flux on ventilation for super efficient houses. When building a house that is so energy efficient, how much energy generating capacity do you put in? Did we need more than oil-filled baseboard heaters? We probably should have done the mechanical systems differently.

Once you get the envelope right, the windows right, and the passive solar right—which we did—the increased cost of those components is offset by a substantially reduced mechanical system. We didn't take advantage of this. Who knows? We could have saved 10 or 15 grand.

Not only Ferut, but the entire team, including Mary and me, agree that the mechanical system is not ideal. We made two notable mistakes on systems installed. Although it was clear from the beginning that we were going to heat primarily with a woodstove on the first floor, Ferut's engineer never factored into any of his analyses that he had to design the ventilation system to accommodate woodstove heating. The engineer did consider individual radiant heating units in the absence of a central heating system, but he did not consider woodstove heating. Watson and I discussed the limited capacity of conventional air circulation to move heat from the upper floors to the ground floor. Failing to take the discussion further, when assessing heating options, was an unfortunate omission. Maybe no good way exists for blending conventional and woodstove heating; however, we didn't explore such possibilities as a supplemental fan-duct system that would take hot air from the top of the great room and move it to ground floor rooms.

Related to this first omission, the second misstep was not zoning the ground floor separately from the rest of the house. Had we done that, we could have heated the ground floor with the heat pump while the woodstove heated the upper floors. In July 2008, Strehle asked me by phone if we wanted to zone the ground floor separately, but he needed a decision within a day. He indicated that it would be tight fitting in the additional ducts and would add about $1,000. I talked with Mary, but we were in Arkansas and I didn't think to call Ferut, who had already signed off on the heating system. Too much was happening too fast. And we weren't on-site enough then.

In terms of how Mary and I live in the house, these two mistakes go mostly unnoticed. We are exclusively on the upper floors, and do not heat the ground floor unless we have guests who are with us for only a few weeks in the cold months. At those times we close off all upper floor vents, turn the thermostat several degrees above the great room temperature, and heat the ground floor with the heat pump. Of course, this is inefficient because the system was not designed or balanced to heat this way.

Ferut, Strehle, and Watson have not lived in Trail Magic to see what does and doesn't swing smoothly. Although Strehle did complain about the number of doors we had, he and the others didn't experience the door mistake as Mary and I have. Watson's final schematic design had three pocket doors, while the construction plans handed to Strehle in April 2008 had four pocket doors. The finished house, however, has just one—the master bedroom closet door. We just love that door: sturdily constructed and likely to function well for decades. Unfortunately, this had not been my experience. I rarely saw a sliding door that didn't come off its track routinely or was not already broken. As a result, the other pocket doors were deleted one by one, with the pantry pocket door changed to a regular door after Strehle had built the wall to accommodate it. My assuming that the past would be the future was a mistake. In our compact house, pocket doors for the pantry and the master and ground floor bathrooms would have been far superior to the regular doors that replaced them. And the doors to the ground floor bedroom closets, too, would have been functionally better had they been pocket doors.

Mary, more than anyone else I've written about here, lived the Trail Magic saga. Her voice is omnipresent in the narrative, sometimes alone, but more often intertwined with events as they played out. Her perspective is, of course, a blend of the unique and the common.

I felt that if we were really going to move to Oberlin and make such a big change, then we should build the home we had often talked about. And we did. We all made our unique contributions, but for me, first learning about Mike when I visited Eastwood Elementary School stands out. That was a bit of good luck, or should I say, "trail magic." Mike did a great job.

The majority of the decision-making fell to Carl because he had a more flexible schedule than my teaching position allowed. However, I came to Oberlin whenever I could, doing whatever needed to be done. I joined Carl for my April vacation and felt like a pioneer on the frontier as we cleared brush and cut trees from the pond site in intermittent snow showers and freezing cold rain.

Once we moved into our garage apartment helping with waste management took a lot of my time. Carl and I did that together, and it was a big help to the project. I also took on the role of getting things for Mike at Loews, Home Depot, and wherever else he sent me. Being Mike's gofer was a plus because finding places introduced me to the roads and the area.

Often Mike worked several hours after regular quitting time, so we developed a routine of having him for dinner at our apartment, or when things got really busy, bringing dinner to the house. The first of many picnic dinners at Trail Magic was in our bedroom with Mike and David Sonner. Our table was a picnic bench, and we sat on lawn chairs amongst paint cans and piles of flooring boards. We enjoyed getting to know Mike better and developing a friendship.

I was concerned about the smallness of our new house as compared to our previous houses. At the same time, it was liberating to find new homes for things we hadn't used in years, and for furniture that wouldn't fit in Trail Magic. We gave away our two nicest couches and kept instead our well-used ones because of their comfort and modest size. They, with slip covers, served us well until we had them reconditioned to be like new.

I've come to love our smaller space. Everything is conveniently located on one floor—our suite of bedroom, bathroom, and walk-in closet; the kitchen with everything conveniently located and with a window behind the sink that offers a view of the front yard; and the pantry with lots of shelves, the freezer, and clothes washer and dryer.

I am particularly fond of our clothes line, which attaches from a corner of the house to a large oak tree a hundred feet away. It's only a few steps from the washing machine. Our clothes smell so fresh. We use the line in the winter, even when it is below zero. Carl is fond of saying that he's an advocate for nuclear power when the reactor is at the right distance, 93 million miles away.

The great room is cozy and warm for the two of us, and cozier still for a dinner party of eight. It took almost two years for us to figure out how to make the great room work with more than three or four guests. I missed not having a big sofa and chairs for everybody. But, when Ficke finished the red oak dining table, we reorganized the furniture making it comfortable for eight. In the warm months, the deck and walkout patio easily accommodate a dozen or more people. Being in the sun and fresh air, listening to the singing of birds and frogs, and watching swallows hunt insects, or deer and other wildlife around the pond and in the meadow is quite special.

I have always admired the look and grain of naturally finished wood; it's warm and welcoming. I love the Douglas fir casements around the Loewen windows; the pine doors and trim; the local Ohio oak, maple, and ash flooring on the first floor, and our ash on the study and library floors [loft above master suite]; and, of course, the stairwell bookcases highlighted with our black walnut.

The box Don and Joe designed on our deck for garbage and recyclables is a great feature that has gotten many positive comments from guests. It is right outside the door and has a top that lifts up so you can put things in a garbage can or recycle bucket. On garbage-recycle day, you open a side door and slide out the garbage can and recycle buckets, which have been out of sight and protected from scavenging animals.

The wood stove in the center of our living space provides warmth on all-too-common cloudy winter days. On sunny winter days, the house warms up nicely. We're getting soft. Sixty five used to be our high. Now, when it drops close to 65, it is time to build a fire.

I never paid much attention to the sun shining into our other homes, but it is pretty amazing to watch. In December, the sunlight reaches across the great room into the kitchen by a few feet. By mid-May, the angle of the sun has changed; the roof overhang prevents direct sunlight from entering the house. When we need the sun's heat, we have it. When we don't, no direct sunlight comes in except as fall approaches. I can read in almost any place during the day without turning on a light. The natural light makes one feel good, even on cloudy days.

Together, Mary and I worked the problems that battered us like endless waves on a turbulent ocean. As known to all those before us who've helped design and oversee the building of their homes, these are treacherous waters to navigate. Reefs and hidden rocks can scuttle your boat. Stormy weather and rip tides put you where you don't want to be. And we were unwise to combine Trail Magic with retiring and moving 500 miles from the place where we had spent half our lives. We now sail calmer waters. With the passage of time we reflect positively on the intensely lived adventure that created Trail Magic. Like my navy deployments to Southeast Asia in Vietnam times, "We had some long days, but it was a short cruise."

Owners Programs

1. Initial Owner's Program, July 26, 2007

We wrote this program in response to Don Watson's request to describe what rooms we wanted in our new home, how we would use each, and the items to be in each. The number, size, and layout of rooms were influenced by how Mary and I had lived in our Troy home since our children had left. The floor plan for the first floor was also influenced by the under renovation house we almost purchased in Oberlin. The items in each were primarily determined by the furniture and other items we already owned because what we had was more than adequate for the new house.

2. Final Owner's Program, January 1, 2008

This was the fourth iteration of the owner's program which coincided with Don Watson completing the Schematic Design. It incorporates all that we had learned during the schematic design process. Most importantly, it reflects our acceptance that size matters: the footprint went from 1,800 square feet to 1,056 square feet, a reduction of just over 40%. This is significant because the most important factor in creating a house appropriate for the 21st century is its size. A comparison of the two plans reveals many other adjustments that reduced the overall cost, environmentally and economically.

A careful reading of the plans also establishes that some ideas that the program considered were incorporated in the house that was built (e.g., size, daylighting, electing to install a heating/cooling system that could efficiently circulate air with or without heating or cooling), while others slipped off the table resulting in mistakes or omissions (e.g., sound suppressing insulation not put in all interior floors and walls, screened window on side of front door, no floor drain in kitchen or pantry, no location for exercise bicycle, no ceiling fan in great room).

I was not disciplined sufficiently to keep a running record of suggestions, ideas, and problems raised in iterations of the Owner's Program, at LEED team meetings, and on other occasions. We did not visit each idea or suggestion or problem on a regular basis until we resolved it, one way or another. As a result, we did not adequately address some items. For example, we never resolved the question about evenly heating and cooling the three floors, as well as heating or not heating the ground floor depending on occupancy. If we had, I believe it likely that the heating-cooling system would have had two zones, one for the ground floor and the other for the first and second floors. I also think it likely that we would have discussed woodstove heating at the time of designing the mechanical systems and incorporated a combination duct system that would allow for substantial, independently-controlled, air transfer from the ceiling of the great room to the far east and west sides of the ground floor, thereby facilitating substantial air circulation in the house, and assisting with the heating of the ground floor by woodstove heat, when needed.

Initial Owner's Program
Carl and Mary McDaniel
495 E. College Street, Oberlin, OH 44074

July 26, 2007

These plans represent current thinking. The general layout is what we think we want, but all is open for discussion and change, especially the details.

General description:
- Two floors, no basement or attic
- Rectangle of about 30 ft by 60 ft
- Ground floor with earth built up on west, north and east sides about to the level of the first floor
- Sufficient window area on south side of ground and first floors for adequate insolation [solar radiation] to heat house on cold winter days (coldest days?)
- Minimal window area on north side
- Some window area on east and west sides to provide daylighting, but limited to reduce heat gain in summer and heat loss in the winter
- South facing roof windows close to ceiling [clerestory] sufficient to provide daylighting in north end of spaces (kitchen, living room, bedroom)
- Deck at level of first floor, extending from middle of east side around 1/3 of south side, with entrances from dining room and north end of east side
- Free standing barn about 20 ft by 30 ft, with space for 2 cars and yard equipment, including small tractor. Storage space above cars with access steps
- Metal roof on house and garage

Rooms on ground floor: dimensions, uses, furniture
- One bedroom (southwest corner; window(s) on south side, perhaps a small window near ceiling on west side for daylighting): 10 ft (wide) by 12 ft (deep); closet 2.5 ft by 6 ft (between two bedrooms); guestroom; 2 twin beds, dresser, table, book cases, hardwood/bamboo floor
- Second bedroom (south side, east of first bedroom, window on south side): 10 ft (wide) by 12 feet (deep); closet 2.5 ft by 6 ft (between bedrooms); guestroom, queen size hide-a-bed, dresser, desk, table, book cases; double as work space, hardwood/bamboo floor
- Full bathroom (south side, east of second bedroom, window(s) on south side): 5.5 ft (wide) by 12 ft (deep); for guests; toilet, shower, sink, shelves, mirror, storage closet, tile floor
- Kitchenette (south side, east of bathroom, window on south side): 8.5 ft (wide) by 12 ft (deep); cooking and eating area for guest who will stay for a few days to perhaps a month; small refrigerator, small electric stove with oven, microwave oven, sink, counter, cabinets, drawers, storage closet; door to outside; part stone floor to store sun's heat
- Hallway (north of rooms running east to west): 3 ft (wide) by 36 ft (long)
- Root cellar (north side): 6 ft by 6 ft; either as insulated, walled-off room or as an extra room built under front concrete porch; cool storage space for vegetables; shelves, cabinets, table
- Open space in rest of ground floor except for a mechanical area or room; general work and storage area; work bench, tables, lots of storage shelves

Rooms on first floor: dimensions, uses, furniture

- Master bedroom (southeast corner): 13 ft (wide) by 16 ft (deep); windows on south end, small window(s) on east for daylighting, south facing roof window for daylighting; sleeping and quiet time; double bed, two small tables on sides of bed; two dressers, blanket chest, small desk, two straight-back wooden chairs, hardwood or bamboo floor
- Master bedroom closet (northwest end of bedroom): 6 ft (wide) by 14 ft (deep); no window, 8 ft ceiling, ladder access to storage space that is above both closet and bathroom; hanging space on both sides for clothes each 8 ft long, 4 ft of shelves on each side for general storage, shoe rack at north end of space
- Master bedroom bathroom (at northeast end of bedroom): 7 ft (wide) by 14 ft (deep); small window on north and east sides for day-lighting, 8 ft ceiling; toilet, separate shower and bathtub, two sinks, two mirrors, cabinets for towels and bathroom supplies, tile floor
- Kitchen area (north side): 15 ft (wide) by 16 ft (deep), small window on north side and south facing roof window for day-lighting, roof is ceiling, counter coming out from east wall to separate kitchen area from dining area, lots of counter space, lots of cabinets for storage, cabinet for clothes washer and dryer, some type of tile floor
- Dining area (south side):15 ft (wide) by 14 ft (deep), sliding glass door to deck, roof is ceiling; eating; table for 12 that collapses to table for about four with two chairs (can be put on west side of room against brick half wall separating dining/kitchen areas from living room), oval table with four chairs in middle of eating area, floor stone to store sun's heat
- Front entrance (north side): 5 ft (wide) by 12 ft (long), west of kitchen, open way into kitchen on east and into living room to south, roof is ceiling, stand-up desk for mail, guest book, stone or tile floor
- Front-entrance closet (west side of entryway): 5 ft (wide) by 6 ft (long), 8 ft ceiling, coat rack and storage shelves
- Half bathroom (south of front-entrance closet): 5 ft (wide) by 6 ft (long), 8 ft ceiling; toilet, sink, mirror, cabinets, tile floor
- Wood stove: in a brick wall structure about 6 ft high running north-south about 2 ft wide and 15 ft long, wood stove platform extends into living room with wood storage in brick structure
- Living room (southwest corner): 20 ft (wide) by 18 ft (deep), roof is ceiling, windows on south side, south facing roof window for daylighting, small window on west side for daylighting; small love sofa, big stuffed chair, platform rocking chair, Hitchcock rocking chair, Lincoln chair, several straight-backed wooden chairs (also used for dining table), piano (spinet), doll cabinet, cabinet for TV and stereo equipment, perhaps book case, perhaps part stone floor to store sun's heat with rest of floor hardwood or bamboo
- Study (northwest corner, north of living room): 10 ft (wide) by 12 ft (deep); small windows on north and west for daylighting; 8 ft ceiling over west 7 ft; step-ladder like access to storage spaces over west 7 ft of study and over entryway closet and half-bath; wooden desk and chair, computer table and chair, reclining chair and separate foot rest, many redwood bookcases (stacked box style) on north wall, built-in book cases with adjustable shelf height on all of east wall, hard wood or bamboo floor

Questions

1. The question of maintaining uniform temperature.

- Between ground and first floors. With no attic, will the first floor be much hotter than the ground floor? How to keep first floor cool in the summer? How to keep ground floor warm in the winter? Or with the substantial insulation in the roof is this solved? Is a door between ground and first floors helpful? Other means for keeping first floor cool in summer.
- On first floor in rooms with 8 ft ceiling and those with the roof as ceiling. How might uniform heating and cooling be accomplished or do we have a poor design that is not advisable?

2. Things we can't accommodate yet

- "Mud" room on ground floor when coming in from working or playing outside; could make entrance not in kitchenette space, but into the open basement spaces near hallway to ground floor rooms.
- Space for exercise bicycle with access to TV on first floor; perhaps store bike in study and roll into living room each night to use

Forgot: 1) Stairs to first floor, 2) file cabinets in study, 3) wide door into ground floor, 4) free standing greenhouse later.

Final Owner's Program

Carl and Mary McDaniel
495 E. College Street, Oberlin, OH 44074

January 1, 2008

The following narrative represents our current Owner's Program and commentary, for discussion during the design and budgeting processes.

The Schematic Design drawings by Donald Watson, FAIA, indicate floor plans, section dimensions, as well as window dimensions that are to be followed and take precedent over any variation that might be noted below.

General description:
- Three floors: Ground Floor, First Floor, Second Floor
- Rectangle of 44 ft by 24 ft (outside dimensions).
- Approximate dimensions of inside spaces:
    ~872 sq ft finished space on Ground Floor
    ~990 sq ft finished space on First Floor
    ~162 sq ft finished space Second Floor
    Total: ~2024 sq ft of finished space
    ~128 sq ft of unfinished space on Ground Floor (work area)
    ~0 sq ft unfinished on First Floor
    ~156 sq. ft. of storage space on Second Floor over Master Bedroom
    Total: ~284 sq. ft. of unfinished space
- Ground floor berms. Berm on entire north side. Berm on west side extends ~ 10 ft from north end of house to just under north end of deck. Berm on east side slopes down to south allowing for egress window in northeast bedroom. Berm on south side extends ~ 19 ft from east corner and is below windows in southeast bedroom.
- Sufficient window area on south side of Ground and First Floors for sufficient insolation [solar radiation] to heat house on winter days.
- Minimal window area on north side, but sufficient for daylighting.
- Minimal window area on east and west sides to provide daylighting, but limited to reduce heat gain in summer and heat loss in the winter.
- Barn, free-standing, 24 ft by 30 ft with space for car, truck, tractor, and yard equipment on ground level and a loft for storage and work space.
- Metal roof on house and garage.
- Put material in the ceilings of the Ground and First Floors and in walls between living spaces of all floors to suppress noise between floors and living spaces.
- PV system to provide 3.12 kW. Clamp mounted on raised-seam of metal roof. This 24 panel PV system will be moved from our Troy, NY, house. Each panel: 26 inches by 57 inches; will be mounted on roof in three rows on south facing roof just west of stairwell tower roof. Roof space needed is ~ 14 ft by ~17.3 ft (available roof is ~16 ft by ~23 ft).
- Solar domestic hot water panels mounted on raised-seam of metal roof to the east of the stairwell tower roof. Roof space available is ~ 14 ft high by ~12 ft wide.
- Consider: On the inside of outside walls, over the vapor barrier, attach 2" by 2" studs on which to mount wall board so that wiring, duct pipes, etc. will be inside insulation and vapor barrier to maintain integrity of the vapor barrier and insulation. Doing this will depend upon the wall system selected.

Rooms on Ground Floor: dimensions, uses, furniture

(The floor will be finished cement slap that is not slippery when wet. Throw rug(s) will be used in living spaces.)

- Bedroom one: southeast corner; ~12.5 ft by 10.5 ft with clothes closet; 3, ~2.5 ft (W) by 3 ft (H) windows on south side for heating, daylighting, and one egress window (Note: 1 operational for ventilation); access to storage space under stairs. Use: guestroom or workroom; Furniture: queen size hide-a-bed, dresser, desk, table, book cases.

- Bedroom two: northeast corner; ~12.5 ft by ~10 ft with clothes closet; 1, ~2 ft (W) by ~3 ft (H) window on east side for day-lighting and egress (Note: operational for ventilation). Use: guestroom; Furniture: 2 twin beds, dresser, table, book cases.

- Full bathroom: center of north wall under First Floor bathrooms; ~6.5 ft by ~6 ft. Use: for guests and clean-up after working outside; Fixtures: toilet, shower/bathtub, sink, shelves, mirror, floor is finished cement slap, floor drain.

- Common room: south side, west of stairwell; ~14 ft by ~16 ft; closet; 3 ft handicap-accessible door to sun patio (with or without window?); and 2, ~2.5 ft (W) by ~4.0 ft (H) windows on south side for daylighting and heating (one operational for venti-lation). Use: cooking, eating-relaxing area for guest(s) who will stay for a few days to perhaps a month. Furniture: storage closet, dining table, 4 table chairs, two easy chairs, coffee table, side table.

- Kitchenette: north side just east of Root Cellar; ~6 ft by ~ 7 ft. Use: cooking area for guests, wash area for garden produce and for after working in yard/garden. Furniture: small refrigerator, small electric stove with oven, microwave oven, double sink, counter, cabinets, drawers, floor drain.

- Stairwell from Ground Floor to First Floor: south side between Common Room and Bedroom One; ~16 ft by ~7 ft with flat area ~6 ft by ~6.5 ft at base of stairs with doors to Bedrooms and Common Room; closet under second half-flight of stairs; set of two horizontal windows each ~2 ft by ~2 ft at landing halfway to First Floor for daylighting and heating (one operational for ventilation).

- Mechanical space: north side just east of Kitchenette; ~6.5 ft by ~7.0 ft. Use: water-in pipe, sewer-out pipe, electricity-in line, solar hot water storage tank, PV electric panel, other mechanical equipment required, floor drain.

- Root cellar: north west corner, ~6 ft by ~8 ft, well insulated from other ground floor space. Use: cool storage space for vegetables. Fixtures: shelves, bins, counter space.

- Unfinished space: west side south of Root Cellar; ~16 ft by ~8 ft; 3 ft handicap-accessible door on west wall to space under deck (with or without window?); and one ~2.0 ft (W) by ~3.0 ft (H) window on south side. Use: general work area and storage area, mud-area for coming in from working and other outside activities. Furniture: work bench, table, storage shelves.

Rooms on First Floor: dimensions, uses, furniture

- Front Entryway: ~5.5 ft (wide) by 6.5 ft (deep); 8 ft ceiling; north side in center of house; 3 ft handicap-accessible windowless door; narrow slit window on each side of door for daylighting and seeing who is at door (Consider as possible alternative: an off-center door with one slit window that is screened and opens); opens into great room with pocket door to isolate entryway from great room (closet for coats and boots in "hallway" before great room). Use: greeting people, taking-off/putting-on coats and boots. Furniture: stand-up desk for mail and guest book, perhaps a chair, stone/tile/other suitable floor material that is not slippery when wet.

- Half bathroom: east of entryway; ~6.5 ft (wide) by ~4.5 ft (long); 8 ft ceiling; one ~1.5 ft by ~1.5 ft window for daylighting. Use: guest bathroom. Fixtures: toilet, sink with counter and cabinet below, mirror, tile floor that is not slippery when wet, floor drain.
- Master bedroom: southeast corner; ~13 ft by ~13 ft (not counting space between bedroom and bathroom; roof is ceiling on south end (~9 ft to ~15 ft) and then 8 ft ceiling with loft storage over rest of bedroom and over bathroom and closet; horizontal set of three ~2 ft by ~4 ft windows on south wall for daylighting and heat (Note: one operational for ventilation); one ~2 ft by ~3 ft window on east wall for daylighting (Note: operational for ventilation). Use: sleeping and quiet time. Furniture: double bed, two small tables on sides of bed; two dressers, blanket chest, small desk, two straight-back wooden chairs, hardwood floor.
- Master bedroom closet: northeast corner at end of bedroom entry way; ~6 ft (wide) by ~10 ft (deep); one ~2 ft by ~3 ft window on east wall for daylighting; 8 ft ceiling; pocket door. Use: clothes/storage. Fixtures: hanging space of ~6 ft long on both sides for clothes, shelves/dresser under window, shelves on south wall as enter closet, hardwood floor as in bedroom.
- Master bathroom: west of closet on north wall; ~6.5 ft square; 8 ft ceiling; one ~1.5 ft by ~1.5 ft window for daylighting (Note: operational for ventilation). Fixtures: toilet; tile shower with curtain (not a glass door); sink and mirror; closet for towels, sheets, and bathroom supplies (door opens into bedroom entry hallway), tile floor that is not slippery when wet, floor drain.
- Kitchen area: northwest corner; ~11.5 ft by ~10 ft; roof is ceiling; horizontal set of two ~2 ft by ~3 ft windows on north side over sink for daylighting and seeing arrival of guests (Note: one operational for ventilation); one ~2 ft by ~2 ft window high on west wall for daylighting. Use: cooking with space for several people to work, floor of some type of tile/stone/wood/cork/other durable surface that is not slippery when wet, floor drain. Fixtures: ~2.5 ft by ~4 ft counter with cabinets/shelves below and on wheels that can be locked securely and that can be placed to separate kitchen from great room, or moved to other places; lots of counter space, lots of cabinets and drawers for storage, microwave oven, conventional electric stove and oven, refrigerator, and dishwasher; consider dedicated space under counter for recycling bins and compost container.

  Note: Appliances in kitchen and pantry are to be very energy efficient and of high quality. Cabinets and drawers are not to be custom made, but rather from Home Depot or other supplier. Cabinets can be middle-of-the-line quality, while drawers are to be top-of-the-line so they work well and are durable. Consider a dedicated cabinet area for garbage, compost, and recycle materials that can be transferred to the larger dedicated space/enclosure on the deck for garbage, compost, and recycled materials.
- Pantry: east of the kitchen; ~9.5 ft (deep) and ~7 ft (wide); one ~1.5 ft by ~1.5 ft window for daylighting; same floor surface as kitchen (tile/stone/ wood/cork/other durable surface that is not slippery when wet). Fixtures: clothes washer and dryer; counters with drawers below and shelves above, stereo system (tuner, CD player, tape player), master panel of outlet wires for stereo system, inlet/outlet wires for cable/internet/ phone. Uses: clothes washing, stereo center, and storage of dry foods, table linens, and various serving dishes, flower vases, etc.
- Great Room (Living/Dining Areas): southwest corner; ~22.5 ft (long) and ~13 ft (wide), roof is ceiling, no sharp demarcation between kitchen and great room other than cabinets/shelves/counter on west wall of kitchen and perhaps flooring type.

  Dining room area: roof is ceiling; 3 ft wide handicap-accessible door to deck at north end of west wall close to kitchen (with or without window?); a ~2 ft by ~2 ft sunset window on west wall above door; horizontal set of two ~2 ft by ~5 ft window(s) on west wall for daylighting; horizontal set of 6 windows on south wall of great room for heating, day-lighting, and grand view to the south. (Note: Each is two windows: top window ~2.5 ft by ~4 ft [does not open] and bottom window ~2.5 ft by ~1 ft. [some of bottom windows open for ventilation, perhaps three of 6].); hardwood floor. Use: eating/gathering. Furniture: a table that can expand to accommodate ~ 10.

Living room: roof is ceiling, south facing windows as described above in dining area. Use: sitting, reading, entertaining guests. Fixtures: small wood stove and wood storage bin at the east end in front of the stairwell. Furniture: small love seat, platform rocking chair, Hitchcock rocking chair, small easy-chair, spinet piano to the south of wood storage bin on east side, movable cabinet for TV, DVD player, and VHS player.

- Stairway from First Floor to Second Floor: 2 half-flights with wide landing (~3 ft by ~6.5 ft); four sets of built-in bookcases in east wall on half flight to Second Floor (each shelf ~12 inches deep, ~11 inches high, ~2 ft wide); horizontal set of two windows at landing for heating, daylighting, and view to south. (Note: Each is two windows: bottom window ~2.5 ft by ~4 ft [does not open] and top window ~2.5 ft by ~1 ft. [opens].)
- Deck at level of First Floor: ~12 ft (wide) by ~22 ft (long), on west side of house for access from driveway and barn.

Rooms on Second Floor: dimensions, uses, furniture
- Study: north side over pantry, entryway, and half bath; ~18 ft by ~10 ft; high windows on inside south wall for daylighting from stairwell and great room; horizontal set of three ~2.5 ft by 3.5 ft windows on north wall for daylighting (Note: one window operational for ventilation.) Use: study and guest room; Furniture: Murphy-type double bed that folds down from east wall, wooden desk and chair, computer table and chair, reclining chair and separate foot rest, two file cabinets, many redwood bookcases (stacked box style), hard wood floor.
- Low storage and loft at north end of Master Bedroom: northeast corner with access door from Study and railing on south end overlooking master bedroom, ~13 ft by ~13 ft, unfinished floor (probably OSB), sheetrock on walls and ceiling, electric outlets.

Barn
- Garage, work, storage space: 24 ft by 30 ft, on concrete slap, west side of house ~1 ft. behind the street-side front-line of house with overhead doors facing NE, ~25° angle to front-line of house, ~3 feet below level of first floor of house, sliding door for tractor on west side, windows on ground floor and loft for daylighting, wide stairs to loft (~3.5 ft); loft doors ~4 ft (wide) by ~6 ft (high) on both ends of loft, in the north end have an extended, overhead beam with attachment for block and tackle to allow for lifting objects into and out of loft. Use: shelter for car, truck, tractor, and other gardening equipment; work area and storage in loft.

Things to consider and resolve:

1. Maintaining uniform temperature.
- With no attic, will the first and second floors be much hotter than the Ground Floor? How to keep first and second floors cool in the summer? How to keep Ground Floor warm in the winter?
- Temperature balance in first floor rooms with 8 ft ceilings and those with the roof as ceiling. How might uniform heating and cooling be accomplished?
- Is the answer a combination of ceiling fans and fans in ducts to move air to adjust temperatures? We do not want to make it too complicated with all sorts of sensors and fans. We are not opposed to some manual turning on and off of fans.

2. **Want to have something like R 40 to 50 in walls and R 60 to 70 in ceiling, subject to energy analysis of cost-effective options.**
   - The Reddi-Wall contractors in Oberlin (Don Daily, Mike Strehle) state it has an R 50, but it is probably closer to R 25-30 for the effective ~4 inches of Styrofoam ® in 10 inch thick wall. Reddi-Wall website indicates that they have a system with thicknesses of 10 to 14 inches. If the 14 inch blocks have 8 inches of polystyrene then the R might well be 40 or more. If so, this would be a good choice for the whole house, because it gives a very tight envelope, is very solid and considered tornado resistant. Reddi-Wall goes up quickly and leaves little waste on-site and can be used for the entire house except for side walls of dormers and for roof.
   - SIPs are quite appealing, as are ICFs. We certainly want to consider them even if we have to use expanded polystyrene or polyurethane foam. It makes the frame go up fast, reduces waste on-site, and makes on-site builder less likely to create thermal bridges or other violations of envelope integrity.
   - Joe Ferut suggests straw bale to get R 50 in walls, cellulose in roof to get R 70, and Superior Wall Construction (ICFs) for below ground walls to give ~R 40 with added insulation (they go on about 8 inches of gravel and then floor is poured).
   - David Borton advocates for an envelope (insulation and vapor barrier) that is not penetrated for piping, wires, etc. He also says it is important to have a vapor barrier inside roof insulation.

3. **Need for supplemental heating/cooling.**
   - We anticipate the energy assessment will indicate that we have no need for a central heating system, but perhaps a need for some supplemental heating-cooling system, especially when the wood stove is not used, and in the summer.
   - Global warming models predict Oberlin to be warmer in the winter and to be hotter and muggier in the summer. Everyone encourages us to consider air conditioning. Your energy assessment will indicate if fans and mechanical circulation will keep the house comfortable, or if air conditioning will be needed. Mary and I do not like air conditioning much (never had it), but we do not like 95° with high humidity either, especially at night. Perhaps on those really uncomfortable times, the solution will be to spend time on the ground floor?
   - Is a better solution to install a heat pump and the duct work to provide heating and cooling on the occasions when needed?
   - We will have a PV system of 3.12 kW. Based on our experience in Troy (insolation [solar radiation] appears very similar but temperatures slightly warmer in Oberlin), we anticipate producing about 3.0 mega watts per year and will use about 2.5 mega watts. Thus, we will have some electricity for heating and cooling and hot water heating. Will it be enough, if the wood stove is not used? I doubt it, but I know you can do the calculation to see how much we need. We await your analysis and suggestions.
   - Some data from the web:

Year	Heating degree days	Cooling degree days
2006	4964	889
2005	6245	887
2004	6110	493
2003	6283	531

4. **Operable windows.**
   - Based on our opening of windows in current and past houses, we do not believe that all windows need to open. If, in selecting windows, the operable windows are more expensive than those that don't open, we think that only some of the windows need

to be operable. Operable windows also are more prone to air leaks with use and ageing. We will want your professional perspective and recommendations on the number and locations of operational windows. We have made suggestions above in the descriptions of the rooms.

5. Thermal shades for windows.

- We have thermal shades for two door-size windows in our current house. They really cut down heat loss and give privacy at night. We would like to consider them for many of our windows. We would like to have ones that have spring-tension for raising and lowering instead of strings. Don Watson suggests that they come up from the bottom for trapping cold and for blocking the sun on summer days. We know string operated ones are less expensive, but the Bortons highly recommend the spring-tension ones.

6. PV system.

- We will have 24 panels that are 26″ by 57″ each. They will be mounted in three rows of eight panels on the southwest part of the roof. The panels can be clamped to the raised seams of the roof. When needed, we can get the website that describes the mounting system, and the force created by a 50 mph wind so the metal roof will be attached appropriately to the roof structure to sustain this wind speed (50 mph is the code speed in NY according to the people who installed our system).

7. Solar hot water.

- We accept Don Watson's assessment that we should install a solar hot water system, subject to cost and local servicing availability. In the late spring, summer, and early fall I suspect insolation will provide the energy to heat our water, but it will not keep water hot enough at other times. We have PV and grid electricity to supplement the sun. Natural gas is also available, but we are inclined not to connect it because the service fees are charged even if no gas is used. In Troy, our service fees are ~$18/month for gas and ~$17/month for electricity. We propose having a propane-fired on-demand hot water and installing a ~200 gallon propane tank. However, we do think we should consider running a pipe for gas from the street to the house for the unknown future of energy needs.

8. Wiring house for cable and speakers, and speakers.

- Cable connections: master cable into pantry and cable wires from pantry to loft study, master bedroom, two places in living room, first floor common room, and both first floor bedrooms. I don't know anything about cable wiring, but someone will. Or do we have one hard wire and then rely on wireless?

  Speaker wires from stereo system in pantry to speaker boxes in second floor study, great room, master bedroom, common room on ground floor, and unfinished space on ground floor with toggle switches to turn speakers on/off in pantry. Each place needs two pairs of wires (one for each speaker) placed to give good sound. Or do we go wireless?

  Consider making speaker boxes in walls to hold speakers in the spaces indicated above. Size of boxes will be determined when we decide on the speakers to use. We could have built-in speakers, but think it better not to have them permanent in the walls, and thus, hard to change/repair.

  We think it useful to consider where it would be appropriate to run some empty wire conduits for future uses.

9. Siding.

- We like the idea of cement, fiberglass siding. We saw a house on the solar tour in October with Cententeed siding that was quite attractive, and apparently easy to install. We are open to your suggestions.

10. Windows.

- We are sure you will consider window glazings with high solar heat gain coefficients for south windows and others with lower solar heat gain coefficients for east and west windows. And perhaps other glazings for north windows. We know windows are most critical and expect we will need top-of-the-line windows to get heat loss-gain right. The Alpen windows recommended by Don Watson are an option to consider, if not too costly.

11. Water and moisture.

- We are concerned about dampness and moisture, especially on the ground floor. Don Watson has considered proper drainage around site and under the foundation, and construction of walls that should eliminate any potential problems. But we need to make sure it is done right.

12. Temperature of concrete floor.

- We assume that the ground floor concrete floor will be well insulated so that it is not cold like a standard concrete floor over the ground. We assume mechanical air circulation, insulation, and insolation will resolve the temperature concerns state above.

13. Piping.

- Don Watson has done an excellent job at reducing the piping needed by putting bathrooms and kitchen very close together and on north foundation wall. To reduce energy for hot water consider direct hot water pipes from heater to each faucet, and thereby, use smaller diameter pipes in order to reduce water and energy in getting hot water to faucet. Perhaps our pipe runs are too short for this to make much difference except to first floor kitchen sink and dishwasher.

14. Use/build with green materials.

- No or low VOC materials.
- No or few toxics.
- Sustainably harvested wood.
- Recycled materials when possible.
- Others.
- But, we are not obsessive.

15. Alarm system.

- Consider putting wiring in windows and doors for a security system that we will probably want because we are likely to be away from Oberlin for extended periods of time.

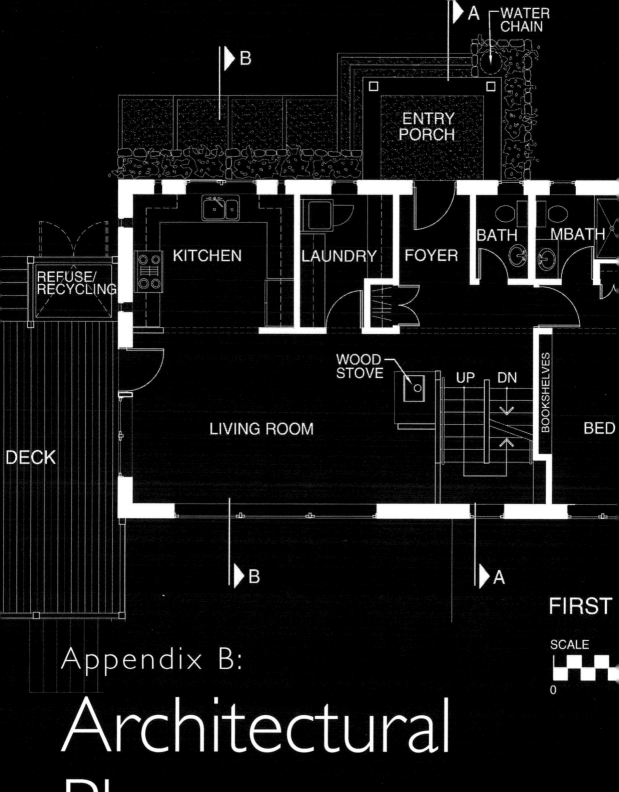

A — WATER CHAIN

B

ENTRY PORCH

KITCHEN

LAUNDRY

FOYER

BATH

MBATH

REFUSE/ RECYCLING

WOOD STOVE

UP

DN

BOOKSHELVES

BED

LIVING ROOM

DECK

B

A

FIRST

SCALE

0

Appendix B:

Architectural Plans

Architectural Drawings

1. Site Plan
2. Ground Floor Plan
3. First Floor Plan
4. Second Floor Plan
5. North Elevation
6. East Elevation
7. South Elevation
8. West Elevation
9. Wall Section
10. Energy Efficiency Strategies, Section AA
11. Energy Efficiency Strategies, Section BB

Architectural Drawings courtesy of Ferut Architects

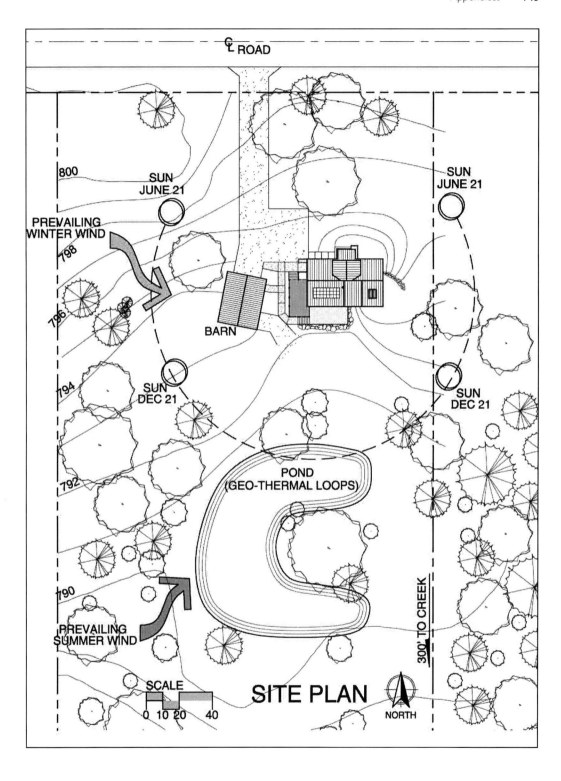

SITE PLAN

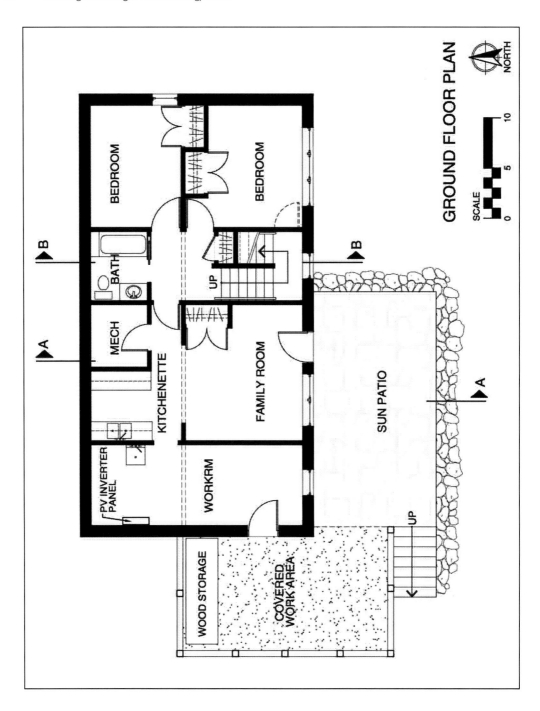

GROUND FLOOR PLAN

SCALE

NORTH

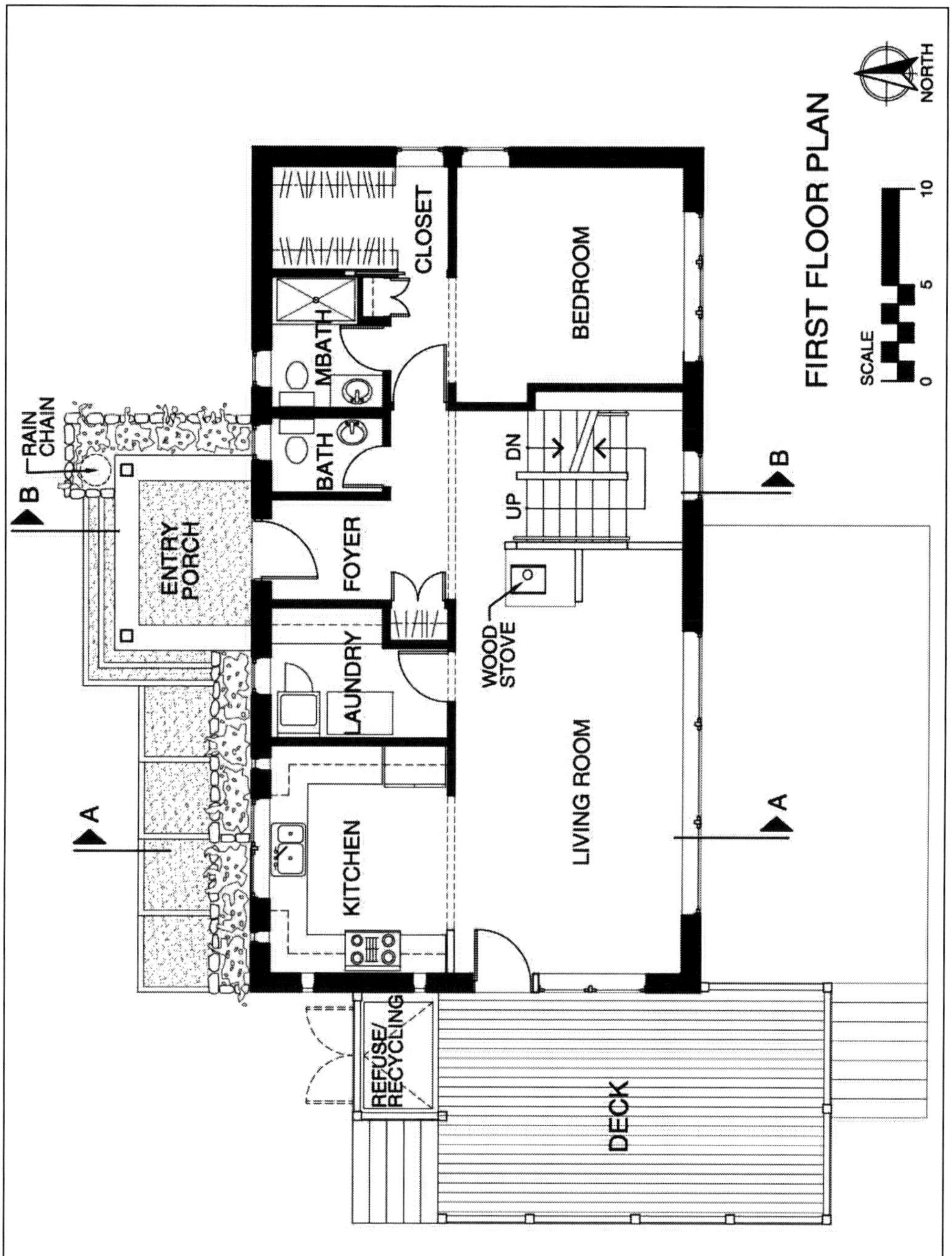
FIRST FLOOR PLAN
SCALE
0
5
10
NORTH
CLOSET
BEDROOM
MBATH
BATH
RAIN CHAIN
B
ENTRY PORCH
FOYER
UP
DN
WOOD STOVE
LAUNDRY
LIVING ROOM
A
KITCHEN
REFUSE/ RECYCLING
DECK

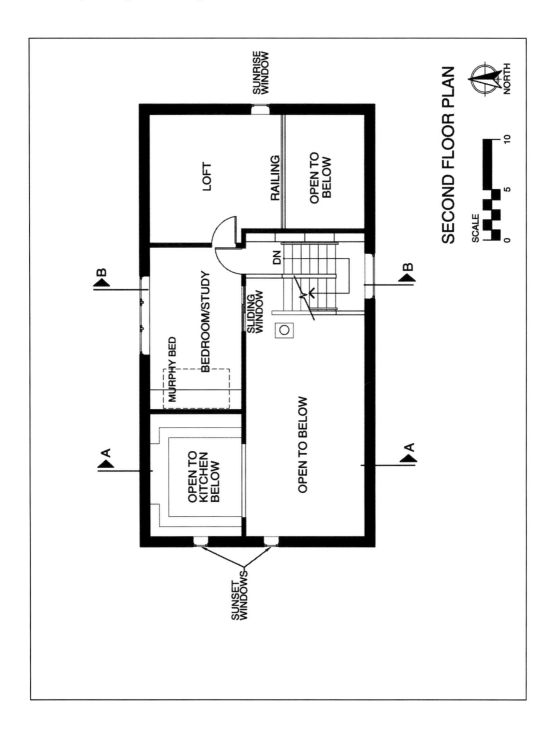

SECOND FLOOR PLAN

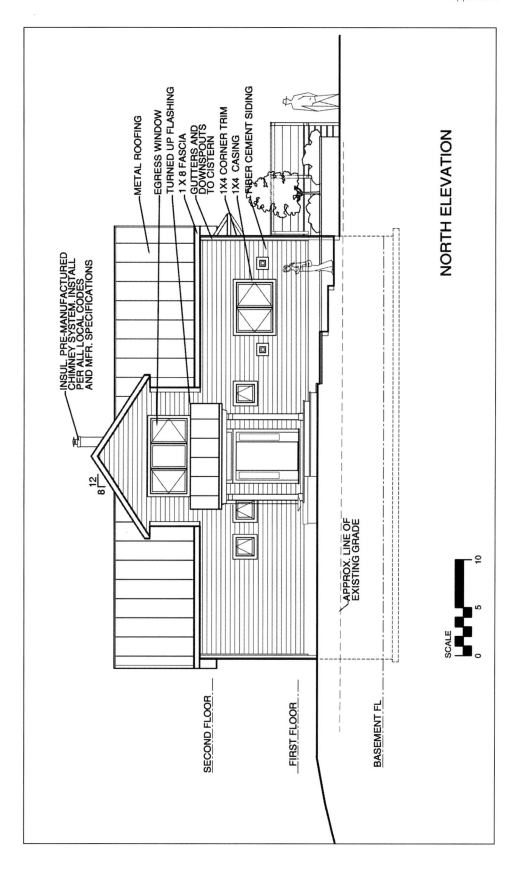

INSUL. PRE-MANUFACTURED
CHIMNEY SYSTEM. INSTALL
PER ALL LOCAL CODES
AND MFR. SPECIFICATIONS

METAL ROOFING

EGRESS WINDOW

TURNED UP FLASHING

1 X 8 FASCIA

GUTTERS AND
DOWNSPOUTS
TO CISTERN

1X4 CORNER TRIM

1X4 CASING

FIBER CEMENT SIDING

NORTH ELEVATION

SECOND FLOOR

FIRST FLOOR

BASEMENT FL

APPROX. LINE OF
EXISTING GRADE

SCALE

0   5   10

12
8

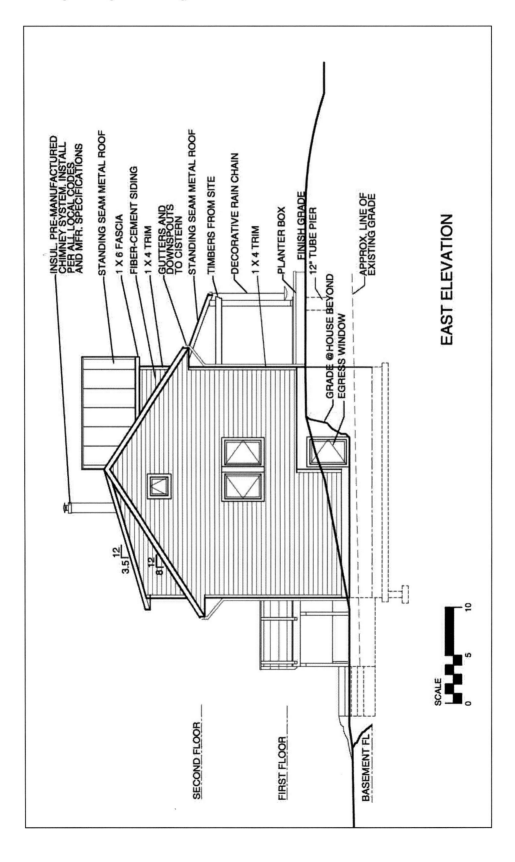

INSUL. PRE-MANUFACTURED CHIMNEY SYSTEM. INSTALL PER ALL LOCAL CODES AND MFR. SPECIFICATIONS

STANDING SEAM METAL ROOF

1 X 6 FASCIA

FIBER-CEMENT SIDING

1 X 4 TRIM

GUTTERS AND DOWNSPOUTS TO CISTERN

STANDING SEAM METAL ROOF

TIMBERS FROM SITE

DECORATIVE RAIN CHAIN

1 X 4 TRIM

PLANTER BOX

FINISH GRADE

12" TUBE PIER

APPROX. LINE OF EXISTING GRADE

GRADE @ HOUSE BEYOND

EGRESS WINDOW

SECOND FLOOR

FIRST FLOOR

BASEMENT FL.

3.5 12

8 12

SCALE

0   5   10

EAST ELEVATION

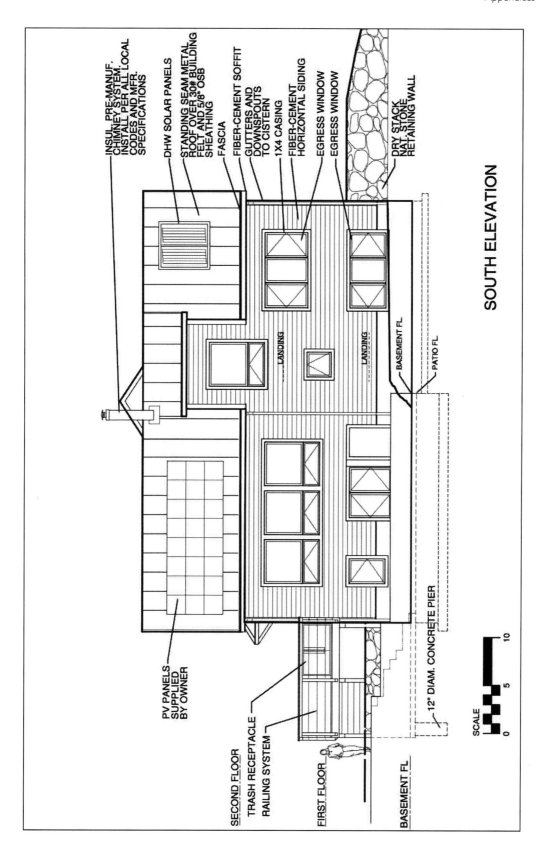

SOUTH ELEVATION

INSUL. PRE-MANUF. CHIMNEY SYSTEM. INSTALL PER ALL LOCAL CODES AND MFR. SPECIFICATIONS

DHW SOLAR PANELS

STANDING SEAM METAL ROOF OVER 30# BUILDING FELT AND 5/8" OSB SHEATHING

FASCIA

FIBER-CEMENT SOFFIT

GUTTERS AND DOWNSPOUTS TO CISTERN

1X4 CASING

FIBER-CEMENT HORIZONTAL SIDING

EGRESS WINDOW

EGRESS WINDOW

DRY STACK NAT. STONE RETAINING WALL

LANDING

LANDING

BASEMENT FL.

PATIO FL.

SECOND FLOOR

TRASH RECEPTACLE

RAILING SYSTEM

FIRST FLOOR

BASEMENT FL.

PV PANELS SUPPLIED BY OWNER

12" DIAM. CONCRETE PIER

SCALE

0   5   10

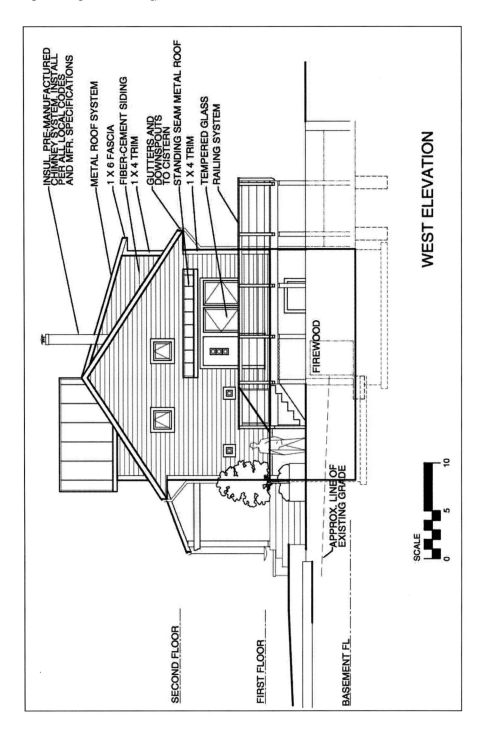

INSUL PRE-MANUFACTURED CHIMNEY SYSTEM. INSTALL PER ALL LOCAL CODES AND MFR. SPECIFICATIONS

METAL ROOF SYSTEM

1 X 6 FASCIA

FIBER-CEMENT SIDING

1 X 4 TRIM

GUTTERS AND DOWNSPOUTS TO CISTERN

STANDING SEAM METAL ROOF

1 X 4 TRIM

TEMPERED GLASS RAILING SYSTEM

WEST ELEVATION

FIREWOOD

APPROX. LINE OF EXISTING GRADE

SECOND FLOOR

FIRST FLOOR

BASEMENT FL

SCALE

0   5   10

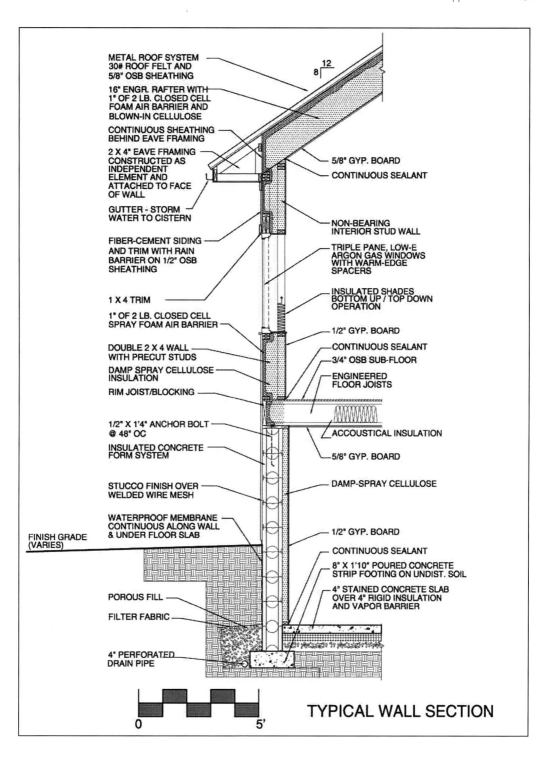

METAL ROOF SYSTEM 30# ROOF FELT AND 5/8" OSB SHEATHING

16" ENGR. RAFTER WITH 1" OF 2 LB. CLOSED CELL FOAM AIR BARRIER AND BLOWN-IN CELLULOSE

CONTINUOUS SHEATHING BEHIND EAVE FRAMING

2 X 4" EAVE FRAMING CONSTRUCTED AS INDEPENDENT ELEMENT AND ATTACHED TO FACE OF WALL

GUTTER - STORM WATER TO CISTERN

FIBER-CEMENT SIDING AND TRIM WITH RAIN BARRIER ON 1/2" OSB SHEATHING

1 X 4 TRIM

1" OF 2 LB. CLOSED CELL SPRAY FOAM AIR BARRIER

DOUBLE 2 X 4 WALL WITH PRECUT STUDS

DAMP SPRAY CELLULOSE INSULATION

RIM JOIST/BLOCKING

1/2" X 1'4" ANCHOR BOLT @ 48" OC

INSULATED CONCRETE FORM SYSTEM

STUCCO FINISH OVER WELDED WIRE MESH

WATERPROOF MEMBRANE CONTINUOUS ALONG WALL & UNDER FLOOR SLAB

FINISH GRADE (VARIES)

POROUS FILL

FILTER FABRIC

4" PERFORATED DRAIN PIPE

5/8" GYP. BOARD

CONTINUOUS SEALANT

NON-BEARING INTERIOR STUD WALL

TRIPLE PANE, LOW-E ARGON GAS WINDOWS WITH WARM-EDGE SPACERS

INSULATED SHADES BOTTOM UP / TOP DOWN OPERATION

1/2" GYP. BOARD

CONTINUOUS SEALANT

3/4" OSB SUB-FLOOR

ENGINEERED FLOOR JOISTS

ACCOUSTICAL INSULATION

5/8" GYP. BOARD

DAMP-SPRAY CELLULOSE

1/2" GYP. BOARD

CONTINUOUS SEALANT

8" X 1'10" POURED CONCRETE STRIP FOOTING ON UNDIST. SOIL

4" STAINED CONCRETE SLAB OVER 4" RIGID INSULATION AND VAPOR BARRIER

0   5'

TYPICAL WALL SECTION

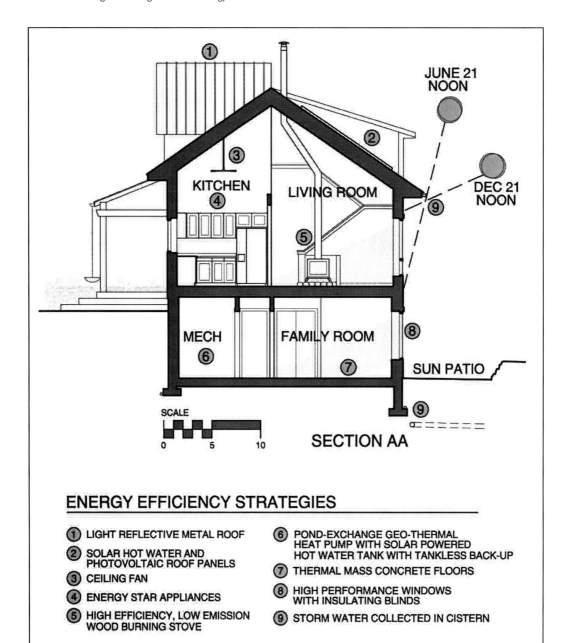

SECTION AA

ENERGY EFFICIENCY STRATEGIES

1. LIGHT REFLECTIVE METAL ROOF

2. SOLAR HOT WATER AND PHOTOVOLTAIC ROOF PANELS

3. CEILING FAN

4. ENERGY STAR APPLIANCES

5. HIGH EFFICIENCY, LOW EMISSION WOOD BURNING STOVE

6. POND-EXCHANGE GEO-THERMAL HEAT PUMP WITH SOLAR POWERED HOT WATER TANK WITH TANKLESS BACK-UP

7. THERMAL MASS CONCRETE FLOORS

8. HIGH PERFORMANCE WINDOWS WITH INSULATING BLINDS

9. STORM WATER COLLECTED IN CISTERN

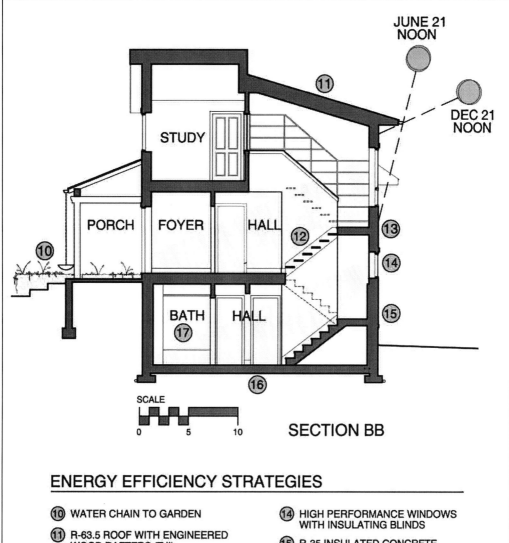

JUNE 21
NOON

DEC 21
NOON

STUDY

PORCH   FOYER   HALL

BATH   HALL

SCALE

0   5   10

SECTION BB

ENERGY EFFICIENCY STRATEGIES

⑩ WATER CHAIN TO GARDEN

⑪ R-63.5 ROOF WITH ENGINEERED
WOOD RAFTERS (TJI)

⑫ OPEN RISER STAIRS FOR AIR FLOW
AND LIGHT TRANSMISSION

⑬ R-48 DOUBLE WOOD STUD WALL
WITH HIGH-PERFORMANCE WINDOWS

⑭ HIGH PERFORMANCE WINDOWS
WITH INSULATING BLINDS

⑮ R-35 INSULATED CONCRETE
FORM FOUNDATION WALLS

⑯ R-20 INSULATED CONCRETE FLOOR

⑰ DUAL FLUSH TOILET AND LOW
FLOW SHOWER HEAD

Appendix C:
Trail Magic
Photographs

Photographs of Trail Magic

1.   Pouring concrete in Reddi-Wall insulated concrete forms
2.   Stairway to first floor taken from study when interior framing was in progress
3.   Stairway wind tower, woodbin/woodstove, and east end of great room
4.   Great room, stairway bookcases, woodstove, and south facing picture windows
5.   Great room, woodstove, and hardwood floor taken from second floor stair landing
6.   Kitchen
7.   North and east sides of house and barn
8.   South side of house and barn
9.   House and barn with reflection in pond at dusk
10. Garden and pond

1. Pouring concrete in Reddi-Wall insulated concrete forms. Pump man, Aaron, and Mike fill polystyrene blocks with concrete. Photo was taken in June 2008. (Photo: Carl McDaniel)

2. Stairway from first floor to study with Mary sitting in southwest corner of great room viewed from western most end of second floor study during construction. Note double 2×4 walls to Mary's left and in roof the 16 inch, oriented-strand-board, I beams for roof insulation. Photo taken in July 2008. (Photo: Carl McDaniel)

3. Stairway wind tower, woodbin, woodstove and east end of great room viewed from front door entryway. Open stairway treads facilitate daylighting of stairs and front entryway and allow air flow for passive cooling. The small woodbin (12 inches wide, 2 feet 8 inches deep and high; stores about 6 cubic feet of wood) holds sufficient wood to heat Trail Magic for two days when outside temperature is 0°F and the sun is not shining. Hearth made from reused cobblestones. Photo was taken on a sunny day in January 2011. (Photo: Carl McDaniel)

4. Great room, stairway bookcases, woodstove, and south facing picture windows. Picture was taken on a cloudy day in January 2011. (Photo: Carl McDaniel)

5. View of great room and wood stove taken from stair landing outside study. The picture was taken in early January. The photo shows winter sunlight reaching across the great room into the kitchen, pantry, and entryway. From mid-May to early August, no direct sunlight enters the great room from the south-facing, picture windows. Sun patio and rock garden are seen through south picture windows. Deck is seen through west picture windows. (Photo: Carl McDaniel)

6. Kitchen taken from the great room showing north facing picture windows and two of four small windows that daylight countertop. (Photo: Carl McDaniel)

7. North and east sides of Trail Magic and barn taken from northeast corner of property. (Photo: Joseph Ferut)

8. South side of house and deck, and south and east sides of barn. Winter wheat is in the foreground. PV panels on west side of roof and evacuated tubes of solar hot water system on east side of roof. Sun shadows on house from roof overhangs illustrate passive solar design feature that reduces warming of house by direct sunshine in summer. Photo was taken in early July. (Photo: Carl McDaniel)

9. Evening image of house and barn with reflection in pond. (Photo: Joseph Ferut)

10. Trail Magic garden and pond taken from the north end of the garden in spring 2010. House and barn are northeast of the garden. The large stump south of the garden is from one of the two, 100 year old, red oak trees that were lumbered for flooring, bookshelves, and dining room table. (Photo: Carl McDaniel)

Appendix D:
Cost Analysis

It is difficult to make meaningful cost comparisons of houses with the single metric of cost per square foot. The first problems arise in defining square footage and in establishing items to include in the cost. The next problems come from the individuality of each house and the features included and their quality. In addition, construction costs vary significantly from location to location and year to year.

For establishing the square foot size of Trail Magic, we used the external size of the conditioned space (heated), the method employed by Energy Star and LEED. For Trail Magic we used the number on the Energy Star analysis: 2,494 square feet. This square foot number is different from the 1,309 square feet listed on Trail Magic's tax assessment because the tax form number does not include conditioned space in the basement. This latter method makes a more valid comparison of the quality living space than the conditioned area method, and is also generally used in real estate descriptions.

We consider the cost for the house to include that which we paid the builder plus the cost for items directly paid by us, but not the cost of the barn or the land. We do not include architect and engineer fees, and expenses for appliances, per convention for custom houses.

Many factors go into the choice of a material or item. In building Trail Magic we elected, in most cases, to use materials and items based upon environmentally and economically measured lifecycle costs as Chapter 8 discusses. In many cases, we "upscaled" our choice for aesthetics, durability, ease of maintenance, or environmental importance. Many features and items that we selected had alternatives that would have given similar performance in terms of operating energy efficiency. These upscale elements added significantly to the cost of Trail Magic.

For the house only, Trail Magic cost $364,200 or $146 per square foot of conditioned space (Table 1). We asked Mike Strehle to identify the upscale features and items that we could have eliminated or replaced without substantially reducing Trail Magic's energy efficient performance. Without these upscale items, Trail Magic would have cost $273,200, or $110 per square foot (Tables 1 and 2).

These numbers for cost per square foot of conditioned space establish that 1) a quality, custom-made house that is high performance and positive energy is no more expensive than a quality, custom-made house that purchases its operating energy and 2) when the upscale features are removed, the cost for making a high performance, positive energy home is similar to that for a development house of equivalent size. We have established, contrary to common belief, it costs nothing extra to build a house that runs on sunshine.

We can estimate ROI (return on investment) for features and particular items in a house for a given time period; ROI is given as a percent = ([gain from investment − cost of investment] ÷ cost of investment) × 100. But, ROIs are fraught with uncertainty because of numerous assumptions. In Sidebar 14, I estimated the 100-year value of making Trail Magic passive solar to be $50,000 or $500 per year. We added little expense to Trail Magic by making it passive solar, because costs are essentially in design features, not in material or labor costs—orientation, size and placement of windows, roof overhang. If we assume it cost $1,000 to make Trail Magic passive solar, the 100 year ROI is 4,900%.

We can estimate ROI for making Trail Magic positive energy by assuming an outlay of $25,000: superior insulation, $9,500; PV system, $12,100; and pond loop for heat pump, $3,400. If we estimate the annual return to be $2,200 or the cost to operate an average home in the U.S. (110 million BTUs × $20/million BTUs) plus the money saved on income taxes not paid on money not earned ($800), the first year ROI would be -88%, and for 30 years (the anticipated life of PV system), 260%: an average annual ROI of almost 9% or $2,250.

We can only calculate these and other ROIs imprecisely; however, if we accept the long term ROI is the important number, then the energy conserving and producing features of Trail Magic pay handsome dividends.

We have provided data and analyses here establishing that it costs nothing extra to build a home that provides income in the form of no energy bills.

Table 1: Summary cost for building Trail Magic, with and without upscale features.

Item	Cost	Notes
Original Contract	347,900	Includes barn
Change Orders 1-56	28,200	Includes barn change orders
Finish Work	10,000	Because site wood had to be dried and milled, the shelves, bookcases, beams, pantry counter and second floor flooring were not ready until spring 2009
Custom Lumber	17,100	Site trees cut, dried, and finished by George Ficke
Owner Cost for PV system	9,100	Cost for system in Troy, disassembly, and additional panels and mounting parts minus tax credits
Light Fixtures and Ceiling Fans	2,000	
Miscellaneous	1,000	Estimate of owner small expenses not recorded
Expenses for Barn	−47,100	Included in contract and change orders
Tax Credits	−4,000	Pond loop and heat pump (geothermal), solar hot water system
Total Cost	364,200	$146 per/ft^2 for 2,494 ft^2 of conditioned space
Extra Cost for Upscale Features	91,000	See Table 2 for details
Total Cost without Upscale Features	273,200	$110 per/ft^2 for 2,494 ft^2 of conditioned space

Table 2: Cost for upscale features of Trail Magic with comparison cost for similar, high performance house without upscale features.

Item	Actual Cost for Upscale Feature	Alternative Item	Approximate Cost for Alternative	Cost Difference between Alternative and Upscale Feature
Custom Grading	3,000	None	0	3,000
Cistern and Rain Collection System	4,000	None	0	4,000
Walkout Patio on Southside	4,000	No patio, retaining wall, or stairs and sidewalks to patio	0	4,000
Landscaping: Sandstone Planters and Sandstones on Sides of Driveway	3,000	None	0	3,000
Central Vacuum System	1,400	None	0	1,400
Pond	8,500	None	0	8,500
Foundation: Reddi-Wall	10,800	Poured wall foundation	9,000	1,800
Framing: Double Wall	28,000	Single 2×6 wall	24,000	4,000
Insulation for double walls	12,900	Insulation for 2×6 walls	7,400	5,500
Roof: 24 gage standing seam	17,000	25 year asphalt shingles	5,500	11,500
Windows: Loewen wood frame and aluminum casing	25,300	Fiberglass or vinyl windows	15,900	9,400
Deck: Tigerwood	9,700	Pressure treated wood	7,200	2,500
HVAC Pond Loop with Heat Pump	15,500	Air to air heat Pump	12,100	3,400
Energy Recovery Ventilation System	1,100	None	0	1,100
Quartz Kitchen Counter Top	4,900	Laminate kitchen counter top	1,200	3,700

Table 2: Continued

Item	Actual Cost for Upscale Feature	Alternative Item	Approximate Cost for Alternative	Cost Difference between Alternative and Upscale Feature
First and Second Floor Flooring: Site Hardwood	8,800	Bamboo flooring	5500	3,300
Stairway Bookcases: Site Oak, Maple, Ash, and Blackwalnut	5,500	Pine	2,000	3,500
Exterior: Pre-colored Hardiplank	22,500	Vinyl siding	14,800	7,700
Closet and Pantry Shelves: Site Ash	2,800	Pine	1,700	1,100
Custom Tiled Shower	3,500	Fiberglass shower	400	3,100
TOTAL	209,200		118,200	91,000

End Notes

Prelude

pg ix   I visited the Anasazi ruins in December 2001 when my family was on its way for my sabbatical at the University of California-Davis.

pg x   Perhaps the most comprehensive discussions of the major environmental issues facing humanity can be found in the annual volumes of *State of the World* and *Vital Signs* as well as the numerous reports produced by the Worldwatch Institute, Washington, DC.

Chapter 1: Deciding to Really Do It

pg 1   Photo is of the western side of Trail Magic's site taken in spring 2008 looking south from where the pond is now located.

Chapter 2: Size Matters

pg 11   Photo was taken in June 2008 facing the southeast corner of the ground floor Reddi-Wall foundation prior to concrete being poured into the wall.

pg 12   Information about Donald Watson, FAIA, can be found at http://www.donaldwatson.com/Index.php

pg 13   McDaniel energy use is discussed in Carl N. McDaniel, *"Positive Energy: A True Understanding of Energy Use Comes only with Hands-On Experience,"* Oberlin Alumni Magazine 102(4):22-23, Spring 2007.

    The annual operating energy and energy uses for the average U.S. home can be found at many sites on the Web. The average home spends $2,200 annually for energy or 110 million BTUs from: http://www.energystar.gov/index.cfm?c=products.pr_pie

pg 21   Alex Wilson, *Your Green Home: A Guide to Planning a Healthy, Environmentally Friendly New Home* (Gabriola Island, BC, Canada: New Society Publishers, 2006); also see Wilson's website (www.greenbuildng.com) for extensive information on green building materials and practices.

    See work of Al Bartlett (http://www.albartlett.org/) for an excellent introduction to the relevant meaning of exponential growth to humanity. "The greatest shortcoming of the human race is our inability to understand the exponential function."—Professor Al Bartlett.

    An analysis of the energy used by hunter-gatherers and by modern humans is found in C.N. McDaniel and D.N. Borton, *"Increased energy use causes biological diversity loss and undermines prospects for sustainability"* BioScience 52:929-936 (2002).

pg 22   Donald Watson, FAIA, and Kenneth Labs, *Climatic Design: Energy-Efficient Building Principles and Practices* (New York: McGraw-Hill, 1983).

Chapter 3: Wants and Needs

pg 23   Photo of the great room was taken December 2010 from second-floor, stair landing.

pg 29   The amount of carbon dioxide released from various fossil fuels is from: http://green-energysaving.com/carbon-emissions/which-fossil-fuels-give-off-most-carbon-dioxide-what-are-the-worst-fossil-fuels/   and http://www.naturalgas.org/environment/naturalgas.asp

Chapter 4: Matching Personalities

pg 33   Photo of Mike Strehle putting-in front porch ceiling was taken September 2008.

pg 34   Provider contractual responsibility to USGBC from *LEED® for Homes Rating System, January 2008* (Washington, D.C.: USGBC, 2008, pg v).

pg 41   Keeling curve was reproduced by Bruce Laplante from NOAA figure (http://www.esrl.noaa.gov/gmd/ccgg/trends).

For information on historic carbon dioxide concentrations see: http://en.wikipedia.org/wiki/Carbon_dioxide_in_Earth%27s_atmosphere and http://www.realclimate.org/

For a discussion of humanity's well being and the principles of the natural sciences see: J.M. Gowdy and C.N. McDaniel, *"One world, one experiment: Addressing the biodiversity-economics conflict,"* Ecological Economics 15:181–192 (1995); Carl N. McDaniel and John M. Gowdy, *Paradise for Sale: A Parable of Nature* (Berkeley, CA: University of California Press, 2000).

Chapter 5: Oberlin Mud

pg 43   Photo was taken May 2008 looking west from what is now the north eastern edge of the pond.

pg 45   Wackernagel, Mathis and Rees, William, *Our Ecological Footprint: Reducing Human Impact on the Earth* (Gabriola Island, BC, Canada: New Society Publishers, 1996) provides the basics of ecological foot printing. Current information on ecological footprinting can be found at the website of the Footprint Network (http://www.footprintnetwork.org/en/index.php/GFN/page/our_team/).

Chapter 6: Where's the Dumpster?

pg 53   Photo was taken August 2008 looking north toward the split rail fence and E. College Street from in front of the house.

pg 54   Ray Anderson quote ("harvesting yesterday's carpets, recycling … into ecosystems [by 2020]".) is from Interface, Inc. "2002 Annual Report" (Atlanta: Interface, 2002).

pg 55   David Orr quote ("On the immediate horizon is … what Paul Hawken calls 'blessed unrest'.") is from a personal communication with permission.

For NY Times article on SEED House see:
http://www.nytimes.com/2008/05/26/education/26green.html

pg 60   LEED requirement for waste is from *LEED® for Homes Rating System: January 2008* (Washington: U.S. Green Building Council, 2007, pg. 83).

Chapter 7: Deadline

pg 65   Photo was taken October 2008 of lumber truck being loaded in the west side driveway of Trail Magic.

pg 70   Carl N. McDaniel, *"Positive Energy: A True Understanding of Energy Use Comes only with Hands-On Experience,"* Oberlin Alumni Magazine 102(4):22-23, Spring 2007.

pg 76   Board feet numbers for Trail Magic trees lumbered were generously provided by George Ficke.

Chapter 8: The Big Decision

pg 81   Photo of the south side of Trail Magic was taken July 2008 from under the osage orange tree that is at the northeast end of pond.

pg 86   See end note for page 97.

pg 87   U.S. uses a total of 100 quads of energy measured in BTUs. With a population of about 300 million, the per capita energy use is about 350 million BTUs (100×10^{15} BTU ÷ 300×10^6 people = 333×10^6 BTU per person)

Percentage of indoor household water to flush toilets is from http://www.drinktap.org/consumerdnn/Default.aspx?tabid=85.

Chapter 9: Performance

pg 89   Photo of the disassembly of the evacuated tube part of the solar hot water heating system was taken September 2010.

pg 91   The plug load of a house is important to electricians designing the wiring of a house, because it is the potential electrical draw, but it is not usually measured after construction and only gets attention when circuit breakers are tripped off. The baseline operating energy minus heating and cooling energy is usually similar day to day. Likewise, the phantom load for a home is more or less constant.

The operating energy for Trail Magic over the first two years was 7.0 kWh/day (5,100 kWh used in 2 years ÷ 730 days), not including the energy in the one cord of wood used each year for heating, and passive solar heating and lighting energy.

To estimate the baseline operating energy and the phantom load of Trail Magic (minus wood heat and solar input), I measured electricity use when the house was unoccupied for several 7-day periods. The baseline operating energy was about 2.0 kWh/day. The only electrical devices plugged in and on during these periods were the refrigerator and freezer that draw about 1.0 kWh/day; thus the phantom load of Trail Magic is about 1.0 kWh/day or 15% of the electricity used by Trail Magic.

A Kill-a-Watt meter is a very useful device if one wants to know the plug load component of his/her dwelling. This knowledge often leads to behaviorial changes that can reduce electricity use substantially. A Kill-a-Watt meter can be purchased on the Web for about $20.00.

pg 97   I made the following analyses to establish 1) the energy (BTUs) required to heat water by the combined evacuated tube solar hot water system & the on-demand hot water system, 2) the solar component of this energy, and 3) the energy used by the on-demand hot water system alone to heat water.

I estimated the amount of solar energy supplied by the evacuated tube solar hot water system to the hot water used as follows.

The electrical energy (kilowatt hours [kWh]) to heat water by the on-demand heater was measured with The Energy Detective that recorded current flow thorough the 2, 240 volt circuits that feed the on-demand heater.

The electrical energy used to pump glycol from to the roof and water from the storage tank through the heat exchanger was measured with a Kill-a-Watt meter into which the pumps were plugged.

The temperature of the water coming into the house was measured with a thermometer twice each a month. For the three periods assessed (summer: August 14 through September 30 [47 days]; fall: October 1 through November 8 [39 days]; winter: December 1 through February 13 [75 days]), the incoming water temperature was taken as the average temperature measured over the period being analyzed.

The hot water temperature at the faucet was measured with a thermometer five times over the 6 month period and the average temperature for the measurements was 111°F (range 110°F–112°F) and used in analyses.

The amount of water used in each of the three periods was measured with a water meter on the water line feeding the hot water, storage tank.

The total amount of energy to heat the hot water used in the period in question was measured in British Thermal Units (BTU; the amount of heat needed to raise one pound of water 1°F) and calculated by multiplying the gallons of water used × temperature difference between the incoming water and 111°F × 8.35 BTU/gallon °F.

The net amount of energy provided by sunshine that was in the hot water used equals the total BTU needed to heat the water to 111°F minus the BTU of electricity to pump fluids and minus the BTU of electricity to heat the water with the on-demand heater. Conversion: 1 kWh = 3412 BTU. Net percent of energy from sunshine = (net solar BTU ÷ total BTU) × 100.

During a period of 161 days between August 2009 and February 2010, 1,107 gallons of hot water were used. Total BTUs to heat these gallons was calculated to be 485,837. Of these BTUs, the on-demand heater provided 156,952 BTUs and pumping of fluids in the evacuated tube system used 293,432 BTUs for a total of 450,384 BTU. The energy provided by the sun was 35,453 BTUs (485,837 – 450,384) or 7.3% of the energy to heat these 1,107 gallons of hot water. The annual dollar value of this solar energy would be $2.80 (485,837 BTUs ÷ 3,412 BTUs/kWh = 142 kWh; 142 kWh ÷ 1,107 gallons = 0.13 kWh/gallon of hot water; 0.13 kWh/gallon × 3,000 gallons/year (annual use) = 385 kWh/year; $0.10/kWh × 385 kWh/year = $38.50/year; $38.50/year × 0.073 = $2.81/year).

The average person annually uses about 10,000 gallons hot water (DeOreo, William B. and Mayer, Peter W., The end uses of hot water in single family homes from flow trace analysis (Boulder, Co: Aquacraft, Inc.).

The theoretical cost for heating Trail Magic's 3,000 gallons of hot water with the on-demand hot water system is $41.00 (3000 gallons/year × 56°F × 8.35 BTUs/gallon °F = 1,402,800 BTU/year; 1,402,800 BTU/year ÷ 3,412 BTUs/kWh = 410 kWh/year; 410 kWh/year × $0.10/kWh = $41.00/year).

The actual cost for heating Trail Magic's 3,000 gallons of hot water with the on-demand hot water heater was estimated to be $36 ([40 kWh ÷ 335 gallons] × 3,000 gallons/year = 358 kWh/year; 358 kWh/year × $0.10/kWh = $35.80). I measured the electricity used by the on-demand hot water heater from October 26, 2010 to February 15, 2011 but used the interval from October 26, 2010 through November 31, 2010 for the above estimate because the incoming water averaged a temperature of 55°F, the estimated, annual average temperature of incoming water.

The average person uses about 25,000 gallons of water annually (http://www.epa.gov/WaterSense/pubs/indoor.html) and (http://pubs.cas.psu.edu/freepubs/pdfs/uh164.pdf).

pg 98   Estimation of the annual energy (kWh) and cost to heat Trail Magic. The average annual degree heating days (DHD) for Oberlin for years 2003 through 2006 was 5,900 DHD. For the 9 day period from February 16, 2010 (9 am) through February 25, 2010 (9 am), I measured the kWh used by the ground source heat pump with The Energy Detective with the first floor thermostat set at 68°F (the only thermostat). The average temperature in the 2nd floor study 70°F (range 68°F to 76°F), on the 1st floor 69°F (68°F to 76°F), and on the ground floor 65°F (61°F to 66°F) while the average outside temperature was 31°F (range 19°F to 42°F). The estimated cost for keeping Trail Magic at a constant 68° F was $210 (108 kWh ÷ 301 DHD = 0.36 kWh/DHD; 0.36 kWh/DHD × 5900 DHD/year = 2,124 kWh/year; 2,124 kWh/year × $0.10/kWh = $212).

pg 99   Estimation of annual energy (kWh) and cost to cool Trail Magic. The average annual degree cooling days (DCD) for Oberlin for the past seven years (2003 through 2009) was 758 DCD. For the five day period from August 10, 2010 (8 am) to August 15, 2010 (8 am), I measured the kWh used by the ground source heat pump with The Energy Detective. During this period the 1st floor temperature was maintained at 75° F (range 74° F to 75° F) with the temperature on the ground floor ranging from 70° F to 72° F and on the 2nd floor study from 77° F to 79° F, while the outside daily low temperature ranged from 67 to 71 and the daily high temperature ranged from 84° F to 92° F. The estimated cost for keeping Trail Magic at a constant 75° F was $91 (88 kWh ÷ 72 DCD = 1.2 kWh/DCD; 1.2 kWh/DCD × 758 DCD/Year = 910 kWh/year; 910 kWh × $0.10/kWh = $91).

pg 100   The average U.S. home uses over 10,000 kWh of electricity (http://www.ehow.com/about_5166858_much-electricity-average-home-use.html).

The annual operating energy and energy uses for the average U.S. home can be found at many sites on the Web. The average home spends $2,200 annually for energy or 110 million BTUs (http://www.energystar.gov/index.cfm?c=products.pr_pie).

The energy used for various applications can be found at (http://www1.eere.energy.gov/consumer/tips/home_energy.html).

Chapter 10: Trail Magic and Oberlin—Gesture and Promise

pg 105   Photo is of Trail Magic's electric meter when it passed zero and went negative as Trail Magic went positive energy.

pg 106   Bob Berkebile's statement is based upon my notes and those of several other people at the ceremony.

pg 110   Quote ("The relative indifference ... difficult to marshal.") is from Edward O. Wilson, *The Future of Live* (New York: Knopf, 2002, pg 40).

Coda

pg 118   Sidebar 16 figure and text courtesy of Donald Watson, FAIA.

Appendix A

pg 129   Image of a page from the notebook in which comments on Schematic Design Option B were made.

Appendix B

pg 141   Image of first floor schematic design.

Appendix C

pg 155   Photo of Trail Magic taken by Joe Ferut in May 2009.

Appendix D

pg 163   Photo of Mike Strehle mounting PV panels on Trail Magic taken by Carl McDaniel in September 2008.

Selected General Reading:

History of solar architecture

Ken Butti and John Perlin, *A Golden Thread: 2500 Years of Solar Architecture and Technology* (Palo Alto, CA: Cheshire Books, 1980) is a look back at the history of solar energy for building operating energy.

Donald Watson (Editor), *Energy Conservation through Building Design* (New York: McGraw Hill, 1979) is an historic commentary on energy use in buildings considering efforts to employ solar and conservation to address the changing environmental landscape three decades ago.

Donald Watson, FAIA, and Kenneth Labs, *Climatic Design: Energy-Efficient Building Principles and Practices* (New York: McGraw-Hill, 1983) is the benchmark book that provides the scientific principles and practical applications of climatic design to building science; that is, illustrates how to create structures that maximize the use of the energy provided by the climates in which they are sited.

See also: http://en.wikipedia.org/wiki/History_of_passive_solar_building_design and http://www.californiasolarcenter.org/history_passive.html

Green home building

Alanna Stano and Christopher Hawthorne, *The Green House: New Directions in Sustainable Architecture* (New York: Princeton Architectural Press, 2005) is a collection of 35 homes in 15 countries considered in 20005 by green architects to be leading examples of sustainable architecture.

Alex Wilson, *Your Green Home: A Guide to Planning a Healthy, Environmentally Friendly New Home* (Gabriola Island, BC, Canada: New Society Publishers, 2006) is an excellent, how-to book on green home building.

Many recent how-to books on green-house-building have focused on energy efficiency: Dan Chiras, *The Homeowner's Guide to Renewable Energy: Achieving Energy Independence through Solar, Wind, Biomass and Hydropower* (Gabriola Island, BC, Canada: New Society Publishers, 2006); David Johnston and Scott Gibson, *Green from the Ground Up: Sustainability, Health, and Energy-Efficient Home Construction* (Newton, CT: Taunton Press, 2008); Bruce Harley, *Cut Your Energy Bill Now: 150 Smart Ways to Save Money & Make Your Home More Comfortable & Green* (Newton, CT: Taunton Press, 2008); Ann V. Edminster, *Energy Free: Homes for a Small Planet* (San Rafael, CA, Green Building Press, 2009); David Johnston and Scott Gibson, *Toward a Zero Energy Home: A Complete Guide to Energy Self-Sufficiency at Home* (Newton, CT: Taunton Press, 2010). These and many other books provide readers, potential homeowners and builders with comprehensive and detailed information on topics and approaches discussed in *Trail Magic: Creating a Positive Energy Home*.

Climate change

Bill McKibben, *The End of Nature* (New York: Random House, 1987) was the first general audience book that focused a bright light on how human activities were radically changing the functioning of planet and climate, and Bill McKibben, *Eaarth: Making a Life on a Tough New Planet* (New York: Times Books, 2010) is a two decade later update on how we have made a radically different planet than the one on which we evolved, including forcing climate change that may very will undo civilization as we know it.

Stephen H. Schneider, *Global Warming: Are We Entering the Greenhouse Century?* (San Francisco: Sierra Club Books, 1989) is among the first scientific-based books accessible to the general reader that over two decades ago presented a solid case for aggressively reducing human-caused, heat-trapping-gas emissions.

Numerous general audience books have been written in the past several years that leave no doubt that the scientific evidence is unequivocal—we have entered a period of climate destabilization and human activities are forcing this destabilization: Spencer R Weart, *The Discovery of Global Warming* (Cambridge: Harvard University Press, 2003); Tim Flannery, *The Weather Makers: How Man Is Changing the Climate and What It Means for Life on Earth* (New York: Atlantic Monthly Press, 2005); James Hanson, *Storms of My Grandchildren: The Truth About the Coming Climate Catastrophe and Our Last Chance to Save Humanity* (New York: Bloomsbury USA, 2009).

Indices

Names

Arrhenius, Svante, 109
Anderson, Ray, 54
Andrews, Geoff, 2, 3
Annabel, Kim, 48, 71
Baron, Richard, 16
Benzing, David, viii, 4, 6-7, 17, 29, 47-48, 50-51, 54, 58, 60, 62, 76
Berkebile, Bob, 106, 110
Borton, David, vii, ix-x, 12, 21, 34, 51, 61-63, 71, 78-79, 83-85, 93, 101-102, 121, 138-139
Borton, Harriet, vii, ix, 12, 83
Bortons, x, 4, 8, 12, 14, 17, 24, 34, 57, 63, 83, 98-99
Brazuinas, Kristin, 54
Buchs, Cameron, 50, 55, 73, 75-76
Carter, Brian, 18, 25, 42
Crowley, Peter, 24-25, 27-28, 39, 69, 84-85, 123
Daily, Don, 18-19, 29, 138
Engstrom, Nathan, 6, 60, 63
Ezinga, Ben, 16, 19
Ferut, Joe, vii, 24-25, and throughout the book; perspective on Trail Magic, 113-126; See also detailed design (Subject Index)
Ficke, George, vii, 56, 66-69, 73-75, 77, 104, 124, 128, 165; See also lumbering site trees (Subject Index)
Frantz, Andy, 110
Frantz, Cindy, 110
Goodman, Lee, 48
Hawken, Paul, 55
Hoberecht, Mark, 122, 128
Jensen, Kirk, vii
Keeling, Charles, 41
Korten, David, 55
Kozusko, Bill, 7
Krislov, Marvin, 54-55, 106
Laplante, Bruce, viii
Laskowski, Marta, 24
Lindberg, Charles, 67
Mac & Sons, 17, 19

Masi, Brad, 18
McDaniel, Carl, throughout the book
McDaniel, Mary, vii, x, 2-5, and throughout the book; perspective on Trail Magic, 113-128
McDaniel, Stuart, ix, 4, 12, 25, 32, 92
McDaniel, Virginia, ix, 12-13, 25, 29, 48-49, 92
McDonough, Bill, 12
Norenberg, Eric, 106
Orr, David, viii, x-xi, 4, 15-16, 18, 54-55, 108
Petersen, John, 17, 50
Portman, Doren, vii, 5, 12, 15, 27, 39, 47-48, 58, 68
Portman, Jo Ann, 58
Rose, Kevin, 70-72
Rosen, Josh, 16
Roth, Nancy, 54
Sabel, Naomi, 16
Scout, vii, 3, and throughout the book; See Sonner, David
Shammin, Rumi, viii, 97
Sigel, Thomas, viii
Smith, Calvin, 24-25, 28, 37-39, 42
Sonner, David, vii, 2-3, 127; See Scout
Stangl, Mike, 70
Stanley, Ken, 24
Stoner, Howard, vii, 63, 101-02
Stoner, Margaret, vii, 63, 101-02
Strehle, Mike, vii, 18, and throughout the book; perspective on Trail Magic, 113-128
Viancourt, Kelly, vii, 78
Watson, Donald, vii, 12, and throughout the book; perspective on Trail Magic, 113-128; See also schematic design (Subject Index)
Webster, Buck, 79
Wilson, Alex, 21
Wilson, Edward O., 109
Young, Danielle, 57, 79
Zachos, Nick, 19, 47

Subject

All Seasons Builders, 27, 42, 67; *See also* Strehle, Mike (Index, Names)

ash borer, emerald, 47-48, 67, 74-75; Benzing, David and, 47-48

American College & University Presidents' Climate Commitment, xi, 55

American Municipal Power of Ohio (AMP-Ohio), 40

Anasazi, ix

Arkansas, 48, 61, 108, 126

baseline operating energy, 91

Bethany, Connecticut (house), 14, 17, 51, 83, 117

bid process, 19, 34, 37-39, 42, 45; cover letter and, 35-36

bioclimatic design, 116-19; diagram for Trail Magic, 118-119

biophysical reality, 21, 41

blackcap jelly, 8, 22, 30, 115

Black River, 5, 97

Black River Café, 26

Bortons' solar home, vii, ix, x, 4, 12, 37, 83, 102

Bluffton University, 17

budget, Trail Magic, 2-4, 15-17, 22, 24, 31, 35, 116

builders. *See* Daily, Don; Mac & Sons; Smith, Calvin; Strehle, Mike; Zachos, Nick (Index, Names)

Capital District Community Gardens, 63

carbon dioxide, 29, 40, 92, 97, 102, 109; parts per million (ppm) and global temperature, 41; increase of, 41

carbon in fossil fuels, 29

Cleveland, Ohio, 18, 29, 34, 38, 42, 52, 59, 64, 77, 99

climate change, 41, 28, 62, 82, 101, 108, 122, 170; *See also* carbon dioxide

climate neutral, xi, 2, 19, 29, 40, 52, 55, 61-62; operating energy and, 62, 99, 102, 108

climate positive home for all energy used by residents, 106-08

climate positive home for operating energy, 62, 79, 96, 102, 110; Trail Magic becoming, 99; Stoner home becoming, 102

climatic design, 22, 116-119

Clinton Foundation Climate Initiative, 55, 106

coal, vii, 13, 29, 40, 55, 107; cost not paid for, 40; *See also* energy

daylighting, 14, 24, 86, 92, 100, 102; photos of, 23, 158-59

decisions, 46, 49, 82-88; criteria (environmental and economical live cycle costs), 87-88; energy value of big three (size, orientation, envelope), 86-87; final, 46, 49, 70, 82-88; preliminary, 19, 30, 46, 55-56, 58-59, 82-88; water use, 87; electricity use, 91; *See also* insulation; orientation, house; size, house; vapor barrier; wall types

degree heating and cooling days, 98, 138, 174

design, detailed, 34, 48-49, 52, 99; architectural drawings, 141-53

design, schematic, 20-22, 26-27, 30-32; architectural drawings, 141-53

earthberming, 30, 36, 117, 119-20, 134

Earthrise: design inspired by nature, 31

East College Street Project, 16

ecological footprint, 45, 82

economic growth, 21, 41

energy: British Thermal Unit (BTU), 13; carbon dioxide and, 29; commercial, 21; equivalents, 13; heat pump and, 79, 98, 100, 125; hunter gatherers, use of, 21; global use of, 21; kilowatt hour, 13; person annual output of, 13; total amount used in U.S., 106; woodstove and, 98, 100; *See also* base load; climate positive home for operating energy; coal; hot water; phantom load, photovoltaic electricity, plug load; positive energy home for operating energy; solar energy; Trail Magic, operating energy

energy recovery ventilation, 119, 125

envelope, 12, 21-22, 28, 38-39, 49, 82-87, 93-94, 103, 124-25, 138; Borton house and, 83-84; Stoner house and, 101; *See also* vapor barrier, wall types

EnviroAlums, x, 54

environmental issues, x, 21, 29, 41, 45, 121-22; *See also* carbon dioxide, climate change

fantasy, 17, 21-22, 41, 111
Florida, 108
garage apartment, 60-61, 69
George Jones Farm, 18-19
Goodwill Industries, 63
ground fault interrupter (GFI), 61
Hardi-Plank siding, 88
heat pump, 98; cooling Trail Magic,
    99, 100, 175; heating Trail Magic,
    98, 100, 174
Home and Garden Show (Cleveland),
    18, 42
hot water system, solar and on-
    demand, 35, 46, 61-62, 86-87, 90-
    91, 96-97, 107-08, 134, 139, 160,
    172-73
initial design and energy analysis
    (IDEA), 20; contract, 20
insulation, cellulose damp-spray, 24,
    35, 66, 84-85, 138; foam, closed
    cell, 84-85; foam, open cell, 84-85;
    straw bale, 18-19, 28-30, 35, 38,
    84, 122-23, 138; Also see R value,
    Reddi-Wall
Interface Corporation, 54
Keeling Curve, 41; See also carbon
    dioxide
Kill-a-Watt meter, 91, 173
Kurtz Brothers, 77
Leadership in Energy and
    Environmental Design (LEED), 15,
    16, 18, 20, 28, 34-35, 37, 46-47,
    51-52, 59-60, 64, 88, 93-94, 96, 109,
    130; appeal of rejected application,
    94; green rater, 34, 52, 64, 93-95;
    LEED team, 51; pre-drywall inspec-
    tion, 64; provider, 34, 51-52, 93-95;
    rejection of appeal (letter), 95
Lewis Center, Adam Joseph, x-xi, 3, 12,
    54-55, 106, 108-109; Tenth
    Anniversary of, 109
light emitting diode (LED), 90, 92
lumbering site trees, 40, 47, 51-52, 66-
    68, 73-77, 124; board feet, 76;
    contract, 68; dangerous, 74-75;
    multispecies hardwood flooring,
    67-68, 77; trees, value of, 67; trunk
    cross-section tables and, 48, 56; See
    also ash borer, emerald
Mauna Loa Observatory, 41
McDaniel dream house, 3-5, 7, 9
McDaniel energy use in Troy, 13
McDaniel Troy house, 13; operating
    energy of, 13

mistakes, 82, 114-15, 125-126, 130;
    doors, 126; kitchen picture
    windows, 58, 115; kitchen
    windows, small, 82; mechanical
    systems, 125-26, 130; project too
    rushed, 124
net metering, 4-5, 8
New Haven, Connecticut, 15, 45
Oberlin, city of, xi, 4, 106; city council,
    xi, 29, 40, 55
Oberlin College, x-xi , 2, 4, 54-55, 106,
    109, 111; environmental initiatives
    of, 15-16, 47, 55; Alumni Council
    Executive Board of, 2, 24, 58, 79;
    See also EnviroAlums
Oberlin Community Services, 110
Oberlin Project, The, 55, 109
owner's program, McDaniel, 14, 129-140
Passivhaus, 28, 125
phantom load, 61, 91, 173
photovoltaic electricity, 4-5, 13, 24, 86,
    62, 86, 99-100, 108, 110; photo-
    voltaic system reassembly, 70-73
Providing Oberlin With Efficiency
    Responsibly (POWER), 110
plug load, 91, 173
Plum Creek, 5-6, 90
Portman property, 5, 7-9
positive energy home, 99-100, 102;
    positive energy for all energy used
    by residents (defined), 106-107;
    positive energy for operating energy
    (defined), 62; Trail Magic becoming
    positive energy for operating
    energy, 107-08
orientation, house, 86-87
R-value, 24
radiant heating, 117
Reddi-Wall, 18, 28, 38, 42, 56, 84-85,
    138; photo of, 157
real estate available in Oberlin, 3-9
Rensselaer Polytechnic Institute, x-xi,
    12-13, 34, 44, 49
Salvation Army, 63
size, house, 14-15, 21-22, 82-83, 86-
    87, 130
solar energy: Anasazi and, ix; passive,
    86, 100; sunshine in Oberlin,
    percent, 99. See also energy; hot
    water system, solar and on-
    demand; photovoltaic electricity
St. Louis, Missouri, 15-16, 61
Student Experiment in Ecological
    Design House (SEED House), 55

sun shading, 117-119
Tappan Square, 3, 6, 8
Trail Magic (495 E. College Street): architectural drawings, 141-53; cost analysis of, 163-67; derelict houses on-site, 5; design suggestions from friends and colleagues, 17, 21, 26; insulation, 85; open houses, 66, 69, 79; operating energy, 100; origin of name, 32; performance (quantifiable), 90-100; performance (not quantifiable), 90, 102-104; photographs, 155-61; spilt rail fence, 3, 7, 18, 39, 78; site of, 5, 7; vapor barrier, 85; *See also* bioclimatic design; budget, Trail Magic; daylighting; heat pump; Leadership in Energy and Environmental Design (LEED); owner's program, McDaniel; size, house
Troy, New York, vii, ix-x, 2, 4, 8-9, 12-13, 17, 21, 24, 37, 45, 48-50, 54, 56, 58, 61-63, 70-71, 73, 78, 82-83, 90-92, 100-01, 107, 130, 134, 138-39
Troy United Ministries, 63
United States Green Building Council (USGBC), 34, 51, 55, 93-95, 106, 109; *See also* Leadership in Energy and Environmental Design (LEED)
vapor barrier, 84-85; Borton house and, 83-84; dew point and, 84; *See also* envelope
wall types, 35, 38-39; diagram and photo of Trail Magic wall design, 151, 157; *See also* insulation
water use, 97, 174
waste, management, 59-60, 69; derelict houses, amount recycled, 16; landfill, amount put in, 60 (Trail Magic), 63 (Troy); photograph, 53; recycled and reused, amount, 60
Winsted, Connecticut, 22
woodstove, 46, 98; installation of, 71-72; *See also* energy

About the author

Carl N. McDaniel is Visiting Professor at Oberlin College in Oberlin, Ohio, and Professor Emeritus at Rensselaer Polytechnic Institute in Troy, New York. He was founding director of the undergraduate environmental science degree program at Rensselaer. For the first three decades of his academic career he studied insect and then plant development. His scholarly interests since have focused on the interface between biology and economics. He has written two books—*Paradise for Sale: A Parable of Nature* (2000, with economist John M. Gowdy) and *Wisdom for a Livable Planet: The Visionary Work of Terri Swearingen, Dave Foreman, Wes Jackson, Helena Norberg-Hodge, Werner Fornos, Herman Daly, Stephen Schneider, and David Orr* (2005).